T0283510

MAD
WIFE

MAD WIFE

A MEMOIR

KATE HAMILTON

BEACON PRESS
BOSTON

BEACON PRESS
Boston, Massachusetts
www.beacon.org

Beacon Press books
are published under the auspices of
the Unitarian Universalist Association of Congregations.

27 26 25 24   8 7 6 5 4 3 2 1

This book is printed on acid-free paper that meets the uncoated paper
ANSI/NISO specifications for permanence as revised in 1992.

Text design and composition by Kim Arney

Library of Congress Cataloging-in-Publication Data
Names: Hamilton, Kate (Author of Mad wife), author.
Title: Mad wife : a memoir / Kate Hamilton.
Description: Boston : Beacon Press, [2024] | Includes bibliographical references. |
Identifiers: LCCN 2024011489 | ISBN 9780807016404 (hardcover) |
ISBN 9780807016411 (epub)
Subjects: LCSH: Hamilton, Kate (Author of Mad wife) |
Abused wives—Biography. | Family violence.
Classification: LCC HV6626 .H2693 2024 | DDC 362.82/92 [B]—dc23/eng/20240429
LC record available at https://lccn.loc.gov/2024011489

*For those who've hurt and been hurt
in these unfathomable ways,
in empathy and solidarity—*

*For those who find such things unimaginable,
so you might choose differently—*

*For my children,
though you don't know it yet:*

This is your story too.

When I dare to be powerful,
to use my strength in the service of my vision,
then it becomes less important
whether or not I am afraid.

—AUDRE LORDE,
The Cancer Journals (1980)

We either die of the past
or we become an artist.

—DEBORAH LEVY,
The Cost of Living (2018)

I will always aspire to contain
my shit as best I can,
but I am no longer interested in
hiding my dependencies
in an effort to appear superior to those
who are more visibly undone or aching.
I'm glad not to be there right now,
but I'm also glad to have been there,
to know how it is.

—MAGGIE NELSON,
The Argonauts (2015)

CONTENTS

Author's Note xi
Introduction: Testimony xiii

PART 1: TUMULT

1. Fellow Creature *3*
2. Love Story *15*
3. Betrayal *25*
4. Stay *39*
5. Voices *47*

PART 2: SEEMING LIBERATION AND PLEASURE

6. Boiling Frog *55*
7. Freedom *63*
8. Control *75*
9. Family *83*
10. What We Owe Each Other *91*

PART 3: DIVORCE IS NOT THE WORST THING

11. Inside/Outside *115*
12. Hovel *121*
13. Cruel and Inhumane *131*
14. Control Redux *147*
15. Banshee *161*

PART 4: SEX IS NOT SOMETHING YOU OWE

16. Mad *185*
17. Disturbing *193*
18. Monstrous *199*

Epilogue: Awakening 203
Resources 207
Recommended Reading 209
Acknowledgments 211
Notes 215

AUTHOR'S NOTE

To make this book as accurate as possible, I consulted every record available to me while writing: letters, calendars, and journals; saved emails and texts; notes on medical appointments and legal meetings and trials; and police reports and court transcripts. When pulling from such material I have quoted or paraphrased to preserve original meaning and intent. I included all details I considered relevant and created no composite characters or events. While I strove throughout to render these experiences with unflinching honesty and thoroughness, I did so in the only way I could— from my own particular perspective. Others whom I write about by way of telling my story have lived their own versions. I have done everything possible to preserve the anonymity of all of these people by changing all names, including my own, and omitting or modifying identifying details.

TESTIMONY

The beginning of things, of a world especially,
is necessarily vague, tangled, chaotic,
and exceedingly disturbing.
How few of us ever emerge from such beginning!
How many souls perish in its tumult!

—KATE CHOPIN, *The Awakening* (1899)

I n the quiet, still space of a late morning in February, one week after my thirty-ninth birthday, I must have been glowing with the happiness of it: straddling the pale middle of a blissed-out man, leaning in, my long hair framing his face. The weak winter sun reached gingerly through his bedroom window, touching that bower of hair that suspended us outside time and the world, turning it gold. I remember the look on his face and his eyes full of love, holding mine, telling me he saw me and loved what he saw.

Bliss turned to terror in an instant, as the banging began one floor below. Then came the yelling, screaming, a barrage of fury. Grabbing for his clothes, the man hobbled to the window and peered down to the driveway below. "What kind of car does your husband drive?" A red Acura, the one parked impossibly in your driveway.

We stood there listening long enough to understand that my husband was not going to stop until he got what he came for. The man, eyes now withdrawn, stepped back, arms hanging, waiting for me to offer myself up and take this violence elsewhere.

I threw on my clothes and ran to the front door, not pausing to hear what my husband was shouting or register that he was out of his mind with rage. When I opened the door, the porch was strangely empty. I entered the yard just in time to see my husband loping awkwardly through knee-high snow around the back of the house. By the time I got there he was, inexplicably, hanging from the edge of the roof by his long arms, swinging. When I called to him, he dropped to the frozen ground in a crouch, then took off in his bizarre caper around the other side of the house. We met at the front, where I found him savagely pitching across the hard lawn everything that was pitchable: Adirondack chairs, potted plants, a baby carriage, which struck the ground with a sickening plastic crunch. Then he whipped around and, spitting with rage, ordered me into his car. Looking into his blazing eyes, I was filled with the surreal and precise knowledge that the man with whom I had had children and shared a life for nearly twenty years simply was not in there. It's impossible to describe the devastation of looking into the face of the person you've loved and seeing a beast you know without doubt will kill you if you let him.

But think of all the women who have done exactly that and the men who have killed them—nearly three every day in the US alone.

It was obviously not safe for me to go anywhere near him. Yet I told him I would go home with him once I had retrieved my bag from the house. It didn't occur to me that I could say no. It didn't occur to me that anyone watching what was unfolding should stop me or—even more unthinkable—should call the police to stop him. When I found that the front door had been locked behind me, I wasn't even surprised, let alone hurt. Of course the man inside was protecting himself from my husband, who was looking to destroy something, someone. I knocked; without meeting my eyes, he undid the latch and retreated upstairs while I grabbed my bag and left.

I climbed into the old red Acura, the car my husband had just bought when we began dating as seniors in college; the car we'd driven to the Garden of the Gods, where we held each other, awestruck by the glory of new love and ancient cliffs; the car where, under a starry Colorado sky, he first told me he loved me. Now it was parked behind my lover's car. My husband was manic, unable to sit still, writhing with rage in the driver's seat. I tried to tell him I did not feel safe, that he should drive home and I would follow separately, but he cut me off, revving the engine while slipping it in and out of gear so that the car leapt forward and back like an animal: "If you so much as open the car door, I will smash his car to bits." I looked at his face and believed him.

On the drive home, along winding rural roads outside our small town, I tried to calm him. I tried to apologize. Every attempt to speak was met with the same response: "If you don't shut your mouth, I will kill you." Then he'd run the car off the road, bringing the passenger side where I was sitting inches away from one telephone pole or tree after another. I shut up.

He took a strange route home, along narrow roads that run by the river and are lined with old stone houses built by European immigrants in the seventeenth century. Taking a curve at a dangerous speed, he drove over a large rock, stalled the car out in the middle of the street, opened the door, and fled—straight into a historic cemetery, where he bellowed amid tombstones whose names the centuries have nearly erased. I climbed into the driver's seat to move the car to the side of the street, by which time he had run across the road again and toward the wide river, limbs akimbo. I thought he might fling himself in. Instead, I found him crumpled at the base of a grand tree at the river's edge, weeping. When I gently tried to encourage him back to the car so I could get him home, he began to run again, back up the hill toward town and the cemetery, screaming at the top of his lungs: "My wife is a postmodernist! That means she doesn't believe in anything! There's no black or white or right or wrong! Nothing matters!"

Somehow I corralled him back into the car and deposited him in the passenger's seat. As I drove the rest of the way home, he opened the glove box and pulled out a nearly full pack of gum, then methodically unwrapped each piece and shoved it into his mouth, eyes and cheeks bulging, spittle dribbling down his face, until I thought he might choke. At home the rage continued. He screamed at me for hours, hurling every insult he could think of while I wept and cowered. At one point, he snatched my computer—my portal to life outside our miserable marriage—and dangled it out the third-floor window.

That night we attended our regularly scheduled couples counseling, as we'd been doing, futilely, for months. This was the latest in a series of marital counselors that stretched over several years and three states. I had initiated all of them, in a series of desperate attempts to salvage what had been a happy marriage but had become absolutely unbearable for me. For years, I had approached the problem of my marriage as I did everything—believing that success was only a matter of applying my whole self completely, of hard work and dedication—and watched our relationship grow more toxic in ways that counseling normalized rather than challenging. I lost all faith in my ability to save my marriage while losing none of my commitment to it. I believed I was stuck for life with a man I could hardly stand to be in the same room with, and I was figuring out how to deal with that. The lover whose baby carriage had just been pitched was only my most recent attempt to cope, one my husband had grudgingly accepted: "Anything, just don't leave me" was practically a mantra of those last dysfunctional years. But just as I could no longer fake my way through a loveless marriage, he could not stand seeing me loved by anyone else.

Perched at the end of the therapist's couch, as far from my husband as possible, I was still in shock from the day's traumatic events. I told our counselor how my husband had threatened to ram our car into another, had stopped just short of killing me with a telephone pole; how he had screamed at me for hours, insulting me, threatening to hit me; how he had thrown things, holding my computer aloft like a Frisbee. I was terrified, I was shaken, I didn't know how to keep living with a man who would do these things. Who was this man? What did it mean that he could look me in the eye and tell me he would kill me, and mean it? How was I supposed to feel safe with him, let alone feel love for him, now? My husband sat like a statue hewn from rage while I spoke. How dare I act like I was the victim, when clearly he was the one who had been hurt by my reprehensible behavior. How dare I ask for sympathy, when he had been so wronged. I had no right to my terror or my tears. Where was his apology?

After nearly an hour of this characteristically unproductive exchange, our beleaguered counselor said that thing that counselors seem to be trained never to say, that no one had said to us over years of witnessing the ruin of our marriage, that ethics should have led someone to say long before we reached this point of mutual destruction: "I can't help you people. I don't think we should meet anymore."

Walking to the car through the freezing dark, I felt enormous relief that someone with authority had finally said out loud what I had known in my heart but refused to acknowledge for years—that there was no help for us, because our marriage had ended long ago. But as we drove home, my husband simply said, "What a terrible therapist. We'll have to find another one."

––––––––––

In the movie version of this, The Worst Day of My Life, my husband's very public exhortation on postmodernism in the midst of such insanity and violence could easily be played for a laugh, absurdity breaking up the terror. And yet, that surreal moment (and his pedestrian misunderstanding of postmodernism) also points to the heart of this story, and of any story. Is there an absolute, objective truth out there, or just a bunch of stories? And whose story is true? Who gets to tell which story? Can one believe, as any postmodernist must, that truth is defined by subject position, context, and experience, and also believe in values, meaning, and right and wrong? Can you be a moral person and also admit that your truth might not be shared by someone else, even someone you love?

More to the point: Was I a moral person? Was I a victim, or just a betraying bitch of a wife? How could I know, and how could my husband know? How can you know? Is this the story of a woman terrorized, emotionally and physically abused, and threatened with death by a man who claimed he loved her? Or is it a story about the unbearable suffering of a man so heartbroken by his cheating wife that he snapped?

Writing this account over a decade later, I can say: it is both.

This is a tricky setup for a memoir. In this story, he suffered and I suffered. If it were possible to scoop out our pain and spoon it onto the cold plates of a balancing scale, I don't know whose side would weigh more. I have never denied my husband's profound suffering. It predated me and in many ways led directly to the nightmare that our lives would become, but I also added enormously to it and hurt others as well. I have spent years barely able to live with the awareness of all of that. But after losing mutual friends and his family, who loved me like their daughter for nearly twenty years before dropping me as if I were dead, I have gathered that he has been telling the story of his suffering and my shame for a long time. Is it my job to tell that story too? Would it be selfish, as he claimed in the counselor's office, for me to tell the story of my own suffering, to share what it was like to be demeaned and dehumanized by my own husband, without also telling the story of his pain?

Who is the monster here?

Until recently I would have said, and sometimes did, that misogyny and patriarchy hadn't really touched me. I have earned the highest possible degree and established a successful career in a specialty dominated by men. I would have said my parents didn't limit my sense of who I could be in gendered terms. I would have said I have never been raped—and so I have been free from the constraints and offenses of patriarchy. But I have said these things because, despite all of that education, I was blind to the myriad ways that our culture, which believes men to be more valuable, entitled, and human than women—misogyny—has shaped everything I believe about what is true, right, and possible.

I grew up in a conservative family in the South and never heard of feminism until college. I'm lucky I accidentally encountered it there. Having written plays as a child, a novella in middle school, a novel in high school, and having spent much of my young life reading, I chose a university famous for its engineering program and entered as a hard sciences major. I knew I was smart, and I wanted to reach the highest levels of smartness and intellectual status, which meant doing what men do, which in the 1990s meant science. Fortunately, fate intervened by way of my required humanities course, where an influential male professor helped me see where my heart and talents lie. He was also the first person to introduce me to feminism.

I used to say, as if it disproved the possibility of patriarchy all by itself, that I'd learned to be a feminist from men. That's true, but now I know that learning feminism in that way has consequences. The few male professors who introduced feminist ideas and thinkers to me did open up a whole new way of seeing the world, and I am grateful for that. But the bits of Simone de Beauvoir I got in college were no match for the lifetime of programming that had preceded it, and the men who gave those ideas and thinkers to me had not had and did not know what life experiences I needed to learn about on top of the philosophy. It didn't help that the one women's studies course I dared to take was taught by a woman who was so off-putting—so uninterested in inviting outsiders into the tiny world she had defined, bitterly, as feminism—that my memory of her publicly shaming me for wearing eyeliner is at least as strong as that of being bowled over by Adrienne Rich's *Of Woman Born*. I clung to the material we read in that class but shunned the vision of feminism my one female feminist professor offered.

In grad school I repeated the pattern, finding myself drawn to what I perceived to be the most difficult literature: experimental fiction wrestling with complex theories of language; massive, obscure, doorstop-thick books written by men. Nearly all of my professors were men, and none of my courses got anywhere near inquiries of gender and power. I chose the most formidable, encyclopedically knowledgeable professor I could find—a brilliant, widely published man—to direct my dissertation, because I wanted to be pushed to do my best work. This meant that I wanted to learn to produce the kind of mastery of canonical literary theory and intellectual history that my adviser produced but in my chosen subject matter. The subject matter I chose to write about was, of course, formally complex novels and complicated theories of language written by men. I wrote a smart dissertation on this topic, soon gained traction in a subfield of studies about a particularly linguistically complex and misogynistic author, and steadily built a successful career around publishing articles, essays, and books about primarily male and often misogynistic writers. Masculinity and misogyny shaped—encouraged, underwrote, enabled—my entire education and career.

In her brilliant and gutting memoir, *Aftermath*, Rachel Cusk, who is of my generation, considers her own complicated relationship to feminism. She realizes that her parents' misguided attempts to teach her how to live something other than a traditional patriarchal life led to her contorted notions of gender and power, which contributed if not to the breakdown of her marriage, then to the painful confusion in which she experienced it:

> What I lived as feminism were in fact the male values my parents, among others, well-meaningfully bequeathed me—the cross-dressing values of my father, and the anti-feminist values of my mother. So I am not a feminist. I am a self-hating transvestite.

Teaching feminist theory and modeling feminist values to my students and children while living a life and career defined by misogyny, I was not anything that colorful. I was just a fake, a hypocrite, a mouthpiece.

But life has a way of teaching you the things you didn't know you needed to learn, if you pay attention. I have been gaslighted, disbelieved, bullied, objectified, used, silenced, and blamed for my own suffering and that of my children. When I started to see these things and defend myself, I was told I am selfish and crazy. I believed that for a long time. I've lived a well-rounded education in misogyny, which was finally made visible to me by women who wrote about their own experiences of it. Now, I aim to use my experience to add new details to the portrait of misogyny and resistance being collectively drawn by so many women.

I drafted this memoir at the end of my fiftieth year, intending to publish it under a pseudonym. During this time, I was transforming. I didn't feel, as Darcey Steinke describes in *Flash Count Diary*, like I was becoming animal or ungendered. But I was undoubtedly becoming something new. The alien body looking back at me from the mirror after another night spent thrashing through heat explosions and fevered dreams confirms it: I am being reforged. Steinke's reformulation of menopause as liberating us from the pressures, expectations, and limitations of patriarchy resonates deeply with me as I write and rewrite my account of how patriarchy first formed me long ago. How empowering, to think of my body and mind as taking it upon themselves to free me from all of these things, to see myself separating from that world, even as I document all the ways in which it claimed me up to this point. First, I transform into a person who is ready to write this book.

Next, I transform into someone who is ready to put my name on it. I begin to feel I am moving toward the kind of radical transformation that led Steinke to identify with killer whales, an unselving that will place me beyond the reach of others' judgment and disappointment, even of their disgust. Meditation teachers talk about the "pressure of the chrysalis," a phrase that for years has been taped to the computer monitor where I do all my writing, where I am writing this book. The quote reminds us that the moment before a caterpillar emerges as an entirely new being—a once-crawling thing taking flight—is the most binding, the most painful.

The pressure that prefaces the emergence of this book brings clarity: my fear of the personal consequences of publishing under my own name can't compete with my intense desire not to be another silenced woman. I do not want to be cowed into quiet anonymity by the knowledge that I will be punished for making public all that patriarchy and patriarchs expect women to pretend isn't happening. I know exactly the vitriol and threats, the public snubbings, the social media slander that would rain down on me in my small town and across the borderless internet if I attached my name to this account. We know what happens in courts and public opinion to women who speak out about male oppression, especially if these women can be construed as anything but entirely blameless. Many of the women who told their stories in the early days of #MeToo were not just disbelieved but socially rejected, fired, threatened, and verbally attacked; one lost custody of her children. But many in the first wave always fall, so we have to keep the waves coming. I want to be a warrior.

Still, I hesitate. It's ironic, a structural conundrum, that it is impossible for me to tell a story intended to communicate empathy and lessen the suffering of readers whom I will never know without causing pain and confusion for the people who are or have been closest to me. I am clear in my own mind that I do not tell this story to humiliate or wound. I am trying to do something much less petty and more important: to make visible the ways in which misogyny shapes relationships, culture, and the legal system; and how marriage, especially heterosexual marriage, empowers misogyny to the point of abuse for women and children, while rendering both the misogyny and the abuse invisible. More than that, I aim to illustrate the myriad ways we cause damage when we deny other people the autonomy of their bodies and our respect for their equal realness, as has been done to me and as I have done to others. But I worry that my children will see this book as a mortifying way for their mom to teach such a lesson. I worry that I will cause their dad the kind of embarrassment that does not lead to growth or understanding.

And yet hiding my identity feels like a cop-out, the opposite of what I meant to accomplish by sharing the excruciating details of these pages. When I agonize about this dilemma in conversation with my partner, who knows me and what I want for this book better than anyone, he suggests a different reading of using a pseudonym: not another self-sacrifice or silencing, but an act of compassion. Compassion that is not cowed.

My name is not Kate Hamilton, but this is my true story. I am a real person who lived these things and is out there, moving beyond them with hard-earned dignity and learning from them, becoming every day the person I want to be, and doing what I can to support others—my children, my students, my family, my friends—in doing the same. Writing this book as a memoir is part of that work, because I need people to understand that these things that I could scarcely believe were happening to me actually do happen, and that they say a lot of disturbing things about the world we live in. Because I hope others can learn from my naïveté and mistakes; because if one woman learns to recognize and avoid the hazards that I couldn't see, if one man learns that some socially acceptable behavior is traumatic for women and becomes a different kind of man, then dragging myself through my ugly past to write this thing will have been worth it. Because however blinkered memoirs inherently are, when you put them together you get visions of the world that didn't exist before. Because reading the testimony of abused women changed my understanding of the world and of my life, and women need to testify to abuses that still remain invisible.

But be warned: mine is not a straightforward story of discrete moral reckonings. All of the hurting is too mixed-up for that. I have done horrible things. I have hurt people I can't even apologize to anymore because it would hurt them too much just to see my face, or to read my name in an email. *And* I have been horribly hurt, damaged, in ways not unrelated to the fact that I hurt others.

I read many memoirs while preparing to write this one. I wonder how people write these crisp dramas, with their delicious villains and heroes, narrative arcs leading inexorably to the redemption of victimized narrators, many of whom emerge not just victorious but—having magnanimously forgiven the villains—saintly. These bestsellers suggest that maybe you don't get to write a memoir—or deserve an audience—unless you can prove that you are the only, or at least the most, victimized person in your story. That any morally questionable thing you've ever done can be explained by the fact that (1) you were young, (2) you were provoked unconscionably, (3) you were on drugs, (4) you are tearfully repentant, or (5) some combination of 1–4.

Fuck that.

How do you write a story in which it is impossible for anyone else in it to rewrite the whole thing with you as their villain? Isn't everyone the villain in someone's story?

Even if I am sometimes my own antihero, I'm going to write my whole messy story: all the things I didn't know could happen, all the things I didn't think anyone would believe, all the ways I suffered that people denied, all the terrible and brave and confusing things I did that I never thought I could do, and what brought me to do them. I am going to testify.

MAD
WIFE

PART 1
TUMULT

He is not a bad man,
and that, I realize suddenly,
is the root of my hurt.
He is not a bad man at all.
To describe him as evil or wicked or corrupted
would do a deep disservice to him.
And yet—

—CARMEN MARIA MACHADO,
"The Husband Stitch" (2017)

1. FELLOW CREATURE

A recent book argues that married people in the US are less satisfied than ever with their relationships because we have come to expect too much from them. We look to our romantic partners for everything, rather than relying on a diverse collection of people in our lives, from friends to family to church to social clubs. Its author, Eli Finkel, a social psychology professor, suggests three methods for increasing marital satisfaction, or what he calls "love hacks": expecting less from our partners; working to see them anew and enrich the relationship; and allowing others to satisfy the needs we have that our partners can't meet, including romantic and sexual ones. As someone who applied herself to making a good marriage with the same passion, dedication, research, and hard work that have undergirded a lifetime of professional accomplishment, only to suffer what my very experienced divorce attorney would call the most vindictive divorce she had ever seen, I am endlessly interested in such arguments. They make so much sense. It seems like they should work. Why didn't approaches like these, which I pored over in books, dutifully explored in therapists' offices, and practiced in my own marriage, work for me?

When Finkel presented his solution to marital discord on the popular *Hidden Brain* podcast, he and its host, Shankar Vedantum, unwittingly answered my question. Each film clip used to illustrate Finkel's ideal "all-or-nothing marriage" featured a long-suffering woman encouraging an egocentric man to cultivate *his* best self and live *his* best life. The clips portrayed men and women as equally fulfilled by these lopsided arrangements, with women even seduced by them. Recent divorce statistics suggest otherwise: a 2015 study found that women initiate divorce

69 percent of the time in the US—90 percent when the women are college-educated—and report being happier divorced than when married. Why are women today unhappy enough in their marriages to choose the personal, social, and financial suffering of divorce so much more often than do men? Certainly many factors contribute to this change, including the fact that more women today are better able to weather the financial consequences of divorce. Still, all other circumstances being equal—which of course they are not—this figure at least indicates that many more women than men are sufficiently unhappy in their marriages to go through the immense pain of ending them.

Perhaps women are beginning to wake from the trance of male entitlement, which our culture encodes as romantic love and experts accept as integral to healthy marriages. Waking up can be slow and disorienting. I spent much of my fifteen-year marriage bound to my husband by our shared conviction that his entitlement to female caretaking mattered more than my own happiness, desires, or pain. When I finally wrenched myself free I did so simply to survive, having held myself in misery so long that I was fantasizing and occasionally plotting my own death. But I did so utterly without understanding. By all appearances and proclamations, my husband loved me more than anything. Friends and family members were happy to remind me of this fact. Yet something secreted and deep moved me away from him, a feeling of disgust and terror that shamed me because I had no rational explanation for it. That inarticulable feeling was the beginning of my long, uneven awakening.

Once I had moved myself and my kids far enough from my marriage's explosive end that I was able to think clearly again, undistracted by constant alarms and the stress of plotting escape, a space opened up that could accommodate understanding. The space sat untenanted for a long time. But it was there when the occasional realization arrived, to welcome it in. It did not ask my permission. Kate Chopin describes this kind of unwilled epiphany in "The Story of an Hour," in which a woman who seems to be happily married, who would have described herself as such to others, reacts to the news that her husband has unexpectedly died in a railway accident. She fixes her "dull stare" on the view from her window: Chopin is careful to describe that gaze as "without reflection," a "suspension of intelligent thought." And yet, "There was something coming to her and she was waiting for it, fearfully." Why fearfully? Because it is entirely out of her control. Because she has no say in what the revelation might be, or whether she must admit it. Once she has entirely "abandoned herself," the revelation comes: "free! free! free! . . . Body and soul free!"

Chopin is also careful to inform us that the woman, who is identified by her married name, Mrs. Mallard, does not experience unbidden glory in her husband's death because he was abusive, for "She knew that she would weep again when she saw the kind, tender hands folded in death; the face that had never looked save with love upon her." Instead, she glories in the knowledge that "There would be no one to live for her during those coming years. . . . There would be no powerful will bending hers in that blind persistence with which men and women believe they have a right to impose a private will upon a fellow-creature." Kate Chopin is visionary not because she wrote in the nineteenth century a story about a woman feeling reborn at the prospect of freedom from her husband. She is visionary because she wrote in any century a story in which a woman who is married to—by her own account—a decent, loving man still experiences her marriage as a cage, a cruelty, a shackling, a structure that granted him permission to bend her. Mrs. Mallard feels this so deeply, and her new freedom refashions her sense of self so completely, that when her husband walks through the door at the end of the story, she dies.

It is one thing to say that many of the abuses and violences of marriage remain invisible to society and to those who suffer them because they do not leave physical marks: emotional battering, threats of physical violence, terrorizing. It is quite another to say that marriage as an institution, today as much as when Chopin was writing, provides a structure in which one's use of a "powerful will" to "bend" the other to suit one's needs is so normalized that an otherwise kind, loving person can commit the violence of denying their partner's autonomy without being considered monstrous by anyone, both spouses included. Literature and culture have recorded many ways in which both men and women seek to bend each other in marriage, using methods deemed societally acceptable for each. Tropes of the nagging or manipulative wife stack up nicely next to tropes of the physically violent or emotionally abusive husband. And all kinds of emotional and physical abuse occur in relationships between all kinds of people, regardless of their expressed sexuality or gender, race, ethnicity, and social or economic factors. But a patriarchal culture such as ours, in which men are taught to exert their will and women are taught to give, to accommodate, to caretake, and to submit, weaponizes male entitlement while normalizing it. The result is unequally armored selves waging grossly unequal battles of will.

Marriage compounds these inequities. In any long-term heterosexual relationship, male entitlement and the power that accompanies it can accrue invisibly over years. Our continued consecration of legal marriage, quite in spite of its continually declining survival rate, further legitimizes the patriarchal power dynamics on which it is founded and which keep it plugging along in a culture whose assumptions about gender, sex, and power are morphing all around it. Heterosexual marriage, then, can easily become a structure in which "good men" feel justified in getting their needs met by any means necessary, and "good women" are those who submit and ignore the resulting injuries and indignities.

Throughout the slow burn and volcanic end of my marriage, and as I picked my way on blistering feet through its smoldering after-years, the story of my marriage was the story of my own abusive power, my disregard for my husband's needs, and my willingness to hurt others to meet my needs. It was the grotesquerie of a woman feeding her appetites while cruelly denying her husband's. My husband wrote that story, and I swallowed it whole, like a Tums chaser sent down to neutralize the sickening fizz of everything I'd had the audacity to eat on my own. Left out of his story were all the ways he had already bent me to breaking, submissions I had blankly allowed, each one sinking unremarked into an unsoundable pit that became a roiling core of bile. Because I could not account for it, I accepted my husband's explanation: the bitterness was essentially mine; it was the bubbling up of all that was toxic and unnatural in me, a gross manifestation of my failures as a caretaking wife.

Years after the eruption, when I had acquired the calm, unreflective gaze of Mrs. Mallard and my soul began to register the gift of its own freedom, the revelations that flooded in unbidden were complicated and sinister. I had loved my husband and he had loved me. He had once been kind and tender. But he had been willing to bend me, and I had been willing to submit, in ways our marriage as we conceived of it could accommodate but that my love for him could not.

Writing about being raped by an acquaintance, Stacey May Fowles notes how absurd it is to ask herself—or to be asked by others—whether she said no enough times, whether she said it properly, whether she was sufficiently convincing. In her mind's obsessive replay of that experience, she counts sixteen times she said no. You would think it would take even fewer repetitions of no to escape unwanted sex from your husband, who supposedly loves you. In the course of our fifteen-year marriage, I'm sure I said no more than sixteen times, including outside sexual situations, such as in conversation with each other and with our counselor, as we discussed our increasingly uneven desire for sex. Once, momentarily emboldened by the presence of our therapist, I screwed up every ounce of my courage and said my deepest, darkest truth: "When we have sex, I feel like I'm being violated." My husband responded to my vulnerable admission exactly as Fowles's rapist responded to her. Addressing the therapist and bypassing me altogether, he declared with a verbal eyeroll, "She's always so melodramatic," dispatching all my pain with one sneering word. When Fowles tried to communicate how violated she felt by her experience, her rapist "accused [her] of being *fucking dramatic*." As my husband did countless times over the nearly twenty years we spent together, Fowles's rapist counselled her "not to be so emotional."

In 2003, when we were eight years married, I dragged my husband and me into couples counseling because I was beginning to register the painful death of our emotional intimacy, while he was complaining about our insufficient sexual intimacy. Weeks of stilted attempts at emotional connection without pressure for sex, recommended by our therapist, resulted only in increased conflict. Finally, my husband offered, or insisted upon, his own solution: "The thing you need is really complicated and difficult and it's not something I can do. I've tried. But the thing I need is quick and easy. Why can't you just give me the thing I need?"

His logic here was airtight, and I was unable to resist it. To refuse him would be selfish and cruel, even irrational, quick and easy as the thing he needed was. Why was I making such a big deal about a few minutes out of my day? I had no context or language for understanding or articulating why the thing he wanted was not at all easy for me to give. So I acquiesced, like Fowles did to her rapist. But unlike Fowles, I acquiesced many times over the years that passed between the death of my desire for my husband and the day I was finally able to leave. I did not say no sixteen times on every occasion. On many occasions, I didn't say no at all. But as Fowles asks of her rape, "Exactly how many times did I need to say no to make what happened to me wrong and worthy of care?"

"Consent" is a fraught term requiring delicate consideration. And yet I think it is fair for me to say without turning equivocating somersaults that I did not consent to a lot of the sex I had with my husband during the last several years of our marriage. It was more that I didn't *not* consent. I had told him in the therapist's office that sex felt violating. We continued to struggle rather obviously with our emotional disconnection. During this time, I did not say "Now I want to have sex with you," or "I no longer feel violated when we have sex; it feels great, hurrah!" I did not initiate sex and blatantly tried to avoid it as often as possible. I waited until my husband was in another room to undress, so as not to arouse him or be available for a drive-by groping. I slept clinging to the edge of the bed, preferring to risk falling on the wood floor rather than make accidental contact with his excitable groin. For years when we did have sex, I refused to kiss him or look at him. That was our agreement: you can fuck me, but you can't kiss me and I don't have to pretend to like it.

Is that consent?

Several years into our marriage, here's what our sex looked like:

I'm reading in bed. This night, I have not heard his footsteps on the stairs in time to turn the light off and feign sleep before his arrival in the bedroom. He undresses and gets into bed next to me, pressing his body alongside mine. I continue reading. He begins to caress my body. I do not look at him or acknowledge him in any way. His caresses become targeted. He knows how my body works; there was a time long ago when I enjoyed having sex with him. I do not want to have sex with him now and have not wanted to for a long time. He knows this. I ignore what he is doing as long as possible, focusing all my attention on my book, the words on the page, the shapes of the paragraphs, the work my brain is doing. I take refuge there, in my mind, while he runs through his little program on my body. He pushes buttons methodically, as if entering a code into a super-special but not very complicated machine. Now I've put the book down, one hand holding it across my chest in a kind of defense posture. My other arm lies still by my side. My head is turned away, lest he forget the no-kissing rule. I do not release the book and put my arms around him. I do not caress him. But I am not storming out: he continues. I need this to end as quickly as possible so I curl up in my mind, eyes shut, far away from the machine of my body. A fly on the ceiling would see a splayed, naked, immobile woman, head turned, eyes squeezed shut, face intensely focused, and a man doing urgent things to her body. (Does this look like consensual sex?) My face is focused because I'm trying to animate the body remotely, like a puppet or an avatar. I'm trying to register the sensations generated in the body by the code as something pure and wholly unrelated to the tenacious operator hunched near the foot of the bed. We both need my body to perceive the impersonally pleasurable output of the code. My husband needs my vagina to get wet so that when he jams his penis in, it will feel good for him and he can come. He needs to feel loved, after all. I need to get wet and sometimes come because I need this not to be rape.

Without digressing into the relatively intellectual question of whether or not this kind of sex is rape, and by which and whose definition, I want to describe what this kind of sex felt like for me. Because no matter what we call this kind of sex—even if you refuse to allow that it is nonconsensual—it undeniably causes profound physical, emotional, and existential suffering. And it is primarily that suffering that I want you to be able to imagine. When my husband entered the bedroom and caught me awake, I felt enormous dread. (Over several years such nightly dread on its own might be considered traumatic.) When he began to touch my body, signaling his desire and expectation, I felt aversion. Aversion gradually intensified to disgust as he continued. I did not want him to be touching me at all, so the longer he stroked and kissed and sucked my most private parts in pursuit of his pleasure and in the face of my demonstrated antipathy, the greater became my revulsion. Way deep down, where I could not even see or feel it until nearly a decade later, in tandem with my revulsion grew my rage. However passive my presence at this event might have looked from the outside, it actually required serious work from me, just not the kind of work one does when sex is fun. Along with the focused effort of casting myself out of my body came the significant work of holding the body still, resisting the urge to slap away hands and mouth and dick and flee, the work of fixing my body in place and allowing the molestation to continue. Anyone who has had their erogenous areas stimulated when they're not willing or ready should be able to empathize with this feeling, if not its intensity: it's like enduring surgery unanesthetized while having to hold yourself in place on the table.

At a certain point, if I had been able to vacate the body sufficiently to let the code do its work, the unthinking space of orgasm sometimes presented itself as the surest escape. It offered the twin benefits of temporarily drowning out my disgust and hurrying my husband along to the end of his pleasure and my ordeal. I took it when possible. After that long animal moment, in which I was not a woman being violated by a man who said he loved her, in which I was more the machine spitting out a rapturous code that had been methodically entered into it, I was cruelly dropped back into the body that had caused the whole fucking nightmare. It was sticky now, the body. I could no longer deny what had happened, or my part in it. My husband was content, glowing, already drifting into a satisfied sleep, like a full-bellied baby in his mother's arms, quietly belching her milk. I was wide awake, equally disgusted with myself and with him and revolted to the point of nausea: once I had to dart directly from bed to bathroom to retch into the toilet. Back in bed, whether or not I had dry-heaved on that particular occasion, I would start to feel enormous relief. I knew I could sleep in the next morning, unmolested. I would not be woken in the middle of the night by a penis prodding me in the dark. The pleasure of anticipating these hours of autonomy over my body and selfhood was what I received in exchange for the minutes in which I was expected to forfeit my right to both.

One of the most wonderful things about my life today—it can still surprise me—is that those years are now themselves many years ago. For fifteen years I have not suffered unwanted, coerced, nonconsensual sex. It is only the space of these years in which I have controlled my own body that has allowed me to begin to comprehend what being denied that control meant back then and how that experience affects me still. Submitting to unwanted sex with someone who knew it was unwanted made me feel— during the sex and, over time, in general—like a thing, a vessel for my husband's needs. A sex doll, made wholly of orifices. It made me feel like I was not a person. I no longer existed, not as a complete human being with needs, feelings, opinions, beliefs, agency, or anything like intrinsic value. I had been replaced by my body, the body he constantly desired, the one that told him he was loved. My body became for me a detested thing that repeatedly betrayed me while serving his pleasure, and at some point I left it to live elsewhere. I no longer attempted to relate to him as a whole person; he didn't need that from me anyway. Submitting to unwanted sex like this, for years, with a man who knew it was unwanted but was emotionally fulfilled by it, broke my idea of everything—who I was, who he was, what our relationship meant, what sex should be, what love is.

It is very difficult to heal from any traumatic sexual experience. Healing from *this* kind of sexual trauma is difficult in particular ways. For starters, it is unlikely that anyone who has lived through such a sexual relationship will initially believe that trauma has taken place. We are taught our whole lives, by our families, friends, the law, and all popular culture, that sex is an integral part of any romantic relationship and required for a healthy marriage. Women are taught that men's drive for sex is biological and important and it is our duty to satisfy that need, especially in marriage. Sex therapists today still advise women to consent to unwanted sex in marriage in the interest of "relationship maintenance," suggesting that your painful unequal sexual relationship with your husband is not just normal but salubrious, like regular visits to the dentist. If at some point you are able to admit that what you experienced certainly *feels* wrong and even traumatic, it will be difficult to figure out why, or who or what hurt you. Without a violent stranger holding you down or threatening physical harm, whom do you blame for your feeling that you've been violated? Not your husband, who didn't physically harm you (outside the unwanted sex) and reminds you—for years afterward—that he loved you more than anything. You are likely to blame yourself, because after all, you didn't fight or flee; you allowed the sex that you found so painful. You participated in your own subjection.

There are, of course, no "better" or "worse" kinds of sexual violation. But there are many different kinds, and they differ in terms of the physical and emotional violence used to get the sex, the relationship (or lack thereof) between perpetrator and victim, and thus the nature of the damage done. Sexual abuse in a long-term relationship happens not one unexpected time but regularly over years, becoming a pattern that will redefine the relationship and the victim's understanding of sex and of themselves. It makes you fear not dark alleys or frat parties but lying in your own bed every night next to your husband—or your future partner.

It conditions you to expect abuse from the person who loves you and re-wires you to experience "normal" sex—sex you used to consent to and that you wonder whether you're consenting to even as you're suffering—as frightening, disgusting, nauseating, emotionally painful, and a source of dread. My experience is typical of women who experience sexual violence inside relationships: studies show that women who are assaulted by a *current* intimate partner experience PTSD, stress, and dissociation at higher rates than those assaulted by a stranger or former partner.

Because you normalize it in order to endure it, you feel the suffering but can't understand why. Meanwhile, part of your inability to recognize what is happening as traumatic will stem from the normalizing efforts of the abuser. The perpetrator—your husband—will construct and maintain from that moment forward, over all the subsequent years, a narrative in which no harm was done. And if, despite all of these normalizing efforts by culture, your partner, the law, and yourself, you do manage to eventu-ally identify the sexual relationship as morally wrong and justifiably trau-matic, you will be completely alone in your suffering. There is no public recognition of sexual abuse within marriage, no one to report it to or gain sympathy from, no hashtag collecting reports of it.

But submitting to unwanted sex in this way *is* sexual trauma, and it scars in deep, abiding ways. My life partner of over a decade is a kind, loving man who has never imposed himself on me in any way, and yet for years having sex with him could trigger traumatic flashbacks in which I felt terrified, confused, outside my body, and unsure who was touching me or where I was. I can't have sex in the dark, where I might lose track of what is happening—am I participating in mutual lovemaking or en-during something torturous? Am I enjoying this or do I need to flee my body and hide until it's over? In the absence of visible evidence, I can end up shaking and weeping without understanding why.

I have regular dreams in which my former husband pursues me slowly, methodically, through the halls of some oppressive house. The house is always changing but the pursuit does not. I back blindly away from him as he presses inexorably toward me, fixing my gaze to him, his face a fea-tureless blank. Even in my dreams, I experience his offense from outside my body: I see myself holding a massive butcher's knife straight out of an '80s slasher film. As he leans into me, I wave the knife at him, and huge, gelatinous pieces of him fall noiselessly away. He doesn't seem to feel their loss or miss them. They do not reduce him in size. He keeps on coming at me, relentlessly, and I know that any house I enter, he will be there. I will never be safe. These are my nightmarish "love hacks," what I did to myself to maintain a marriage that was truly a nightmare. I bound myself to a monster and became murderous myself in my attempts to evade him.

That dream, and the others like it that I continue to have, reveals more about the long-term effects of those years than do my fraught sexual experiences with my current partner: My former husband did not simply damage my sex life. He damaged my sense of who I am and of my place in the world. He demonstrated that I did not have the right to choose what happened to my body, to protect myself, to assert my own needs and limits. He persuaded me not to participate in sex so much as to participate in my own subjugation and unselfing, to consent to my own dehumanization, to willingly give up my autonomy and integrity—almost literally, considering how much time I spent outside my body during sex—in order to oblige him and demonstrate my care. He taught me that marriage, love, and domesticity in general are sites of power and control, where he could do whatever it took to force my compliance, and I was still expected to love him, that love was meant to contain such things. And I did love him, for as long as I possibly could, despite and through the coerced sex. Which means that he forced me to learn not only how to lie still when I wanted to run, through rage, aversion, and nausea, but to equate these feelings and what I was doing, and what was being done to me, with love. He ruined love for me.

2. LOVE STORY

Beverly Gooden begins her talks about domestic violence and #WhyI Stayed, the hashtag she originated in 2014, by projecting her wedding photos so that they loom enormously behind her. When I saw her speak at my university, a student asked in the Q&A if it was painful for her to look at those pictures now. She said she hadn't looked at the photos since she built the talk a long time ago; she knows when to click to advance the slides. I thought about how important it is for her to begin with those wedding photos, her younger self smiling, so in love, radiant next to the man who would later threaten and beat her. I thought, students need to see that abusers start out as men we love. No one ever teaches you that.

You think that women who wind up in abusive relationships must not be very smart or are tragically imperceptive. Or perhaps—let's not blame them—they grew up in abusive families and don't know what love is, or how to recognize abuse. They're unaware, in denial, naïve—not thoughtful, sensitive, well-read, and wise for their age, like you.

Watching Ms. Gooden speak about her abusive husband without meeting his gaze over her shoulder, I wondered: How do I show readers that once I was in love, once he was kind and treated me like I was a real person, once we were genuinely happy, without turning to look, without describing what I see when I do?

I wish I could, like Bev Gooden, insert some photos here from our happy years to show you that we had them. I could spend one day on a hell-bent archeological dig, rooting out photo albums from the depths of my closet where they lurk beneath artifacts from my current life because I can neither get rid of them nor bear to look at them. Taking care not to cut myself on their sharp edges, I would sift through the photos for representative moments. I'd convert treacherous images into digital information, beam them to the publisher, and never look at them again. For a crazy moment, I indulged the fantasy and its poetic justice: I could put little black bars over my former husband's face to protect his privacy, like he did when he posted photos of me on swinging websites without my knowledge. But that would be wrong.

One of the many tragedies of a vitriolic divorce, especially one that extends the dysfunction of the marriage into more than a decade of punishing postmarital years, is that the continuing fear and anguish of the divorce make it impossible to remember the happiness and love that founded the marriage. I hope that one day the part of my brain that contains those joyful memories—for they must still be there, neurologically speaking—will unclench, unbox, come online again. I'd like for my history to contain fewer blank pages; I'd like to move through the rest of my life as less of a fragment of myself. Those missing years contain many of the most exciting and meaningful parts of my life: traveling around the world, earning a PhD, becoming a mother. The first several years of each of my children's lives are mostly lost to those blank pages. How to remember the intoxicating scent of my babes' downy heads, the peach fuzz of their pudding thighs, their serious eyes locked on mine—our animal bodies the universe entire—without also remembering the man who was and was not also there, and all that led up to their invention? This protracted trauma makes of my life a hackneyed time-travel story: change one thing and you risk erasing your whole past. Or a real-life version of *Eternal Sunshine of the Spotless Mind*, with one crucial difference: my children persist beyond the reprogramming to remind me of all that I have lost of them and of myself, and of a deep love I once treasured.

So, as much as I want to write for you a narrative of my marriage before the disaster, to remind us all of the dangerous lie of "happily ever after" and the terrifying truth that good people can do terrible things, I can't. But I can translate into narrative the artifacts of those years; I can share with you the story I was telling myself when I created all of those photo albums.

———

HANDWRITTEN TITLE PAGE: "OUR FIRST YEAR TOGETHER"

Opening photo: Our senior year in college, the two of us posing with friends of mine we'd gone dancing with. He was on my campus for a debate tournament and, remembering me from high school, had called me up. The next day we'd build a conversation that would take us straight into dinner and keep us up all night. I'd share my dream of finding a man who'd treat me as an equal, and he'd declare himself a feminist. Just before the sun would begin to peek through the hotel blinds, he'd reach out to barely brush his fingertips against my electrified cheek before asking if he could kiss me. No man had ever treated me with such respect.

Photo of us dressed for a Roaring Twenties college party: He stands behind me in a comically oversized zoot suit, trying to look grown-up and cool. I'm sitting in a flapper dress on a low bench, all legs caught up in fishnets, showing off my garter belt with holster and tiny plastic gun. Later that visit, or the next, I will invite him to have sex with me on that little bench in my dorm room. I am experienced and he is not, so I teach him, and we work at it till we get it right.

Photos of his parents' hundred-year-old cottage on a New England coast: The screened porch where we ate late breakfasts after long mornings of lovemaking, the couch where we lay entangled and reading on rainy afternoons, the little table where we worked on a thousand-piece puzzle all week, cracking each other up with silly jokes. The tiny bathroom where I begged for privacy through the closed door till he burst in and sat down, laughing, right on top of my lap. A mortifying violation. I shook it off and told myself it was romantic: he couldn't suffer any barriers between us.

A page of only captions: These continue the fairy tale I've been writing throughout the album, starting with "The Night We Re-Met" and progressing to "Our First Anniversary," which I will document at album's end. Ignoring all digressions—like our brief breakup—my captions resolutely unfurl that universal story, the one Rick and I didn't write but were only stepping into, in which the person you meet in your twenties is the one

you follow forever and moments of romantic and sexual intensity prophecy permanent compatibility. "You held me in the summer's moonlight
and asked me to rejoin your life," intones the album. "Whether for right
or for weakness or for romance, the decision had been made." By whom?

<h2>ENGAGEMENT ALBUM</h2>

Photo of the engagement ring I designed for him: Two separable but in-
terlocking bands, reminding us that in becoming one we would remain, in
some significant way, two. Painfully sundered by his job training, we were
living over a thousand miles apart, and the distance had clarified the am-
biguity that had fogged his departure. I arrived for one much-anticipated
visit planning to propose to him. I was proud of myself for being so bold
and liberated in taking the lead, choosing my own marital fate.

Photo of the engagement ring he designed for me: Two loops combining
into one solid, undividable whole. Soon after I arrived, I intuited that he
shared my plan. I carried the ring I'd brought in my pocket everywhere
we went all weekend so I'd have it ready for his big moment. Heading to a
restaurant for dinner, I stuck it in my purse and waited to see what would
happen with dessert. In a hot tub under a starry sky, I stashed it in a towel
and tried not to lose it in the dark. All the while, I held my breath and
hoped he would not choose such gauche locations for our life-defining
moment. It didn't occur to me to choose the time and place myself.

Photo of the moment he orchestrated, at the top of a massive granite dome
on a bright and windy day: He prefaced his proposal with a poem he'd
written, which I later glued on the inside cover of our wedding album.
Now I see that even as he was asking me to join my life to his, he was acknowledging that I had already been struggling to feel his love: "What
is it I love about you? You ask me to tell," he wrote. "You wonder what
I see, what I feel." The moment that began our happily-ever-after in the
story of this album was also the original iteration of a pattern we would
repeat, with increasing futility and distance, until I left: "Please express
your love for me in a way I can feel," I'd say. His response increasingly
echoed this poem. "You must know with absolute certainty that your love

is matched," said the poem. Must I? "I may never answer completely, but that is the beauty." Is it?

Photo of us kissing, newly engaged: After he put his ring on my finger, I removed the uncomfortable lump from my shorts pocket and produced my ring for him, laughing and blushing a little with embarrassed pleasure. We noted the similarity of our ring designs, marveling at how connected we were, our minds thinking exactly alike.

WEDDING ARTIFACTS

Photo of me in my wedding gown approaching the gazebo, where he waits: I refused to be "given away," not caring whether it broke my father's heart. In the photo, my sister is behind me, holding my long, creamy train, and his sister walks in front with a pillow bearing his ring, her hair wreathed in tiny white and yellow flowers. My sister's pink dress blooms against the deep green of the forest around us. The chiffon flowing down from my shoulders to meet at the base of my spine looks like wings. We are a trio of fairies emerging from the sacred wood.

Wedding video: I draw the line at watching it now, even if I could find a VHS player, but I remember it well—how we told the story of our meeting, *When Harry Met Sally*–style (a requirement for '90s weddings), shaping our lives up to that point as fairy tale, as fate, everything leading to this. Just before the ceremony I look straight at the videographer and say, smiling but not joking, "Whatever you do, don't call me 'Mrs. Rick.'" I had been adamant about not changing my name and never tired of explaining why to anyone who would listen. Our families were well aware of my reasons. When the video finally reached us in our far-flung first marital home, I was heartbroken to see the record of our beautiful day capped off by what felt like my own violent erasure: *Congratulations, Mr. and Mrs. Rick!* Rick called his parents, who had received their copy weeks before. Had they not noticed? we asked. They did, and they thought it was hilarious. They couldn't wait to hear about my reaction.

————

The spines of the next few albums I unearth are cracked and distorted, their pages bursting with photos of us posing for each other all over Asia, Africa, and Europe. Every time I look back at this chapter, I feel remiss about one or another photo I've left out. Here's one of the more important ones: Rick, sunburned and bearded, sitting in the sun in Arusha the day we came down from Kilimanjaro, where he had saved my life by dragging me out of that blasted crater when I was black-lipped and nearly unconscious with altitude sickness. But I don't think you need to see any more to get the picture: we loved each other and had a healthy sex life for a long time.

Also, these albums are difficult to deal with. Seventeen years after our fairy tale began, Rick tore them up and tried to light them on fire.

––––––––––

The first time I read Carmen Maria Machado's "The Husband Stitch," it totally overwhelmed me. I had never seen anyone, in fiction or nonfiction, communicate something so close to my own experience: how the nice guy, the man you love and who loves you more than anything, can become the monster who kills you. Essentially it's a story about stories, primarily fairy tales. Our narrator knows them all and tells many of them to us, pointing out how stories teach women how to be, what we are and are not permitted to do, what to fear, how we will be punished if we misbehave. Most of these stories are about what we are and are not allowed to do with and decide about our bodies. Our narrator is a liberated woman who defies these stories and their warnings even in her youth. She chooses and initiates her first sexual relationship, even bringing herself to orgasm when the young man she has chosen doesn't yet know how. She teaches him how to please her; their love grows alongside their passion. Married, they become even more insatiable, even while she's pregnant, even after their child is born. Her husband is also a loving father.

It can seem like Machado has written just another fairy tale, a happily-ever-after story in which the characters' lives become a cornucopia of impossibly perfect pleasures (the awesome pregnancy sex being especially dubious). Students want to read it that way: The couple is really happy, so what's the point? My work in the classroom is to help them see that the point is exactly how hard it is to find the point. The nightmare at the heart of the fairy tale can be difficult to see, and every fairy tale contains a nightmare—an oppression whose repression enables the fairy tale. The narrator's husband loves her so much, and she is so happy. Except for a couple of things.

Our narrator has a ribbon around her neck, which her husband tries to touch the first time they meet. She tells him very clearly he cannot; it belongs to her. Over the years of their happy marriage, he repeatedly asks to touch it, accuses her of "keeping secrets," and begs for access to every part of her, including this. When he holds her down and fondles the ribbon, she feels "as if he is massaging my sex," violated, like he is raping her. Exhausted after years of saying no and being pressed and vaguely bullied, she finally gives in and tells him to "do what you want." It is the end of her.

The other thing is that he has already done what he wanted with her body, even before he pulls the ribbon. After the birth of her son, without consulting her, her husband accepts the doctor's offer of a "husband stitch"—a medical procedure in which a doctor extends an episiotomy repair past what is necessary, to leave a woman's body "nice and tight" for her husband's pleasure. It can also leave the woman with chronic pain, which is why it's called "the husband stitch" and not "the mother stitch."

In thirty-one pages of bliss, these two briefly mentioned exceptions can get lost, just as a few intensely significant moments of overrun boundaries can get lost in fifteen years of an otherwise "happy" marriage. But what do these two exceptions in the story mean? That however much he loved her—even if he "truly" loved her, in his own mind—he never actually saw her as a separate, autonomous self. He never acknowledged her right to decide which parts of herself to share or hold back, or her right to decide what happened to her body. He confused love with the right to trespass, to consume, to invade. Even once students see the significance of these details, they find the end shocking: Why does she have to die? I try to get them to see that of course she has to die; he won't stop until he owns all of her, and she knows that. The more interesting question is, why does she let him pull the ribbon?

A few years ago, after publishing a short piece on sexual abuse in marriage on Vox.com, I agreed to speak to my colleague's class in a course about domestic violence. This was the first time I spoke about my experience publicly. As I walked across the quad toward the classroom, it hit me, what an enormous thing I was about to do by talking about my personal experience of sexual abuse at my own university. I was essentially outing myself in some way, as someone with a history I had barely begun to admit to myself. I felt vulnerable and afraid, of things I didn't even have time to identify. But I was committed to using my experience to help other women avoid it, so I kept walking, then sat down in the large circle of my colleague's students and told my story.

I shared with these young people a very short version of what I detail in this book: what my sex life in my marriage felt like to me, how damaging it was, how I couldn't understand that damage until I learned about sexual violence from other people and from other women's stories. I quoted statistics about domestic violence, sexual assault, and rape, figures they must have known better than I, at the end of a semester spent studying these topics. I explained how my experience felt like a version of all of those things, even though it has yet to be recognized as such in our culture or even academically. I shared more of my own feelings than I have ever shared with students, hoping to impress upon them how damaging this societally acceptable behavior is and that we need to take it seriously. I tried to speak in a way that these young people, full of hope and romantic expectations for their sexual and emotional relationships, as I had been, might hear and remember. I hoped they might be empowered to see and react to the signs as I could not. My colleague and I planned for me to speak for about ten minutes; prompted by students' earnest questions, I wound up talking with them for about an hour and a half.

I left the classroom feeling completely wrung out but satisfied, even a little exhilarated. I had been brave and set aside my own vulnerability to help young people go through life a bit more clear-eyed than I had done. From the moment I decided to write the article for Vox.com, that was all I had wanted to do: Use my experience to help others. Make a difference.

So it was shocking, and devastating, to see how profoundly misheard I had been. The next day, I received an email from a student in that class, thanking me for my "moving talk" and "honesty." The student, a woman, spent the rest of the email offering me insight and advice for fixing my sexual problem. "Many conditions affect cisgender women and cause dyspareunia," she wrote. "These cause painful sexual intercourse and other health and psychological issues. They are underdiagnosed and characterized by women taking part in sex despite serious chronic pain. I believe this happens because of the lack of emphasis on female pleasure in heterosexual intercourse." The student ended the email with several links about living with vulvodynia, one of those painful conditions.

At no time during that hour and a half did I mention painful sex (which I have been lucky never to experience). I also didn't talk about my whole sex life, how supremely healthy and enjoyable it had been for a very long time, as this did not seem appropriate in front of students, some of whom I might see in my own classroom one day. My focus had been simple: I had not wanted to have sex for a long time during which I submitted to sex anyway, and this damaged me and my marriage. It had not occurred to me how students—young people—might fill in that lacuna: Why would she not want to have sex with her husband? Of course there are many reasons why a woman who had once been happily married might stop wanting to have sex with her husband, but these are primarily reasons that people who have not weathered a long relationship are unable to imagine. This student, for all her kind intentions, was telling me that it was simply not possible for her to imagine that a loving relationship with a healthy sex life could become the *emotionally* painful thing my marriage and sex life became. She could not imagine that love could die so completely that enacting its forms could feel like rape. In her mind, it must have felt like rape to me because I was being physically injured and was too embarrassed to speak up about it.

Contemplating how seriously this student had misunderstood my message, I realized that I could not have imagined these things at her age either. In my twenties, I might also have looked at the middle-aged woman sitting and speaking at the top of the circle with pity: She had never been wild as I was; she had never been free. She had never learned to enjoy her body. Poor thing. And now her vagina was broken and needed to be fixed. Or maybe—and here's the misogyny worming its way into even the brains of self-styled young feminists—she needs help with her "psychological issues." I get it; this student is young. She has no idea how violating it feels when the man you love keeps fondling your ribbon.

What's funny about this whole depressing misunderstanding and all that it says about the myopia of youth and the pervasiveness of misogyny is that, in writing this bit, I discovered that "dyspareunia" is actually the perfect word to describe what I suffered. Doctors use it to mean "painful sexual intercourse," but its Latin roots mean something altogether different. *Para*, to lie beside. *Euno*, combination of "bed" and "to have, to hold." *Dys*, bad, abnormal, difficult, failure. It felt difficult and bad, a failure, to lie in bed beside this man who was no longer able to hold me without killing me.

3. BETRAYAL

When Rick and I had been married for about three years, in 1998, our friend Alex had a brief affair that absolutely set her on fire. Alex and her husband James were our closest friends, so we experienced every step of the exhilaration and devastation that unfolded. While it nearly tore them apart when James found out about the affair, her electric awakening was something to behold. She had confided all of it to me—her struggle, her excitement, her eventual decision to plunge in, her rapture. When I communicated to Rick the sexual awakening she was experiencing, it piqued something in both of us.

We had just emerged from our own long stretch of adventures: living and traveling in Asia and Europe, climbing Kilimanjaro, skiing Austrian slopes at Christmas, backpacking around Thailand till we ran out of money for beer. Back in the States for my PhD program, we found that all the charm of our new home paled in comparison to pulmonary edema in Kili's crater or camping in the Schwarzwald so impulsively that we forgot our sleeping bags. We were restless. Rick was not nearly as good at philosophical conversation as he was at adventuring. And I was discovering that I wasn't so interested anymore in the nearly constant sex that had glued us together in the early years. We discussed solutions to our different dissatisfactions. Mine was quite a bit more conversational and emotional than sexual, but the Venn diagram of our desires only overlapped on sex: it was good to want an active sex life with my husband, but I was absolutely not allowed to want or demand a fulfilling emotional life. After receiving Alex's missives from the electrifying land of extramarital sex, and reaching for something that would shock us back to life, Rick and I began to discuss the possibility of pursuing a new adventure together: swinging.

I've always been a bit of an adventurer. It was my idea to climb Kili and to make a pilgrimage to Isak Dinesen's house in Nairobi, where we were mugged in the street. I wrote a "Things to Do Before I Die" list when I was twelve and had ticked off several items by my early twenties. Many of them involved transgressing boundaries: living abroad, scuba diving. And then there was the delicious transgression of discovering sex at seventeen with my first love—on stairs, on a ladder, in cars, in the closet of the church choir room, with props and narration—despite my parents' fierce attempts to ruin every facet of it and shame me into compliance. My mother called me a whore decades before my husband did without killing my sexual openness. Rather than altering my behavior or beliefs around sex, my parents taught me how to perform acceptability so I could endure their pressures and judgment while holding space to make my own choices. Nearly twenty years later, I would fall back on that learned proficiency in splitting to preserve myself in the face of Rick's pressures, and he would exploit it in securing my compliance. But before all that, when I was newly married and my sexual desire had been owned and contorted by my parents but not yet by my husband, sex still felt to me like an avenue for expansion and exploration. So I wasn't shocked at Rick's suggestion, in our little grad-school cottage, that we give swinging a try. I played along with only minor trepidation—until I heard the voice of a man we were interviewing for the part on the phone. My stomach dropped; I left the room. I told Rick no. I said, we have this precious, pure thing between us, and once we break it, it's gone forever. I recall he was not entirely convinced by this argument. But he didn't push me. Not yet.

Seven years, one PhD, two children, and much unhelpful couples counseling later, the idea of swinging would enter our increasingly ailing marriage again. By then I would have discovered, first, that Rick was unable to be emotionally moved by his own children, and then—like the *drip, drip* of water torture—that what I had taken for his deep love of me was dangerously superficial. That he loved me desperately, like a starving lion loves the gazelle that stands between it and death: it doesn't much matter that it's a gazelle; and the gazelle can't survive it.

The man with whom I had in the beginning stayed up all night talking about urgent ideas turned out to be a gifted talker and a preternaturally gifted faux listener. He could mime attention only to a point, which we reached with the arrival of our first child. I had the uncanny experience of watching Rick relate to our baby as he related to me: *as if* he loved him, *as if* he would do anything for him, but with little discernible emotional bond. After an exceedingly long day during which I had comforted our wailing baby, taken him on an expedition to Whole Foods, occupied him while making organic baby food, played with him, insisted on the detested "tummy time," read to him, sung to him, and lined up his cars and trucks on the street-themed carpet approximately one hundred times, Rick would slouch through the door after an exhausting day of graduate school. Having recently completed that stage of grad school myself, I knew exactly how exhausting it was compared to a day alone with a crying baby. I would hand the baby to Rick, desperate for a few minutes during which no one was grabbing my breast, screaming in my ear, or vomiting down my back. Rick would sit down on the couch and turn on the TV, baby in his lap. Or he would sit in front of the computer and play video games, baby facing the screen. Or he would lie down for a little nap with the baby—who had cried most of the day, so of course he was exhausted—and make the most adorable picture of loving fatherhood you could imagine. What I cannot remember seeing him do is look in the face of his baby with love, talk to him like a person, or express the kind of care and attachment that builds into real bonds between human beings.

He was so good at *acting* like a loving husband and father. I didn't understand why watching my husband with our baby made me so sad. Nor could I figure out why I felt so alone in this parenting onslaught, since people constantly applauded Rick's impressive parental efforts. When he took the baby to the grocery store so I could clean the house with both hands, total strangers—women—would stop him in the aisles to shower him with praise and gratitude, as if on behalf of all the world's beleaguered mothers. Not once did a stranger in a store, or an airport, or in a restaurant or doctor's office or mall compliment me for my impressive calm, patience, and selflessness as I comforted my baby in his second or fourth or seventh hour of crying. Nor did Rick express praise or gratitude that I did this heroic thing daily on next to no sleep for over a year, while doing all the other required things, minus some trips to the grocery store. I was just really good at my job.

What had begun as a true union, something we built and made anew together every day—our marriage—had become an arena in which I scrimmaged for resources with an opponent who was becoming a stranger.

Being a mother, however trying, meant something profoundly vital to me. I could not tell what being a father was to him, outside certain required actions and the oppressiveness of having drawn from the universe a shockingly difficult newborn. That the equal coparenting model we had promised each other failed to materialize was exhausting but not itself estranging: I suppose I never fully expected him to manage it. But his emotionless performance of fatherhood echoed and magnified the alienation I already felt from him but could not explain. It triggered something in me.

A year after our first son was born, in 2002, I spent marathon training runs with my closest friend trying to explain why I wanted a divorce. That I sincerely wished no harm for Rick but needed him to cease existing. Confused and ashamed about my feelings, I was unable to convince my friend that my reasons for wanting to end my marriage were sound. So I was also unable to convince myself, or to even consider actually leaving. But I remember the clarity of the feeling: I was married to an automaton who looked like a kind, successful man but was empty on the inside. The man kept his hungry eyes on me, and I could not leave. If I left, he would die. I'm not entirely sure I felt that only metaphorically.

I did tell Rick about my unhappiness, or I tried. I'm sure I stumbled and confused him too. But I was unhappy enough that I insisted we start couples therapy when I was just a few weeks pregnant with our second child. I described to the therapist how Rick routinely left the room in the middle of my sentences, as if I wasn't even speaking, and how he'd often reply to me by shifting to an entirely different topic. He fell asleep when we watched movies, and when we'd try again on one that moved me, at his suggestion, he'd fall asleep again. When I tried to discuss my writing or a novel that was blowing my mind, his gaze would drift away, and I'd know he was gone. He repeatedly asked questions about things I had just told him. Nothing that interested or moved me could hold his attention. *I* couldn't hold his attention. The therapist suggested he take medication for ADD, with which he had been diagnosed. I thought it helped; he stopped taking it because he disliked the side effects.

I came to feel as if I wasn't even there. And unless I was needed for some domestic chore, I really wasn't. There seemed to be nothing he needed from me and nothing I could give him that he wanted—until we went to bed. I told the therapist (and Rick) that I found having sex under these circumstances deeply disturbing. She suggested that we abstain and schedule weekly "emotional sharing" sessions instead. These were supposed to provide Rick with regular opportunities to make his emotional self visible to me and to build a bridge between us made of something besides body parts. Maybe scheduled emotionality works for some people, but I found the therapist's program worse than absurd. Watching my husband strain to concoct a little quasi-affective speech every week only made the gulf between us more apparent and his performance of intimacy more pronounced.

Meanwhile, a real and urgent opportunity for emotional sharing presented itself. At our first meeting with that therapist, I shared the overwhelming news that I was pregnant with twins. Rick and I were both graduate students with minimal income in an expensive city, and we had just started to recognize the enormous energy our high-needs first child was going to require. After the doctor showed me the two heartbeats on the ultrasound, I had gone home and gotten immediately sick. I could not imagine how I was going to write a dissertation, teach, take care of my demanding toddler, manage my disintegrating marriage, and take care of newborn twins, all at the same time, with no family help and little money. Before long I was tackling this problem in my usual way: doing research, finding resources, making a plan. I started imagining us as a family of, gulp, five. We'd probably need a different car, for starters. How would we afford that? But we would; I'd figure it out.

I spent the next week transforming the terrifying revelation into an occasion for excitement and joy. Once I could envision the necessary practical steps, I could allow myself to be overwhelmed not by fear but by the wonder of bringing two human beings into my life and my son's life. I imagined the boundless love I felt for my toddler multiplied by three, and it staggered me. So the doctor's report at my next ultrasound was a new kind of shock: one heartbeat, where two had been only a week before. My life as a mother of multiples was over before it had begun, and one of those lives I had been excited to meet would never exist. Worse, the loss of the fetus—there was a dead fetus in my body; that was another realization that was dawning—imperiled the life of the one that was still alive.

Women have miscarriages all the time. I had had one before the pregnancy that resulted in my first child. I do not mean to suggest that in losing the twin I suffered in any remarkable way. I suffered only in a way that women suffer every day, and like them, I suffered this privately and without support, because women still do not talk enough about what having a miscarriage can feel like. The banality of a miscarriage does not make it unremarkable to the woman who suffers it. For her it can be an enormous loss, of a future she'd imagined and a person she had already begun to relate to. If you wanted the pregnancy—a big "if" in a world where women are inhumanely forced by laws, culture, circumstances, or partners to have children they did not want to create—your body's transformation into an alien thing sparks a corresponding transformation in your sense of self. By the time your baby is first placed on your belly, you've had a months-long relationship with it. Losing a pregnancy, even early, even if, like me, you fight for women's reproductive rights and don't confuse a mass of cells with personhood, can mean letting go of complex narratives of self, future, and world.

If I had thought Rick would care, or even just listen, I would have told him all of these things during one of our weekly "emotional sharing" sessions. I tried to communicate some of it, but I could not elicit a single connected conversation about the fact that we had lost a future baby and might lose the other. He barely registered the fact, much less any emotional reaction to it, and this grief became, like so many others before and to come, a profound thing that had happened in the context of our relationship but that only I would carry. It might have brought us together but instead illustrated to me how absolutely alone I was.

Eventually, I gathered my courage and admitted my darkest truth to my husband in front of the therapist: "I have been thinking that I want a divorce." It was very hard to say that, especially with a new baby precariously in my belly. Rick stared straight ahead and said nothing. The therapist prodded, "Did you hear what your wife just said?" "She doesn't mean it," Rick explained. "She's exaggerating."

We had had a good sexual relationship in the early years. I had had my adventures with my first love, and he had had none, so we had done a lot of discovery together, and we were close. But that intensity fell off, as it does, so soon we were trying desperate things to rediscover the early passion. We took a sex game to the castle on the Rhine where we celebrated our first wedding anniversary—as if a bedroom in the converted turret of a real castle weren't enough—and then flirted with swinging a couple of years later. By the time our second child was born and my desire for Rick had disappeared with his ability to express care to me, things were dire. My defunct sexual desire was my fault and my problem—he was happy—so off I went to the doctor for hormonal testing (all was normal) and to the bookstore to read about sex after pregnancy and making marriage last. And I pulled us into couples counseling and timidly squeaked my truths: "I want a divorce," "When we have sex, I feel violated." When they had no effect, I blamed myself: I should have been more forceful, I should have made him understand how I felt. Only twenty years later, seeing all of this materialized in language, do I wonder: Who hears his wife say these things, even once, even timidly, and sleeps well that night, much less insists on sleeping with her?

In late 2005, ten years married and now with a baby and toddler, we were hanging out with our good friends Alex and James on the last night of their week-long visit. All the kids were sleeping—their one and our two—and we were a little high on the intimacy of all the shared years behind us and a lot drunk on the seven empty bottles of wine that had appeared as if out of a fog on the coffee table. We wound our way through the evening with increasingly charged talk about music and movies and sex, dallying in displacements of desire, in an intense version of the game played at many middle-aged dinner parties. The idea bubbled up: old friends, new configurations, why not? We had all been married long enough and were poorly matched enough to have reached the point at which marriage had become an endurance sport. The idea wicked off our skin, and Rick and James became giddy with anticipation. We were sprawled on the carpet by then—all that wine—and I remember James holding his toes and tumbling around like a toddler on Christmas morning. I was thirty-five and drunk to the gills, so of course I was aroused, but I was less giddy—now you'll start to see the train coming—than I was moved. In the pre-children years, James and I would sometimes end our dinner parties reading poetry aloud, with our bored spouses snoring next to us on the couches. I can't tell you what Rick was looking forward to with Alex or what had James so excited he couldn't sit still, but for me it was clear: It would be very nice to be physically intimate with a man who loved poetry. It would be very nice to have sex with a man who had a palpable soul.

Our grand transgressive plan exploded when Rick got alone with Alex and discovered she was not on board at all. Apparently, the three of us had been too drunk to notice that when we jumped aboard the magic carpet, she had decidedly remained on terra firma. She was shocked at the very idea, and hurt, and—here's another train car—she clearly felt threatened. We talked her down and she went to bed. Rick looked directly at me and said "Do whatever you need to do," then went to bed as well.

I was elated. I had carte blanche! James, however, had not read Rick's remark quite the same way I had and had gotten no such permission, snide or otherwise, from his wife. And however daring we liked to think of ourselves, we were bourgeois to the core. So James and I huddled on the couch and leaned dramatically on each other against walls and furniture till sunrise as we did the least offensive of the things we needed to do and analyzed why we must not do them. Lying down would have been the end of us.

The next morning, we four sat and discussed what had happened and not happened and why. Alex and I cried, James obfuscated, Rick sat stone-faced, and the kids went utterly neglected. Thus we struck the tableau in which we'd all be stuck for the next several years. After they left for the airport, I found myself sneaking into my own guest room to inhale the scent James had left behind on the pillow. It was weeks before I could bring myself to wash the sheets. I found myself emailing James to pass along some article on a shared intellectual interest. I found him confessing how overwhelmed and confused he was about that night and his persistent feelings for me. I found myself confessing the same as we emailed about art and ideas, our kids, our work, and our lives.

Into this tinderbox of inchoate desire for every kind of intimacy, a new marital crisis landed like a lit match.

In early 2006, with two small children, I was on the academic job market for the first time. During a fantastically successful campus interview, hiring committee members toasted me and "new beginnings" and showed me where my children "would go to school," then followed me home with an emailed birthday card. They all but handed me the contract. The next Monday, when the committee would make their decision, I took my work to a café to avoid waiting by the phone. I hadn't yet heard others' bitter stories that would have tempered my expectations, so I was optimistic enough to spend the morning working happily there. But something else distracted me: my period was several days late. As I had done many times before, I dropped by the pharmacy on my way home to pick up a pregnancy test so I could stop worrying.

You can see where this is going. I did not get the call that day, but I did find out that I was pregnant. Even now, having thought about this many times, I can't name the emotion I felt. We don't have a word for such a collision: shock, terror, wonder, grief. I was in the throes of the same baby lust that had attacked when my older son began to move out of infancy, a physical yearning that was emotionally profound. But Rick and I had planned to have only two children for many practical reasons, not least of which was my desire to be a present, involved mom to my children while building an academic career. Suddenly I was on the brink of that career, expecting any moment the phone call that would launch me into the profession I had spent nearly a decade training for. How could I move across the country in August, start a demanding new job, and have a baby in September? It seemed impossible, and yet there it was, the pink plus sign on the stick.

The thought of not having the baby didn't enter my mind until my dear friend and former marathon-training buddy suggested it. She was the first person I called, dazed, from my bathroom, and she simply said, "Well, you don't have to go through with it." Her Catholicism somehow legitimized the suggestion in my mind. At that point, I had a decision to make rather than a fate to stolidly suffer—a decision that depended from its inception on receiving that call from the university. And so the decision felt monstrous to me. I was not simply deciding what was best for the future of my family, of all the people who depended on my care. I was deciding what was best for *me*, in the context of my career, which everything I had been taught about being a good woman, wife, and mother told me I had no right to do.

Memories of my mother's vitriolic criticism of "working mothers" punctuate my childhood. During a recent visit, I sat at the kitchen table while she and my child-free sister mocked a working mother right in front of me. It's like they forget I'm one of the bad ones. That's easy to do: my work is rarely acknowledged by my family. I have struggled for decades to get out from under the guilt my family taught me to associate with mothers who choose to work (the many who are forced to work by economic or social circumstances provoking little discussion). My guilt only began to fade recently, as my children turn into young adults I'm enormously proud of and who are proud of me and the work I do in the world. Ironically, I suspect that some of my worst parenting habits—modeling female self-sacrifice and the superpowered ability to do it all without complaint—stem from my constant anxiety that I am not being a good enough mother because I am also a devoted teacher and scholar. In 2006, with two little ones in daycare so I could work while trying to secure a tenure-track job, I was painfully well-versed in this career-motherhood conflict. So to perceive my decision about having another child as coming down to whether or not I was offered an academic position—to read the job offer as a death sentence for the pregnancy—manifested that conflict in terms so stark that I could hardly bear it.

As the days passed and our phone refused to ring, other factors grew in prominence alongside that silence. Rick's reaction to the pregnancy was clear, unnuanced, and unchanging: he did not want another child. He stated that fact so aggressively that it felt a little like an attack: *no more children.* In that moment, the onerousness of his fatherhood to our existing children flashed out. His best approximation of reassurance vanished in his own contradiction: "I'm not saying I won't support you and do my part, but I am saying I do not want anything to do with another child." What I heard was, "You're on your own with this"—if not materially, then certainly emotionally—and I had already been discovering the extent to which that was already the case. So the question became: Do I want to, am I able to, is it right to, is there any argument for having a third child with a man who vehemently does not want to so much as see another child in this house, presumably while I am also moving across the country to start a new career?

Rick's palpable antipathy combined with the anticipated job offer moved me from confusion to clarity, making the decision not to have the baby seem obvious, though not easy. A day after the pink plus, I was calling Planned Parenthood, wanting to schedule the procedure as soon as possible. Having been pregnant three times before (the first ending in a miscarriage), even at this very early stage—less than five weeks into the pregnancy—I could feel my body doing the things it did when it was growing a life. My breasts were sore, my belly ached. My connection to that clump was intense; I intuitively identified it with the two little ones who had so recently been in its place. I could project out from those visceral sensations and imagine all that would happen if I did nothing. So it was not merely an intellectual decision for me. It was a decision I had to make about my body and about another potential body that was very real to me. What I "should" do was clear, but it was agonizing, and I hated everything about it. Even as I was grateful that it was my decision to make, I hated myself for making it.

That week was the worst in my life to that point. Every day I expected the phone call from the university; every day it did not come, and I wept for the baby, the son or daughter I would not have. I cried every kind of tear in the world; it was my Greatest Hits of weeping. During the day I talked on the phone to my girlfriend, who allowed me to express my pain uncensored. With my children I was quiet but still wet-faced, a small boy on each side of me on the couch, their stubby arms reaching around me in concerned incomprehension. Rick and I didn't talk about it much after that first deciding day. He quickly grew exasperated with all the "melodrama"; he could not understand what the big deal was. He scolded me for putting on such a show. I stopped trying to explain. Finally we had come upon a chasm between us so vast I didn't even try to cross it. I stayed on my side and wept, and I don't think I ever really tried to cross it again.

Given the outpouring of misogynist rhetoric about abortion provoked by the overturning of *Roe v. Wade*, I want to clarify the particularity of my grief. It was about the loss of a future I would have welcomed under other circumstances, not the loss of a particular baby, which did not yet exist. It was about the loss of intimacy and care in my marriage, which up to that point I had not been forced to fully recognize. It stemmed in part from what I felt as my own heinousness in contemplating the decision in relation to my professional life. That is to say, it emanated from my own situation and training in misogyny. Abortion is a safe and common medical procedure that many women undergo without significant grief. Studies show that not having access to abortion is far more damaging than undergoing it, just as childbirth is much more dangerous than any legal abortion procedure. Like the vast majority of women who choose it, I never regretted my decision. If it changed me, it changed me into someone who started showing up to rallies for abortion rights, donating money to agencies that support women seeking abortions, and volunteering at Planned Parenthood. Making that decision, the right decision for me, broke my heart, but not having the right to make it would only have further proved how little I owned my own body. My fraught experience is an argument not against abortion but against the stigma, patriarchal norms, and lack of support that made it so fraught for me.

That Friday in 2006 I went to the clinic, and all the week's grief and confusion intensified into surreality. I had received no word from the university, but the signs had been so clear that I remained perplexed rather than pessimistic. Rick sat blankly by my side as I waited simultaneously to be called back for the procedure and for a message announcing my professional fate. A stopwatch seemed to tick away in the corner of my vision as the calamity of waiting unfolded. Since this was pre-smartphones, Rick had brought his computer to the clinic so I could check my email, which I did neurotically, feverishly, over the many hours we sat there. The information I thought I needed in order to decide whether to go with the nurse when called refused to arrive. If I had discovered that I hadn't gotten the position, would I have fled the clinic? Without the pressure of the move and a new career, would I have decided to have the baby despite Rick's stern opposition? Or would the prospect of raising three children, one of them already rejected, with that man, in that marriage, have been enough to keep me there? I will never know.

I was called back, a sonogram was performed at which I did not look, I was questioned to make sure this was my unforced decision—its own little farce—and I was handed the pills that would stop the pregnancy's development. Sitting on the edge of a gurney, with a nurse looking down at her clipboard and a doctor bustling out the door, I threw the pills into my throat violently, as if afraid I would falter at the end. As I swallowed them, I burst into tears again, stopping the doctor in his tracks. He and the nurse looked at me quizzically, with neither cruelty nor compassion. I don't know how other women react to initiating an abortion, but maybe it's not like that. Or maybe it's exactly like that, but no one knows what to say.

That was it. I rejoined Rick in the waiting room, and we headed to our preplanned, post-abortion lunch. The tears that had begun with the pills had not stopped or slowed, and I sat silently in the restaurant booth as they poured out of me. By this point Rick had no idea what to do, think, or say. And he was tired of my tears. Clearly nothing in his mind or heart could comprehend my unreasonable sorrow. I have to imagine he thought he was being kind, but what he said chilled me to the bone and made that deep well of hatred erupt: "We can always have another one."

That statement felt absolutely monstrous to me. It contained the depth and breadth of his ineptitude; his utter inability to imagine how I was feeling in that moment, or all week long; his total ignorance, after sharing half our lives, of who I am, what matters to me, how I feel and why. It was the chasm in a sentence, one that communicated nothing so much as how profoundly alone I had been, again, through the whole experience. In that moment, faced with his complete disconnection from me, another thing broke inside me: my belief in Rick's ability to understand, value, and love another human being. After all we had gone through together so far, and then *this*, how could he say such a thing and think I would be comforted? When I recovered my wits and replied to him, it was through gritted teeth: "If we aren't going to have this one, then I don't see why you'd think we'd have another."

The next morning, I inserted the medication that causes the cervix to open and expel the clump. When that happened and I recognized it, there was a wailing and gnashing of teeth of biblical proportions, and I did not care whether Rick had any understanding of it; he was no longer a part of any of it. Weeping in our bathroom with blood on my hands, I looked up at Rick as he came through the door, so baffled and exasperated that he couldn't even fake adequate concern. At that moment he seemed to disappear from our marriage altogether. Or maybe it was the marriage that flickered out around us, the thing I had thought we were jointly living in.

A couple of hours later, still cramping and bleeding, I checked my work email to see if any of my students needed me. There, I found a voicemail as an email attachment, a message that had been left on the office line that, as an adjunct instructor, I rarely used. Naturally, I had not given that number to the university who interviewed me for the job. I can only imagine why they found and called it rather than use the phone numbers I'd provided them. The voicemail said that I had not gotten the job.

Weeks later, Rick would apologize. Not for his heartless treatment of me that week but for waiting so long to put on a condom—prolonging his pleasure, increasing my risk—the night he got me pregnant.

4. STAY

One of the earliest things I understood about the world was that my parents were miserable with each other and would remain so until one of them died. As a small child, I'd lie at night on my bed or, if the yelling was particularly scary, underneath it, riveted on my mother's screeching or keening pain. Or I'd crouch at the back of my closet, reading by flashlight to escape into a different world altogether. Those nights, I'd yearn with all my heart for that thing I'd heard of but was still unthinkable in the suburbs of the 1970s South: a divorce. My mother's loneliness and disappointment filled every crevice of our lives, as piercing as her fury. They permeated the house like sour smoke. Some nights, she left. Always she came back, which I knew because I'd lie statue-still, ears searching the dark until I heard the dog's jingling collar at the front window, then her car door. By the time I was in middle school she'd stopped leaving, instead dragging herself into sleep via pitchers of gin and tonic. Through all of this, my dad said little, stoically enduring her rage and tears. But he did make the gin and tonics.

The night of their fiftieth wedding anniversary celebration, my uncle's wife greeted my mom with a huge bouquet of flowers—an extravagant gift for frugal country people. "Any woman who can survive fifty years with a Hamilton man deserves flowers," she explained. It was a weird moment of female solidarity between two women who had never been friendly with each other. The party my sister and I threw for our parents was genuinely warm and full of love, the guests awed by their accomplishment. People gave speeches about my parents' amazing fortitude and perseverance, as if they were just back from summiting K2 minus a few digits each, lost to frostbite. In her speech, my sister tearfully thanked my mother for "always being there" for us, unlike so many otherwise occupied moms. I was a divorced working mother by then, fulfilled by my career, proud of my kids, and in love with my new partner, all of whom were sitting with me at the table while my sister spoke. Still, I felt terribly conspicuous, a failure at everything we were there to celebrate that night. The feeling wasn't new: the most my taciturn father ever said to me was in admonishing me for leaving my husband, which "a woman should not do under any circumstances."

I only ever knew of one divorce in our extended family. I wasn't privy to its particulars—it wasn't the kind of thing one talked about in "polite company"—but it was clear that the ungrateful wife was to blame. I didn't know anyone outside our family who was divorced either, so all I knew about divorce growing up came from pop culture, in movies like *Kramer vs. Kramer* and *The War of the Roses*. Women who leave their husbands, I learned, are selfish and hurt their poor children, and divorce is a nasty business in which greedy parents hurt the entire family. By the time I was contemplating divorce myself, I saw it as a shameful and terrifying thing that respectable people didn't do, and I had no one to consult about it who might have told me otherwise.

And then there was this: my parents approved of Rick. A clean-cut former military man from a good family with a very good job, Rick represented my good judgment to them. So much else about me—my work, my social values, my intellectual life, my stridency—made me the "black sheep," or the stork's mistake, designations my family reinforces regularly through an assortment of family fables. In my mother's favorite, the nurse told her I was a boy when she woke after my heavily medicated birth. It was hours before she knew she'd given birth to a girl. When we got home from the hospital, she found that the numbers on our identification bracelets didn't match. Pause for dramatic effect. Sometimes she adds that my birth certificate says "Baby Hamilton—BOY," corrected to say "GIRL." (This bit is definitely just for kicks.) This story gets repeated every time I do or say something that marks me as outside the Hamilton clan, which is a lot.

Divorce was for whiny quitters and bad women. It would ruin all of us, including our children. As a devoted mother of two married to a good man, though, I was finally doing something right. Rick made me belong. I was not going to leave Rick.

———

When the abortion happened, James and I had been emailing for about a month. We'd acknowledged the impact of the charged night of the near-swinging but had so far carefully remained in friendship territory. I didn't tell him about the abortion, but he perceived my deep sadness in my writing voice and offered what comfort he could. His noticing and respecting my grief after it had been so aggressively denied meant the world to me.

Soon, our email conversation expanded into lengthy, near-daily missives that began to feel dangerously crucial to me. We discussed art and ideas, wrote elaborate fictions, poems, and songs for each other, gloried in the glow of being seen and heard by a kindred soul after our long years of married solitude. I felt creative again, visible, alive. I blazed through life like a Catherine wheel, throwing off sparks.

Equally unhappy, equally committed to staying married, and thousands of miles apart, we thought we were the perfect adulterous pair. We could fulfill all the emotional and intellectual needs our spouses demonstrably could not, plus enjoy the sexual frisson of someone new and far away, safely prohibited from crossing serious lines by those thousands of miles. In the ugly end, I would discover the error in my concept of "serious lines" and how alone each of us was in the experience. Social media has now taught us that the exquisite intensity of virtual relationships derives from the *absence* of the real beloved; their perceived intimacy depends on it. But when your relationship with an absent person feels infinitely more intimate than the one you have with your physically present husband, the "virtual" easily displaces the "real." I gladly let whatever was between us grow into a powerful salve, one that paradoxically enabled me to stay married to a man whose presence had become loathsome in all kinds of large and small ways. If I could feel loved and seen by one man, I could continue to feed myself to another, doling myself out in small enough bits that I could live for a while.

We carried our conversation into electric all-night instant-messaging sessions when we could manage it. After one stretch of particularly exhilarating hours, James sent a giddy email declaring his love for me. Finding it in the bleary morning was like entering a ball of light. The world went Technicolor after years of being mottled gray. On nearly no sleep, I took my kids to the zoo—a daunting endeavor even for the well-rested—and every detail overwhelmed me with its beauty. I was in love with my kids, the elephants, the big blue sky. I felt like I was tripping on Ecstasy. I was not just back in my body; I was plugged into senses that had been turned up to 11. That was the first serious line crossed, and perhaps the most important, because I believed James when he said he loved me. I loved him too, or I loved the electronic version of him I was allowed to know. Stuck in a marriage to a nonperson, I found the virtual love of a virtual person to be enough. It felt like everything.

But soon that electronic love wasn't enough. I made many entreaties for James and me to get our bodies together. The more I felt like Rick's sex doll, the more I longed to merge my body with my online affair. I wanted to have emotional, intellectual, and physical intimacy all in one place, to experience sex with my living body, rather than with my dead one. James and I managed a couple of days together only once. It was rapturous, it was heartbreaking, it was confusing. It changed nothing. We returned to our unhappy marriages and clandestine conversation, with the addition of shame and urgency so agonizingly intensified that it stopped the shame from stopping us.

I doggedly continued the virtual affair even after Rick discovered photos James had sent me and the chocolates I had hidden to send him, and even after he figured out who I was typing to all of those late-night hours. Each time, Rick expressed his hurt and disapproval, and I cowered and apologized. But my nocturnal typing continued. One night, when he finally realized how emotionally enmeshed James and I were, he stormed out of the house. A couple of hours later he returned and announced that, since he was not able to give me the emotional connection I needed, he would allow me to have it with James. I was thrilled: no catastrophic reckonings required! I could not see the tragedy of it, his inability to covet this thing he could not fathom, my intense emotional connection to another man.

When Rick found out over a year later that I had had sex with James, his rage was truly terrifying: it was the first time I feared he might hurt me. He was also eerily self-righteous. While he had been happy to allow me to have sex with James as part of a deal in which he got to have sex with Alex, my decision to do it on my own cheated him out of something he felt he was owed. That thing was not my sexual fidelity, which he seemed more than happy to part with in an even exchange: the night of the near-swap had inspired Rick, and he'd been badgering me to have sex with other people ever since. But he was infuriated to learn that I had broken our sexual marital bond on my own. He had wanted to break it together, he said. I had betrayed him and our marriage.

What he said was patently true: I had betrayed him. But I didn't feel it that way. I had felt a great deal of *fear* that Rick would discover my secret, and I felt despair over the state of my marriage. But throughout the affair, I felt no guilt. I spent a lot of time trying to make sense of that fact. Many years later, I read a book that finally helped me do that.

In her 2017 study on infidelity, Esther Perel, a psychotherapist who has witnessed the effects of affairs on marriages for three decades, devotes a chapter to the kind of affair I had with James. It arises in a marriage already characterized by "marital sadism—neglect, indifference, intimidation, contempt," along with lack of intimacy and an inability to communicate. In this context, the affair for which the "faithful" partner will gladly vilify the "betraying" other is, she says, only one injury in a long-shared history of them: "Betrayal comes in many forms, and sexual betrayal is just one." In such a marriage, Perel claims that an affair can be "a gesture of bold defiance" and the "necessary doorway into a new social order."

My affair with James was the only place in my life where I acted on my real feelings and desires rather than disappearing into the contorting character imposed on me and sacrificing myself to someone else's desires. It was the only place where I felt engaged and acknowledged as a full human being. The power of that kind of acknowledgment, especially when felt in the vacuum of denied selfhood, is immense and dangerously moving. While Rick was trying to control me, while he was pressuring me to have sex I didn't want with him and with other people, I made a choice with my self and my body. This choice was selfish in the worst way, but also in a necessary way: it was an early act of resistance. It was me attempting to be faithful to myself rather than to a man and a marriage that were slowly eradicating me. I don't consider this to be "unfaithfulness," "infidelity," or "adultery." By that point in the marriage, I had nothing and no one to be faithful to. The marriage I was escaping through my affair with James could not be adulterated.

After feeling nearly unbearable shame about the affair for years, I also found it revelatory to discover that my experience is sadly common and my choice was entirely understandable. In the US, we condemn marital "infidelity" more than almost any other behavior, while living amid constant evidence of its ubiquity. We publicly and privately shame "adulterers" for behavior we deem inexcusable, while ignoring the fact that extramarital sex simply is part of the fabric of marriage itself, in this and every country. Perel points out that affairs happen in every kind of marriage at extraordinarily high rates, all over the world, even where adultery is punishable by death. Meanwhile, we often condemn the behavior when others do it while committing it ourselves, a fact that's true in culture at large and in my own story. Like miscarriage, abortion, and divorce, extramarital affairs are as common as they are devastating, whichever side of them you're on. After reading an early draft of this book or hearing my story, several women I'd known for years admitted to committing some form of adultery. Yet we rarely talk or write about it outside the cloak of fiction. We should be holding out hands to each other, shining a light.

In explaining my affair to myself or others, I don't excuse it. Though it felt like and acted as my salvation for a time, it unquestionably brought out my worst self. Throughout these months of discoveries, confrontations, and negotiations with Rick, I lied—about James's visit, what we were doing, the extent of my feelings—while assuring Rick that I would never leave him. Only that last bit was never a lie.

From the time we met until shortly after I left, the story Rick told me about himself was of a child who had been neglected or abandoned by every caretaker in his life. When he was an infant, his twenty-year-old mother moved across the country to reclaim her interrupted youth. His father, a medical resident who was rarely home, found a woman down the street whom he barely knew to look after the baby. When Rick was eight, after years of cross-coastal back-and-forth, his father remarried and decided that Rick would live full-time with him and his new stepmother. The stepmother had not been consulted. She was not keen on raising what turned out to be a challenging child and abdicated the responsibility once she had her own children, to whom she devoted her time, attention, and affection. Rick's father, by then a successful specialist surgeon, continued to be rarely at home. So Rick essentially grew up parentless, taking care of himself, spending hours after school wandering the streets while nobody noticed or cared. I know these things because he told them to me as we began to get to know each other and then reiterated them over the years of our marriage. And I know these things because his stepmother told them to me in moments of vented bitterness, guilt, and regret.

These facts of Rick's childhood dictated how we fell in love. I used to say—failing to see the ominous mothering analogy—that when we met, he imprinted on me like a baby duck. His attachment to me was immediate and fierce. When things became dire and he entreated me to do "anything" rather than leave, I took that plea to heart. His story articulated his need of me in maternal terms, and I accepted that formulation; leaving him felt as unthinkable as leaving my own child. And when I finally did marshal the strength to try to leave, he'd hook me back into our dysfunction like a fish on the line: "How can you abandon me like my mother and stepmother did?" In this context—inside this story that Rick had written for us—the course I chose felt kinder, more loving than leaving.

Shortly after I moved out, Rick reattached himself to his family and seemed to have written a new narrative in which they have always been there for him. If the new story he tells about himself to his family, friends, and the string of girlfriends who have occupied him over the past fifteen-plus years contains an abandoning mother figure, it's me. Because we share children and he earns the kind of money that can transform the legal system into a mechanism for control and punishment, the gaslighting he used to hold me in bed and in relationship with him when I desperately wanted to leave both didn't end with the marriage. Since we divorced, his family participates, casting me as the black-hearted bitch who betrayed and abandoned their loving son.

I suspect only I remember the letter his stepmother sent him after he started college and before we began dating, a letter I accidentally found while separating boxes that got mixed up after the divorce. In it, his stepmother, a therapist, poignantly articulated her guilt and regret at his neglect by parents who were consumed by other children and careers. She expressed her concern that he had never learned to forge real intimacy and emotional connections, because no one had forged them with him. She worried that his future relationships might suffer from this lack, from his parents' collective failure. I do not remember the letter suggesting a way to prevent such potential future suffering. Reading the letter soon after the divorce, and caught in a nightmare that was unfolding exactly according to her concerns, I saw what she'd written as a horrible, impotent prophecy. It was Cassandra crying out unheeded about the future fall of

Troy. The analogy is terribly apt: For refusing to have sex with him, Apollo cursed Cassandra with the power to deliver prophecies that no one would believe. Later, as Troy fell, Cassandra was raped.

It is an oversight of the English language that we do not have separate words for expressing care and responsibility. We can only say "I'm sorry" and let people assume we are accepting all kinds of blame. I am sorry for my affair with James. I care that it hurt Rick. I regret enormously that I hurt Alex. But ultimately I am most sorry that I was not able to be clear-eyed and brave enough to leave him before I did terrible things in order to stay.

5. VOICES

A certain light was beginning to dawn dimly within her,
—the light which, showing the way, forbids it.

—KATE CHOPIN, *The Awakening*

Falling into ecstatic love with a man I could never be with zapped me back to life as effectively as electrodes to a flatlined heart. But birth and self-awareness are not simultaneous, even the first time around. My rebirth led inexorably to the long, dark death throes of my marriage. I couldn't see at the time that my rebirth was the path to both marital death and selfhood, because I had to pass through the first to get to the second. I would not be able to save myself until the marriage was good and dead. As Rick and I played out the slow and agonizing demise of our marriage over the next several years, we enlisted several desperate life-saving measures. Every one of them advanced the disease that had already taken hold.

In 2010, four tumultuous years after the abortion revealed our unbridgeable chasm, I went to my annual writing retreat intent on deciding what to do with the instrument of mutual destruction that my marriage had become. By then I had gotten myself out of the house but had been unable to get Rick to cooperate with any humane form of divorce. I was stuck—on a precipice but unable to take the step that would cast me into the new kind of hell that commenced my path toward freedom. No one had been able to offer any clarity about where I was or how I'd gotten there. Those who knew the alarming state of my life were either as confused as I was or unwilling to nudge me in any particular direction. I was hoping that the retreat would do its usual magic.

That June, as I have done now for over a decade, I spent two days and nights in an austere room overlooking acres of lawn that sprawl along the east bank of a great river. Days, I gloried in uninterrupted hours of writing, which sometimes meant typing and sometimes meant looking at the river, waiting for thoughts to come. I've written parts of many academic books and articles in such quiet rooms over the years. Always I find that other thoughts arrive too, about things I don't know I'm thinking until I become still enough for them to find me. Every evening after dinner I sat by the river while the sun set over my left shoulder and the sky sang out symphonies of color. These moments are the most magical, the most likely to produce unexpected revelations like rabbits out of hats. I always bring a book that I hope will participate in that year's incantation. In 2010 it was Kate Chopin's *The Awakening*.

Published in 1899, *The Awakening* was Chopin's last published work, but it is the one for which she is most remembered. Until culture caught up with her forward thinking, it ruined her reputation as a writer. Reviewers called its main character, a woman who dares to make her own choices in life and sex, "shocking," "sickening," and "selfish," and they called the book "unhealthy," "poisonous," and "nauseating." During my decidedly unfeminist education, I had never read it. On that retreat, as I contemplated my inability to tolerate the life I had once chosen and what I had done in my attempts to break free—things that shocked even me—it seemed like the time had come to make its acquaintance. The novel tells the story of Edna Pontellier, who slowly awakens to the myriad ways her life and identity are dictated by the roles of wife and mother that society has thrust upon her. The world of the novel, and the society it reflects, offers a woman of Edna's social class two choices: to become a "mother-woman" who gladly subsumes herself into her husband and the babies she produces every two years like clockwork, or to remain single, socially marginalized, and condemned to limited financial means like the unmarried artist Edna pities as much as she admires.

Edna's awakening begins when she falls in love with a man, Robert, who sees and appreciates her as a separate person and an artist, unlike her husband, who regards her as merely his pretty possession. Robert also teaches her to swim, which empowers her physically and psychically and begins her transformation. Her awakening is a process of discovering that she has a self quite apart from the roles she plays in society and the parts of herself she gives to her family, and of learning to claim it. She stops following social rules and doing her husband's bidding. She begins to speak her mind and assert her wishes. She takes off her wedding ring, moves out of her husband's house, and chooses her own lover, Alcée. In the end she is as unwilling or unable to play the role of the downtrodden single woman as she is to sacrifice herself for husband and children. Because her world presents no pathway forward in which an adult woman can keep her autonomy and her dignity, her awakening inevitably ends in her death.

It's amazing how thoroughly I lived a twenty-first-century version of Edna's life, having never read Chopin's book. It's more amazing that I could encounter Edna's story while immersed in my own rendition of it in 2010 and see none of the similarities between them. Recently I've taken great pleasure in teaching *The Awakening* to literature students. The lesson plan for the novel pretty much wrote itself. I start by raising—or letting students raise, as they often do—the questions that exasperated me when I first read the book in 2010. Then, informed by the sympathetic reading that I came to years later, after I had moved through my own realizations and transformations, I help them see how the book answers those questions.

Why is Edna, a privileged woman with a seemingly doting husband, so unhappy? Chopin immediately gives us all the information we need to answer this question, but the reasons can be hard to spot. Late one night, Edna's husband comes home from the club and talks to her about his fun evening with the lads. He then goes in to check on the kids and asks her to look in on one whom he suspects has a fever. The next day, he gives her some money before he leaves on business; a few days later, a box for her and the children arrives from him, full of exotic and delectable treats. She shares them with her neighbors, and "all declared that Mr. Pontellier was the best husband in the world." Edna is "forced" to agree with them.

While her husband has been performing the roles of loving husband and father for the neighbors and for himself and his family, he has been using his wife and children to feed his own ego. Attention to the details tells a different story than the one the public sees and that her husband is performing. When he comes home chirpy from the club, Edna is in a deep sleep, exhausted. He wakes her up to provide an audience for his "bits of news and gossip." He's forgotten the treats he promised to bring for the kids and assuages his guilt by heading into their room to do a little unnecessary caretaking. They are, of course, asleep. By raising the alarm of a fever he creates a need for action, making himself feel useful, at which point he orders his wife to take over and then goes off for a smoke. She checks the child; there is no fever. Now she's wide awake and agitated, whereas he has slipped into an easy sleep.

It's no wonder that "she could not have told why she was crying," or that the "oppression" she felt was "indescribable." None of her husband's behavior is cruel or abusive. It is only uniformly selfish and controlling. It tells her at every step what she must do, what she must accept, and that he has the power to dictate these things. In exchange for giving up her autonomy she gets a marriage in which "no trace of passion or excessive and fictitious warmth colored her affection." She's married to a role, not a man, a role that is also an overlord, a parent, a cage.

Why does Edna get involved with that cad, Alcée? His reputation as a womanizer precedes him, and he is brutally honest about the insincerity of his courting gestures. Edna's entanglement with him can seem to cheapen her and the awakening of which Alcée is clearly a part. Except for this: Edna gets to choose him, and in doing so, she chooses to follow her own sensual desires. Alcée himself "was nothing" to her, but he offers her the "first kiss of her life to which her nature had really responded." Perhaps the kiss is even more empowering because the desire she responds to is *not* the desire for love but simply desire itself, unbidden and unforced, which Chopin calls "the cup of life." Responding to the sensual desire she has chosen, rather than forever submitting to a man's desire foisted upon her, revitalizes her in an essential step of her awakening.

Why can't Edna end up with Robert, whom she loves? Though triggered by love for one man and enacted in part through sex with another, Edna's awakening is not about either of those men, or about any man. When Robert declares his love, he insinuates that she is a possession to be handed from her husband to himself. She casts herself away from him. Ultimately she awakens to desire not for another but only for her own self. It is an existential transformation: she was "beginning to realize her position in the universe as a human being, and to recognize her relations as an individual to the world within and about her."

The novel's second half is full of Edna's fierce resolutions. Resolving "never to take another step backward" leads her to decide "never again to belong to another than herself." But Edna can't see it so clearly, even as she feels herself propelled along the course of a great change. In her final moments, as she takes herself to the sea to be reborn into the only freedom available to her, she remains "mechanical," "not thinking." It makes perfect sense to me now that we can trace the progress of an awakening that moves Edna even while she can't understand it. For one thing, her world has provided her no framework for such understanding. Chopin frames the mechanisms of her awakening as elemental rather than intellectual: Edna is called by "the voice of the sea," not any idea about autonomy or freedom. She knows nothing about the systems of oppression that have contained her and doesn't need to understand them to perceive them. She senses them and her means to escape them in the fabric of the world.

Her movement without understanding also makes sense to me now when I think of myself all those years ago, reading Edna's story while living my own version without understanding her story or mine. I was also being moved to change. I was grasping at the vitality of love and sex; I was transgressing social dictates, asserting my own desires, and bristling at the ways my husband imposed his will on me—some subtle, some appalling—while performing his deep love for me. I was rebelling against oppressions I did not understand, in ways I could not understand. I didn't have the language to identify the power structures at play, but I knew in my gut that I had to find a way to elude them. Like Edna, I had been called to my own unthinking, elemental awakening.

On that writing retreat, I resolved never to take another step backward and never again to belong to another than myself. Driving home, while crossing that river on a gorgeous, blue-skied day, I was filled with that year's revelation: whatever new misery it brought, I had to file for divorce. When I reached my hometown, I pulled over, called my lawyer, and told her to file the petition. She noted that the paperwork would be filed the next day—our fifteenth wedding anniversary—and I nearly balked. Another unintentional cruelty. But I was in the predicament because I had been denying my own needs to protect Rick from pain for too long as it was. I told her to file.

In 2006, I fell in love with a man I could not have shared a life with even if we hadn't been married to other people. But it wasn't about him; it was about me. I came back to life. I remembered what it felt like to be a fully realized self and recognized as such. It was simply not possible for me to go to sleep again.

PART 2
SEEMING LIBERATION AND PLEASURE

A democratic morality should judge sexual acts by
the way partners treat one another,
the level of mutual consideration,
the presence or absence of coercion, and
the quantity and quality of the pleasures they provide.

—GAYLE RUBIN,
"Thinking Sex: Notes for a Radical
Theory of the Politics of Sexuality" (1984)

6. BOILING FROG

Here's something I never expected to be able to say: it was New Year's Eve in 2007, and I was dancing topless in a cage above a mob of writhing people, some openly kissing or fondling each other, some grinding in a kind of standing foreplay. I didn't recognize much of the music blaring through the massive sound system; I was thirty-seven with two young children asleep at Grandma's house, my clubbing days long behind me. Neurotically fixated on my weight and appearance, I was lean and fit with plenty of long, highlighted hair to fling around. I had worked my way up to the cage by first dancing more demurely in the shadow box, mirroring my girlfriend who danced across from me in another one. She had given me the fancy beaded bra that matched my raspberry silk thong, the bra I'd ditched about a half hour in, after relaxing into the scene. Later that night I would take a turn at the pole, gyrating with inexpert gusto until another woman asked me to move out of the way so she could climb it.

Every time I teach Susan Bordo, I think of that night and of so many moments like it:

> I view our bodies as a site of struggle, where we must *work* to keep our daily practices in the service of resistance to gender domination, not in the service of docility and gender normalization. This work requires, I believe, a determinedly skeptical attitude toward the routes of seeming liberation and pleasure offered by our culture.

I always ask my students, what does Bordo mean by "seeming liberation and pleasure"? What kinds of women's experiences feel empowering but really keep us in the service of patriarchy by reducing us to our bodies, to passive objects of the male gaze, to things that men desire and feel entitled to take? And while I am saying these learnèd things, I think of myself in the cage, on the pole, how I felt like a lightning rod absorbing the energy of all of those admiring, hungry eyes, like I could illuminate a city with the power of it.

Then I think of myself as a teenager, grocery shopping with my mom, how her inability to reach something on the top shelf was my cue to demonstrably try, hopping cutely while tossing my hair and stretching my arm up prettily. Help always magically materialized. My mom would joke that it didn't work anymore when she did it.

I think of the boy in high school who pestered me for weeks before some holiday, begging me to list ten things I wished for in my wildest dreams. Having developed enough sense to suspect he'd try to give them to me, I listed impossible things to make him stop. On that holiday, there he was with a givable version of each thing. I had to lug the loot around school all day while kids snickered at me, as if I had done something foolish. I wondered what the boy thought I owed him and felt guilty for all the money he'd spent on me when he wasn't going to get anything back.

I think of the long, handwritten letters full of poetry and declarations of love, which I received several times a week all summer from a boy I had briefly dated before requesting that we stay just friends. The unsolicited onslaught was so confusing—why doesn't he stop? And are we still friends?

I think of my cherished friend when I was fifteen and he was eighteen, stealing a tiny teacup from the Chinese restaurant where he'd taken me so he could down the vodka he'd stashed in his car to embolden himself to say he loved me. I think of how angry he was when I didn't return his love, how he stopped speaking to me, how his eyes cut into me every time we crossed paths at school, as if I had intentionally wronged him.

I think of another friend with whom I spent Senior Skip Day, drowsing contentedly in the sun, then finding weeks later that he had taken rolls of film of me in my swimsuit, his camera lingering over every part of my body, lens peeking out from some foliage somewhere. I remember him asking me to the prom and threatening suicide when I declined, how guilty I felt. Then at college, there he'd be at every party I went to, furious with me for dancing with other guys, following me back to the steps of my dorm and screaming at me across the quad, calling me whore and cocktease, crying that I was breaking his heart, I was a monster, in scenes that would make the later ones with my husband seem like all of a piece. In private, hanging out together before a party—I was trying to give him something of what he wanted, this boy who loved me so much he threatened to kill himself—he'd run his fingers over my arms, my face, and I would not find the courage to stop him until he pushed his fingers into my mouth. I remember looking into his face then and seeing his own mouth watering and feeling disgusted, like I was dirty.

I think of the rare Southern snow when I was sixteen, the footprints we found the next morning leading from the sidewalk to the side of my family's house, straight up to my bedroom window.

I think of the condoms dangling from the doorknob and strewn across my family's front porch, crude drawings of dicks on the sidewalk in pastel children's chalk. I hadn't had sex yet, had seen neither dick nor condom before. It seemed like my house had been marked, or I had been, claimed for some future visit and purpose.

I think of the man on the beach in Florida who materialized by my side when I was fifteen and boldly took a walk alone along the surf. Not wanting to be alarmist like my parents, I allowed him to follow me farther and farther away from the hotel and its crowds, refusing to be afraid, committed to being polite by giving him my attention, aware of the hold I had on him, like a magnet drawing him along in my wake. When he bent down to kiss me, this older, homely man I had not invited but whose feelings I was loathe to hurt, I was stunned.

Is this power?

I try to use Bordo to explain to my students why such things can feel like power but are actually patriarchy's seductive way of convincing us to give power up—to become all body, in service of another's desire. But having not yet learned this myself by the time I was thirty-seven, I wonder what I might say now to these young people to explain it. If I could, if it were permitted in such a setting, I would describe to them how at thirty-seven, emboldened by what felt like the power of all of those desiring eyes, I climbed down out of the cage and into the orbit of a man I had noticed noticing me. As we danced, he stared at me in awe like he had just won some gigantic prize. Though I had been drawn to something about him that suggested wry intelligence, his awe or drunkenness or both reduced his enticements to versions of "You're so fucking beautiful."

Further emboldened, I asked him to guess what I did for a living. After he'd tried "model," "actress," "dancer," and "stripper"—delighting me with each wrong try—I allowed for a dramatic pause before delivering the line I'd been waiting to say: "I'm a professor of English literature." That brought, as planned, more histrionics of amazement, pleasing me enormously. "See," I thought, "I'm smarter than you can imagine *and* as sexy and beautiful as you could hope for. That makes me the most powerful woman in this room." I imagine the humiliation of my confession to my feminist theory students making Bordo's point quite nicely.

Rick and I were at the club that night to ring in the new year alongside hundreds of other couples who had been led—out of boredom, adventurousness, or desperation; for sheer fun; or some combination of these—into the strange and exhilarating world of swinging. Of all the things we did to sustain our dying marriage, my swinging experiences have remained the most difficult to comfortably place in my story of myself. How could I have been both a professor who routinely taught feminist theory and literature and a woman who so thoroughly confused her own objectification with power? How did things I refused to do for years become an avenue for what at times brought real pleasure? Why does remembering that New Year's Eve, and so many nights like it, still conjure such a confusing mixture of ecstasy and embarrassment, empowerment and submission, fondness and regret? The things I did while swinging, and the forces that convinced me to do them, raise every thorny issue around sex, desire, choice, consent, gender, and power.

Here's how I got into swinging.

In the spring of 2007, I arrived home from the airport after four demanding days at an academic conference. It was late on a weeknight, and I had to teach the next morning. I wanted to tiptoe into my kids' room and watch them sleep for a few minutes, then fall into bed. But before I could even set down my suitcase, Rick was upon me, shoving a sloshing glass of wine into my hand. "Sit down and read this," he said. "Try to have an open mind. I'm really excited about this. I've been working on it for a long time and I really need you to give it a chance. I think it will be great for us." He directed my body, still clad in my finest conference attire, into a chair in front of his computer and pointed my face at the screen. There,

I found an email—a sales pitch, really—from a couple Rick had been corresponding with, whom he wanted us to meet. It took a moment for me to realize that the three of them had been communicating for a while. Dates for our get-together were already being discussed. I didn't even have the wherewithal to wonder how Rick had found these people or why he had been busy arranging a sexual encounter on my behalf.

For the previous year or more, he had been pressing me to join him in finding people to swing with. It seemed to be the solution he could offer to our marital problems, which means he saw our marital problems as reduceable to the amount of sex we were having. This conversation, his sales pitch, slid between pathetic entreaties and sinister implications of what I owed him. It usually took place on date nights, when my parents watched the kids so we could have quality time together—you know, maintain a healthy intimacy. Each time he brought it up, I felt disgust, but not as I had at the beginning of our marriage when I wanted to protect what still felt like our precious, pure thing. That thing was dead. By then, though Rick was unaware of it, I wanted to protect the love that felt real and meaningful to me, my love for James.

James and I believed our affair could sustain us through our whole lives. In late-night chats we'd fantasize a future in which we continued the enlivening conversation of our youth while our old bodies were contentedly confined to porch rockers. Whether our spouses were dead or still miraculously ignorant about us was never specified. But our solution to surviving unhappy marriages could not in fact work forever. In early 2007, Alex became pregnant with their second child, reigniting James's shame and responsibility. He removed himself from our conversation for long stretches of time. I was devastated. Without that space in which my real self could live, I became a zombie in my own life: undead and untenanted, open to occupation.

There's a haunting scene in *The Rapture*, in which the camera lingers on Mimi Rogers's prone body, her face an apathetic mask, while a man has sex with her from behind. The man fucks her body; she's no longer there. That disturbing image was the only notion of swinging I had until I entered the world myself. When Rick sat me down in front of that computer screen, I felt like that vacated woman already. It was hard to imagine that lying down to be fucked by somebody else would make much difference. Simone de Beauvoir describes the effects of patriarchy on women like this: "Her body does not seem to her to be a clear expression of herself; within it she feels herself a stranger."

Like all gaslighters (like all narcissists), Rick has several superpowers, one of which is boiling frogs.

After he'd carefully adjusted me to one tiny part of his plan after another, leading me step-by-step to agree to something he knew I was absolutely opposed to, I discovered that he had opened an account for us on a swinging website. He created our portfolio, in which "we" expressed "our" desire to meet a nice, hot couple to have sex with. He added several photos. Some of them included Rick: both halves of couples who are shopping for other couples want to get something nice. But most of them featured me. He'd selected snapshots that showed off my body, like a few of me smiling in a tailored bridesmaid's dress after a friend's wedding. Innocent photos from our life together became ugly echoes of those bikini pictures from Senior Skip Day. My husband, my stalker. Thoughtfully, he added rectangular black bars over my eyes. To protect my privacy. To protect the privacy of a woman who had not consented to having her photos posted on the internet in an attempt to find someone to have sex with her that she did not want to have.

Rick had been advertising me and my body online for months. This couple he was trying to sell me on was only one of many (with some singles and throuples thrown in) with whom Rick had been communicating. Eventually he showed me some of the correspondence to prove how lucky we were to find the couple he'd chosen.

It's difficult to explain in any way that would make sense to you how I got from that point to the next. How I looked at those profiles, those pictures, and got to the moment when I agreed to participate. I can't fully explain it to myself. I was exhausted from resisting the urgent onslaught of Rick's exhortations. He made me feel terribly guilty that our marriage was so bad (that our sex life was so bad) that he had to resort to this. I knew he would not stop till he got what he wanted. As in my dream, he would keep coming at me, inexorably, and any knife I waved at him would be useless.

I let Rick pull my ribbon.

A week or two after that night, we met the couple for a "date." It was, after all, date night; my parents had the kids for a sleepover. Though the couple had suggested we book one hotel room, assuming we'd all end up together anyway, I insisted that Rick and I book our own. We had things in common with the couple and had begun friendly chatting with them. Still, the fact that we were agreeing to (possibly—we could always back out!) be intimate with total strangers was not only unsettling to me; it was frightening. Anything could happen. Rick chided me for being paranoid: I had nothing to be afraid of.

We met Ivan and Vanya at a restaurant in a neighboring town where we didn't know anyone. Even swingers don't usually just jump into the sack; there's a swinger version of getting to know each other, of foreplay over dinner and drinks, in which all the awkwardness of a first date is multiplied several times. You've got a couple sizing up another couple, two men sizing up two women, and then, as always, the women looking at each other and wondering whether they can pull it off.

Swinging—married or partnered couples meeting others for sex—is only one type of consensual non-monogamy (CNM), which includes poly-amory and open marriages and is practiced by more queer people than heterosexual ones. But in my experience of swinging, the men were het-erosexual and acted as such while swinging, while the women were nearly always expected to be sexual with each other, even if outside of swinging they were heterosexual too. These lesbian overtures always felt vaguely performative for me, a ritual that had to happen to unlock the space in which the swapped het action for which everyone was waiting could be-gin. I wonder how the women I had sex with felt about it. Did they enjoy it? Were their moans, passionate caresses, and long, searching looks real? I find it easy to imagine that some of them might have looked forward to the lesbian foreplay, which always seemed more tender, however fake, than the pornographic het scramble that came after. Or maybe, like me, they put themselves away somewhere and acted their way through all of it.

But even that's not quite right. I'm trying to be honest, and yet it's hard, now, to say how much was performance and how much was plea-sure. My mental record of swinging is a film reel I can watch, if I force myself, like a spectator. I can't inhabit the body I see doing those things. I can't remember how I felt when doing them. That part of the memory was not laid down or has been erased. My body certainly registered diverse sexual pleasures, though not always. Sometimes I felt like a sex worker, dutifully performing tit in exchange for some sort of delivered tat. It was an economy of sex acts that felt neutrally transactional rather than trau-matically so, as in my marriage. In that context and with those people, I owed nothing outside of sexual pleasure. Engaging in that sort of matter-of-fact pleasure exchange actually felt like a bit of a relief. But what was the rest of me feeling, the non-body part? When I press my mind's eye to the milky membranes that wall off those memories from the rest of me, all I can see is this: Power. Choice. Control.

Something was happening—not what I wanted—but it would most certainly change everything.

7. FREEDOM

That first night of swinging, I wasn't sure what I should be assessing from cocktails to dessert with these people I was supposed to have sex with later. They were, it turned out, kind, interesting people, fun to talk with, wide-ranging in their conversation, funny, smart. Vanya was working on her master's degree, and Ivan had completed his master's at the same college and was directing one of its facilities programs. Both had emigrated from Russia, which would later make for a lot of interesting postcoital conversations. At one point we'd develop a group fantasy about the four of us traveling on the Trans-Siberian Railway from Ivan's western hometown to Vanya's far-flung eastern one, fucking in various combinations all the way, in the strange hypersexual family we would become.

By dinner's end, I had no idea what I did or did not want to do. I did know I was expected to move on to the next step. And I was no longer afraid of Ivan and Vanya. In fact, I was genuinely enjoying their company, and we had a whole free night ahead of us, a rare opportunity for parents of small children. The four of us headed to Ivan and Vanya's hotel room, allowing Rick and me to decide when to leave. At first we sat around the room awkwardly, the magic spun in the restaurant by the food, wine, and conversation dissipated. But soon Ivan pulled out bottles of something and poured drinks for everyone, and the soft-focus thrum started building again. Probably one of the least surprising things I discovered about swinging is that a lot of alcohol is involved. Drugs can be a big part of the scene, too, but one of the things we four shared was a strict no-drugs policy. Ivan and Vanya were, we ascertained, almost fanatically healthy and determined to stay that way. Early on we all exchanged results of new STI and HIV tests, with Ivan and Vanya providing theirs before we even met them.

The Russians were very clean. Ivan's face was always immaculately shaven, and I never encountered a trace of chest hair, while Vanya kept her legs and armpits as baby-smooth as she did her regularly Brazilian'd vulva. Both were always impeccably groomed in every way: fresh haircuts, neat clothes, teeth that shined white against their perpetually tanned skin. They both spent a lot of time in the gym, Ivan to maintain his impressively muscular physique and Vanya to stay delicate and slight. They were models of traditional masculinity and femininity, both in their physical prime and always slightly glowing from the tanning beds they used regularly.

Rick and I felt pressure to keep up with all that youthful perfection. The swinging years overlapped with a period of body obsession that enabled me to maintain the extreme leanness that looked good not just in person but on camera. I began to be on camera a lot. It was, ironically, the time in my adult life when I drank the least—outside weekends—in order to cut calories. Taking my cues from Vanya, I maintained a year-round spray-on tan and perfect Brazilian. Once, I was so determined to get my required tan that I went to the salon in the rain, leaving my arms and legs unsexily splotchy till it wore off. Ivan loved to take photos of me and Vanya, and he would proudly share the best ones when we all IM'd between dates, keeping in touch. By the time we parted ways with Ivan and Vanya, Rick and I had an extensive collection of creatively shot photos ranging from *Playboy*-style dressed and semi-dressed to full-on pornography. Occasionally the other three of us took pictures as well, so we had photos of everyone in all combinations and an impressive variety of poses and positions, some of which took entire evenings and much futzing with furniture to pull off.

After the swinging was over, after the marriage was finally really over, when I had abandoned the self-punishing behaviors that produced my picture-perfect body, I found it hard to let go of the photos and videos from that period. I knew I'd never again be so magazine beautiful, and I wanted to hold onto proof that I had been. Even when I could not bear to look at those photos, could not bear to remember what I'd been doing when they were taken, still I held on to the photos. I just moved them digitally farther and farther away from me, burying them first in folders within folders, then transferring them off my computer onto an external hard drive. Finally I traveled far enough out of the fog of that time to see myself in it—the topless woman dancing in the cage, the thinnest version of myself tottering on stilettos in a photograph—as something entirely other than beautiful. I saw the photos as a record of something painful and deeply sad: how I had reshaped my body through obsessions that sprouted from my fear and powerlessness before the swinging and then fed on the self-loathing that grew alongside it. I saw the images as shameful and embarrassing, something my children must never stumble across. Knowing I didn't know how to wipe the hard drive absolutely clean, I asked my partner to do it for me. I left the room while he did.

I don't know what Rick, Vanya, and Ivan used the alcohol for, but I used it to deaden the part of me that didn't want this, that wanted a different kind of marriage, that was swinging as a way of giving up on that. And I used it to wake up the part of me that was dead: my passion, my libido. I don't mean simply my sex drive but "libido" in its original Freudian sense—the drive to extend myself to others, the drive to engage, the drive to live. It's the opposite of the death drive, or the pull toward stasis and withdrawal from the world, the drive to disappear that I knew so well at the time.

When you habitually ~~are forced~~ ~~submit to~~ participate in sex that you don't want, your passion—the part of you that normally wants to open up and greet the other person, to expand and explode—must find some place to hide. It figures out it doesn't belong and withdraws somewhere you do not get to pick. You'll be lucky if you can locate and retrieve it someday. The splitting I'd grown so adept at through my relationship with James returned to serve me during the swinging. But this time, rather than enabling my deepest self to wake up, it allowed that part to go to sleep. Just as I had agreed to try swinging out of guilt, desperation, and apathy rather than excitement, I entered many swinging sessions not drawn by desire but passively floating, inhibitions smothered, inebriated and tranquilized.

Presented with a bacchanalia of some sort, I drifted in with utter surrender. I became wholly body, a collection of delicious sensations. The mind that attended was all id. Swinging required me to move not just outside social norms but beyond relationship altogether, beyond even my sense of personhood. Sex with Ivan, and with Vanya, and with Ivan and Vanya, and with Ivan and Vanya and Rick, and eventually with others, had nothing to do with any of them. It's almost as if they didn't exist any more than I did. In their place was sensation without thought, without

feeling, without self. I slipped into this abandoned version of myself easily. It was my usual nonself + pleasure. Who wouldn't want to go there
now and then for a little escape?

The first time took the most coaxing. As the female half of the rookie pair,
I became the focus of everyone's attention. I was the one who had to agree;
I had to move us from flirting to hands on skin. Displaying the same creativity and planning that would characterize all our future get-togethers,
Ivan and Vanya had brought music along with the booze to create the
right mood. They had also brought a stunning array of sex toys and lubes
but wisely kept those out of sight until we arrived at the moment when
we'd be excited by them rather than alarmed. Soon cocktails and dancing turned into people dancing in various combinations on the bed, as if
we were building an innocuous bridge between the usual vanilla fun and
the chocolate we'd driven all that way for. Then I was dancing on the bed
by myself, with Ivan and Vanya gazing up at me from one side of the bed
and Rick watching from the other.

At some point I decided, or some less conscious version of that, to
let them seduce me. I'm not going to pretend that three beautiful people
seducing you is not exciting. I was wearing a hot pink wraparound blouse
purchased for the occasion, just as Rick was in a specially-purchased
button-down shirt, whose print we thought was vaguely cool. He wore his
"cool" shirt so many times with Ivan and Vanya, and later to other swinging events, that I came to think of it as his "swinging shirt." I'd paired my
blouse with a black miniskirt and heels that I'd kicked off before climbing
on the bed. With impeccable timing born of her considerable sensitivity,
Vanya registered the moment I crossed from playfulness to desire and
reached up to pull the bow at my waist. In an instant my blouse opened
up, leaving me dancing in my hot-pink bra and skirt. Then Vanya's delicate hands were on my ankles, my calves, my thighs, tentative and slow,
as if leaving me time to stop her. This added to my desire not to. I felt safe
with Vanya. I don't remember how we got from the two of us in this quiet,
seductive tableau to the sweaty, athletic, no-holds-barred sex in nearly every possible combination that occupied the rest of the night, but I'm sure
we transitioned by way of a prologue between me and Vanya.

Vanya wasn't the first woman I'd kissed, but that night she became the first I'd had sex with.

I know that is the correct term, "had sex" with, but it doesn't feel right. This is not because I hold a phallocentric concept of sex that requires penile penetration; once we got to the part with the strap-on, even that sexist definition would apply. But it never *felt* like sex, the things I did with Vanya. And I did many things, a full gamut of what must have looked like lesbian sex. I remember the slight roughness of Vanya's soft folds of shaved skin against my tongue, the tidiness of the whole apparatus, the frustrating hunt for her clit, which I was never sure I found. I remember the salty-bitter taste of her, which I did not like as much as I wanted to. I remember what it felt like, strapped up, to drive into her like a man, and discovering something of the power a man must feel. I remember kisses and caresses ranging from tender to slightly painful. I remember Vanya making me come—*she* knew where the clit was—while Ivan did other things. I remember, on another occasion, licking Vanya from navel to breasts in a game we all played, each of us sprawled naked in turn on a kitchen table and anointed with salt, lime, and tequila. I remember climbing on top of the table and on top of Vanya to extend my turn of the game into the full-on sex that would kick off the orgy they were all expecting; I remember knowing this was my role. These things happened, and I remember them. But in my memory they do not feel sexy, or sexual. They feel varying degrees of uncomfortable, a part I never chose to play.

How to explain this without sounding homophobic, or resolutely heterosexual, neither of which I am? In fact, my unresponsiveness to the lovely Vanya—and to all the women I had sex with as part of swinging—only becomes meaningful in contrast to the times I have felt intensely drawn to women.

Fifteen years before I first had sex with a woman, before I was married, before sex became so confusing that I didn't know what desire was anymore, I connected with a woman so exquisitely that it sent me searching for more. I had just graduated from college and was out at a trendy club with two roommates and my new friend Alex. Her date was also there, a guy she'd met a couple of weeks earlier at a different club, James. It's so interesting that I always forget that.

Days later, Alex and I would discuss that electrifying moment and agree: neither of us had seen it coming. We were pleasantly tipsy on white Russians but not drunk. Rick and I were still in the hyperattached portion of our relationship, and with him back at our condo I didn't have sex on my mind in the least. I was there to dance with my friends, have a bit of fun. How to explain it then: Alex and me, standing in front of the thronged bar with people streaming around us; me asking to borrow Alex's lipstick; then Alex gently placing one hand on my arm and the other flat against my lower back, brushing back my hair, leaning in; our lips meeting in perhaps the sweetest, sexiest, most exciting kiss of my life? A fizzing current awoke under her touch, gathered, then streamed to my wrists, breasts, belly, and pulsed. It didn't last long. Alex remembered James and took a step backward. The earth resumed its rotation.

Describing the whole thing to Rick later, I realized the depth of desire stirred by that kiss. I'd wanted Alex to come home with me and spend the night, even though I didn't fully know what that would entail. I knew we'd work it out. Alex later confessed that she'd had the same wish, though tinged with guilt and regret: James had felt betrayed by the kiss. Rick's only regret was missing it. He'd eaten up my play-by-play like candy. So I began the conversion of all my unsanctioned desire into fuel for my sanctioned sex life. Though Alex and I would remain close friends for nearly twenty years—right up to the point when she found out about my affair with James—she and I would never finish what we'd started. As our relationships with Rick and James grew increasingly solid, our treasured what-if became increasingly surreal.

A year or so after the kiss, I found myself thinking about that moment more and more. The softness, the sweetness. I had no concept then of the fluidities of sexuality and desire, so I couldn't see the longing as a part of myself I had stumbled on. Rick didn't mind my desire for this new escapade; he encouraged it. Experiment away, he said, as long as you tell me all about it.

These were the days when the internet was new, email was primitive, and social media had not been dreamt of outside science fiction. Labor and patience were required. I placed an ad in a newspaper's personals section— "girl seeking girl," that kind of thing—and was assigned an anonymous voicemail number. I had to phone periodically to see if I'd gotten any messages. It was a bold move for me: I was still a girl barely delivered from the clutches of her conservative childhood. Only a couple of years before, I'd been proud of myself for being brave enough to meet my one gay friend in the one gay-friendly bar near my college campus. My heart pounded as I listened to the few messages that materialized in response to my ad. I felt like someone was watching me as I pressed the kitchen's wall phone to my ear, straining to hear something enticing, having no idea what that might be. One woman struck me as quirkily intriguing, and we agreed to do dinner and a movie, but feeling unmoved, we did nothing else. A couple of years later I married Rick, which meant I was not allowed to feel anything for anyone else, ever. So I stopped thinking about that desire.

What I do know now is this: when I began to break free from the prejudices of my upbringing, I discovered a desire that was waiting there. Then I put it away somewhere to squish myself into the heterosexuality and monogamy that I believed marriage demanded. Even now, I think it was the right decision for the moment: Rick and I loved each other, and we wanted a monogamous relationship. We managed a good one for a long while. Thirty years after making that decision, after all I've seen and done, I still prefer monogamy and am grateful to share it happily with my partner of over a decade. But everything I've learned about marriage and sexuality has taught me the lie and destructiveness of mandating heterosexuality and monogamy. Refusing to allow oneself or others to express desires outside of them can convert avenues of seeming liberation and pleasure into forced marches back to those killing mandates.

When, after I had lived fifteen years of heterosexual monogamy, swinging ostensibly allowed me to plunge into those forbidden pleasures, I could not feel my desire. Or, I could not feel it unadulterated; I could not feel it pure like I did when I kissed Alex in the bar. I could not feel these things because I had not chosen them, so they were not mine; they were things being done to me and things I was reluctantly agreeing to do. They were things someone else had carefully curated and was doling out to me. Desire doesn't work like that.

Jack Halberstam's analysis of faux lesbianism in popular films explains the absence of my desire while swinging in a larger, systemic way. "The heroine's bisexuality is merely a sexual ruse that amplifies her heterosexual attractiveness," he wrote about love triangles in 1990s films, in which the heterosexual couple always wins. Ultimately, we were all there to feed male heterosexual desire and to confirm and enact men's right to that desire. There was nothing lesbian or self-actualizing about it.

Our first night of swinging became the first time we'd do much of what can be done in swinging. Later, Ivan and Vanya would laugh admiringly at how unfettered we were, which they said was unusual for newbies. In some ways this is not surprising: Rick and I were both relatively free of sexual hang-ups and had done plenty of our own experimenting at the beginning of our relationship. And we were immediately comfortable with Ivan and Vanya. By the end of the night—which is to say, when the sun came up—we were exhausted, famished, and bonded by a shared amazement at this strange new thing we had done together.

Ivan and Vanya quickly became the solution to our enervated marriage. Just home from the first encounter, we started scheming to arrange for more. Handily, we had a getaway on the calendar already, a precious three-day weekend when my parents were scheduled to take care of our kids. For our upcoming twelfth wedding anniversary we had booked an isolated, romantic adventure in a luxurious tree house, nestled in a forest and accessible only by a series of zip lines. Meals would be zip-lined in; otherwise, we'd have that bit of forest to ourselves. It was exactly the kind of experience that would have thrilled us in the early years, equal parts intimate, exciting, and athletic. But in 2007, I think we both wondered what we would do with ourselves for all of those unbroken hours together. We'd waited a long time for the opportunity, which had required us to book a year ahead. A few days after meeting Ivan and Vanya, I found myself calling the tree-house people to ask if we could bring two friends. The question was ridiculous. No, the tree house could not accommodate four people. The tree house was for couples only, for their solitude and intimacy. The tree house did not recognize that some couples could only create intimacy by bringing another couple to have sex with instead of each other.

The long line of couples eager to book secreted tree houses for their healthy private intimacy meant that we were able to break our reservation without losing the enormous fee we'd paid to keep it. Now we were free to find a place that would allow us to celebrate our anniversary in the only way we seemed to be capable of celebrating it—without having to interact too much with each other. We booked a large suite at the place where we'd stayed on our previous anniversary, a casual B&B in the country. From the first stay, I remember the hiking trails, massages, and the kind man who made and served our delicious meals. From the second, I remember the thrill of entering the cozy dining area holding hands with Ivan and wondering if the kind man noticed, if he knew what we were doing in his quiet country inn. Early on, my enjoyment of transgression, the feeling of breaking out of the small space I felt shoved into, became something I genuinely enjoyed about swinging and clung to.

That weekend we four established patterns that would characterize most of our future interactions. We had an enormous amount of vigorous, creative sex in multiple combinations, but primarily in swapped pairs. Our drinking shifted from careful cocktails to sloppy shots as the night wore on, and eating leaned toward dense, high-calorie snacks, like we were athletes grinding their way through an Ironman. Sessions would begin with Vanya and me enticing the guys and each other—perhaps a joint striptease that we'd planned the week before, with Vanya supplying the wild lingerie from her extensive collection—then they'd devolve into sex on beds, chairs, and tables, involving toys or food, feathers or candle wax, with intermittent showers and rest as required. Those in-between moments became the times when our friendships grew in all combinations as well. Once at the B&B, while Rick and Vanya had sex nearby on the big bed, Ivan and I lay spent on the little lounge where we'd wound up, talking like a couple on a third or fourth date, sharing life stories. Another evening, Vanya invited me to join her in the shower while she prepared for the night's festivities. I sat naked on the tile next to her and we chatted, like friends in a dorm room, while she methodically shaved her vulva in short, careful strokes in preparation for having sex with my husband.

As with all respectful sex, ground rules are essential for swinging. Rick's and my inability to agree on these made swinging a reiteration of the marital dysfunction that had led us to swinging in the first place. Initially, we all agreed to Rick's demand in the B&B that we remain in the same room during all sexual activity. But Ivan and I wandered off pretty quickly to have sex in a neighboring room. This is when I discovered what swinging could be for me: a chance to get away from Rick and his sexual demands, to actually *leave the room* when he wanted sex and know that he would have those needs met in a way that had nothing to do with me. All I had to do was have sex with this other person who was, if not someone I was emotionally connected to, at least not someone I expected to be emotionally connected to but wasn't. He was someone who was perfectly nice and extremely technically talented, who found me sexy and was happy to tell me so, and from whom I expected nothing but pleasure and to be treated with respect and kindness. He was fine, and I was, in some weird way, free.

There's a moment that has puzzled my memory for so long that I couldn't figure out where it belonged in this story, what it meant then or now. I was washing my hands in a bathroom at the B&B, alone and quiet. Something bubbled up in me—pure joy, a happiness so powerful that I could not remember having felt its equal for a long time. "I love this so much!" I whooped into the hollow of the bathroom. I stood at the window looking out at the night sky without thought, without reflection, allowing this peculiar revelation to flood in. I have never taken the kinds of drugs that replace your sense of self with ecstatic explosion, but I imagine that this is what it would feel like: every kind of suffering blasted away by a torrent of bliss. When I related this feeling to Rick later, as I did all swinging things, I tried to explain by comparing it to riding the most thrilling roller coaster 24-7. The Hulk at Universal Studios for three days straight.

For a long time, I remembered that moment in the bathroom and the telling of it with deep shame: How could I experience sex with near strangers, sex I had not wanted to have in the first place, and sometimes did not want to have as I kept having it, as blissful? But it wasn't the sex that made me ecstatic; it was the freedom. That moment of exultation in a big, empty room materialized neatly what swinging gave me, at its best: a space for myself, apart from Rick, in which I could move unmolested by him. A space in which no one imposed anything on me or my body that I didn't in some way desire, a space I could fill with my own choices. The fact that Rick had pushed me into the territory in which I was allowed to make those choices did not stop me from feeling the pleasure of my power to choose. It was so much more power and choice than I had in my relationship with him. But it was a terribly qualified freedom, an ex-hilaration of one part of me that relied on the dormancy of another and a freedom to choose among things I would not on my own have chosen.

Deborah Levy: "If we cannot at least imagine we are free, we are living a life that is wrong for us." I needed to at least be able to imagine I was free; then I could bear the rest a while longer. Also Levy: "Freedom is never free. Anyone who has struggled to be free knows how much it costs."

8. CONTROL

I imagine, and media images confirm, that there are places where swinging occurs by the light of day, or at least by the light of Main Street bars and clubs. But we became swingers while living in the conservative, Republican, hyperreligious South, so from the start swinging felt intensely taboo and shameful, something that must remain hidden at all costs. The one and only swinging club we found in our hometown was housed in a strip mall, its blacked-out glass walls sparing unsuspecting, God-fearing passersby from the knowledge that consenting adults were allowed to mingle in all sorts of creative ways just down the block from a Dunkin' Donuts. Every time I opened my wallet, I worried the flimsy little membership card would fall out, exposing my debauchery. I started keeping it buried in the glove box of my car. The club's interior was like any other, dominated by dance floors, bars, and seating areas, with a few significant additions: lining the walls were rows of curtained hideaways where couples or threesomes or multiples of any number could extend the action begun on the dance floor. Since the vast majority of swingers are not only middle-aged but of child-rearing ages (thirty-six to fifty-five), providing ways for swingers to "get a room" without going home makes a lot of sense.

Like every subculture, swinging has its own carefully maintained rules and procedures. On our first visit to the club, we nursed overpriced drinks under strobe lights while extrapolating its customs like anthropologists. Women *always* approached first. It was absolutely unacceptable for a man to express interest in another man's wife or date before the couples had met and decided ("mutually," it was assumed) that they were all interested in interacting with each other. The only way the interaction could happen was for the woman of one couple to approach the woman of another. Over nearly two years of swinging, I saw this ritual play out at clubs, parties, and dates across the country. Years later, while teaching, I'd see it referenced in Lisa Taddeo's *Three Women* and feel the odd sensation of my old and new selves exchanging a glance over the heads of my graduate students. It was an odd performance of chivalry, intended, I think, to make women feel empowered—that we were making the choices and were in control—whether or not we actually were.

It saddens me now to realize that those curtained beds lining the walls of the swingers' club, that all the beds at clubs and houses and hotels where I had sex with all of those supposedly liberated people offered none of the transgressive freedom I found years earlier in a dorm-room bed where I got to have an adventure while keeping hold of myself.

One aimless Friday night in college, enacting a tipsy bravado that would never be repeated, my roommate and I teased our male friend up to the roof of our dorm. While gazing down on the mass of students assembling after classes in the quad below, we took turns kissing him. I was more agog at my straightlaced roommate's participation than I was at this mildest of threesomes we were having in relative public. An absolute gentleman, our friend took what was offered with bemused pleasure and asked for nothing else. I could lose several digits in a brush-clearing accident and still count on one hand the number of men who have behaved with such grace in a sexual encounter.

Back in his room, adventure concluded, my roommate and I prepared to leave. In a moment of pure, unreflective impulse, I slipped my ID onto the corner of his desk. Once my roommate was elsewhere engaged, I returned to retrieve the ID—whereupon I led the young man through a wholly unscheduled, unasked-for romp during which, again, he took only what was gleefully offered and gave boundless pleasure and appreciation in return. When I left, after a sweet kiss at his door, I felt entirely clean and wholesome, my boundaries untrespassed. He looked like he had received a gift from God. We remained casual friends; nothing changed between us, except that our delicious secret bubbled under every future conversation. How many sexual experiences like that have I had? Times when I got to choose, absolutely, what I would or would not do, when I was not bullied or guilted into a performance I wanted no part of, when

I emerged with my autonomy intact? Few enough to have learned that sex was usually a battle I would lose.

Underneath its chivalrous façade, swinging was, in my experience, just another iteration of patriarchal norms designed to control women while giving us the illusion of power. There we were, perfectly groomed in our sexy clothes and stilettos, putting on shows on the dance floor and catching men's eyes, then slinking to the bar area to close the deal with the other wives and girlfriends. An outsider looking in, watching all these women reeling in men like Sirens—women navigating dark spaces with husbands trailing behind them, approaching strangers in sleek jackets to broker serious exchanges—might see a swinging club as one of the few places in America that could rightly be called a matriarchy. But how many of these women had initiated the swinging? I was immersed in the culture and read blogs and listened to podcasts about "the Lifestyle"; I know that many women express enthusiasm equal to their male partners'. I also got to know women whose own expressed enthusiasm should more accurately have been attributed, like mine, to their male partners. So I wonder how many of these women whom I met at the club had, between meetings and car pools, with the insufficient energy remaining after a long week, announced that night, "Honey, what I really want is *more* sex, more complicated things to negotiate, more people to manage"?

Most swingers are middle to upper class, well educated, and well into their marriages, having been married an average of eleven to twenty years. What most swingers are not is young enough to be entirely unencumbered by the things that sap our energy and libidos: demanding jobs, mortgages and other financial responsibilities, domestic work, and children. While swinging often results from the desire to bust through such drudgery before it can consume any remaining passion, my experience and that of many women I met confirmed statistics: we weren't usually the ones with the energy and drive to initiate swinging.

Sometimes when Rick and I were dancing at the club, I would give his chest a playful push to send myself spinning off into my own piece of dance floor, where I would bust out what I considered my sexiest moves. I did it with a coquettish smile, hoping to convince him that the maneuver was part of the dancing we were doing together rather than what it obviously was—my way of getting rid of him for a minute and pretending I was performing solo on a stage that had misplaced its pole. Temporarily alone and giving it my all in my transparent peekaboo heels, I registered every head that turned my way. This part of clubbing I enjoyed very much. After briefly tolerating my rudeness, Rick would deliver a lordly "Stop it!," at which point my fun would be over for the night. As with our dates with Ivan and Vanya, the pleasure of clubbing for me was being my own sexual self and making (or fantasizing I was making) sexual choices that did not include Rick. That was not at all what Rick wanted from swinging.

So began the pattern that would repeat and intensify until peaking on the day of the busted baby carriage. Rick wanted me to swing with him. He *insisted* that I do it and emotionally manipulated me into doing it, which means he bullied me into having sex with other people. Since he clearly didn't care about *my* sexual desire, for him or for whomever he was pressing me to have sex with, he did all this to revive *his* sex life, that one thing he needed: he pimped me out. But his need had to in part be satisfied by me.

When Ivan and I wandered off to have sex by ourselves, as we did increasingly often, Rick became depressed, morose. The first time, at the B&B, Rick sat Ivan and me down to lecture us about how I had hurt him, how selfish I'd been, how important it was for me to understand that we were here to enjoy this experience *together*. This was about our *marriage*; we had to share *all* of it. Often at the end of a swinging evening I was entreated by Vanya or expected by Rick to return to him to finish things off. Swinging thus became, like couples therapy, another thing we were doing in a desperate attempt to stay together that just revealed how far apart we already were. For me, it was a vehicle to get away from him and his sexual demands that cared nothing for me, to gain some sense of control over my body. For him it was, at least in part, another vehicle back to me and my body and another way to control me.

This became increasingly clear the longer we were swinging. Months after we'd moved away from Ivan and Vanya, Rick orchestrated our attendance at a swingers' party. Once things got going, I left him naked in a hot tub full of women, several of whom were obviously angling for his attention. Though my stated mission was drinks procurement, I was also on some unacknowledged level absenting myself from him ahead of the oncoming sex. As if in a movie, perhaps a slightly less misogynistic re-make of *Eyes Wide Shut*, I stumbled into a full-blown orgy. In its other life, the space must have been the living room, but now it was filled wall-to-wall with mattresses and lounge chairs where twining people made a sea of limbs, torsos, and hair. Of course I was drunk and had initiated the required unselfing before even donning the harem garb required by the party's theme.

In that dark place of non-relating, free from self-possession, where I and everyone who touched me was all and only body—this place my mar-riage had trained me to build and seek—I did what the occasion called for: I dived in. But it didn't really take any diving. I simply signaled my willingness somehow, and the writhing mass engulfed me, incorporating me into a multiplayer version of the first night with Vanya: instead of one pair of hands gently stroking my thighs, pulling the tie on my blouse, it was many. I was being kissed, caressed, and undressed somewhat simulta-neously, and I don't know if even in the moment I could say exactly what I was doing to whom or what was being done by whom to me. If dissolu-tion of self had become the balm that sex could provide me, I had found the ultimate method of it.

I didn't notice Rick enter the room, and I don't know what he saw before he reached me. I remember his hands on me, yanking, screaming. I recall startled yelps of confusion and displeasure from those around me as he extricated me from the mass. I remember people expressing offense on my behalf and concern for me. Then he marched me into the back of the house, where we retrieved our clothes and things. It was about 3 a.m., and we were both blisteringly drunk; we had planned to spend the night. But his rage was so keen that it seemed for a while to cut through his in-ebriation. He pulled me outside and berated me loudly while we waited for someone to retrieve the car. It arrived minus his new iPod, adding to his fury and somehow to my shame. The drive home would have taken about three and a half hours under optimal conditions, which do not in-clude being blind drunk in the middle of the night. As he blazed down the highway, struggling to read signs and stay between the lines, I was terrified. I imagined the headline: COUPLE KILLED IN HIGHWAY ACCIDENT AFTER FLEEING DISGUSTING SWINGER PARTY WHERE WIFE ACTED LIKE TOTAL WHORE.

While writing this account, I found a very different portrait of that night in an email from a woman I'd met:

> I am assuming you remember me . . . we met at a party. . . . I know your husband was grumpy at the end of the night so that might have taken away from the happy warm memories you have of me. . . . I thought you were strong, pretty, smart and fun which is a rare find . . . so I had hoped to keep in touch.

How had I managed to strike this woman as "strong" and "smart" that night, dressed as the sex slave I felt like when Rick removed me from the party and shamed me into our car? I hadn't kept in touch; I was embarrassed enough by the swinging that I didn't allow its world to cross into the one where I was an English professor and mother of two. Yet somehow this woman had discerned the me under the costume and the posing, and had liked me and wanted to know me. She saw me, even the swinging version of me, as a valuable person apart from the sex, something Rick had not been able to do for years.

And what had I been thinking when, in all sobriety, I chose, purchased, then donned clothing and accessories that marked me as a sex slave? Maybe I was thinking something similar to what my parents and teachers were thinking when they dressed me as a "slave girl" when I was eight to sing and dance in *Joseph and the Amazing Technicolor Dreamcoat*: what a fun costume! The gaudy bangles and earrings I wore in that Christian musical at my Episcopalian school weren't that different from the ones I wore thirty years later to have sex I didn't really want because someone else really wanted me to. In both contexts, at both ages, nobody, including me, found my being dressed or treated as a sex slave unusual or offensive. Like that child of eight, I kept the jewelry from the party for a long time, as a symbol of my exotic boldness. It took me years to admit the truth: My costume wasn't a mask at all. It was the revelation of who I was—a woman with tenuous rights to her own body.

That terrifying, interminable night was, it turned out, a preview of The Worst Day of My Life, confining all its elements to a car hurtling dangerously through the dark. As Rick drove, he screamed accusations and insults at me: I was selfish, shameful, disgusting; I didn't care about his feelings. Perhaps he realized that however fine he was with killing me, he wasn't ready to die, because eventually he pulled off the highway and into a motel parking lot. We got a room and collapsed into drunken comas on separate beds. But before I knew it he was shaking me awake and ordering me back into the car so we could get home to our happy life.

9. FAMILY

Many people report deriving considerable pleasure and increased marital satisfaction from all forms of consensual non-monogamy. Women say they feel empowered by real sexual freedom. Philosophy professor Carrie Jenkins's *What Love Is* (2017) compellingly argues that CNM makes romantic love more sustainable, personally fulfilling, and equitable between men and women. Today, far removed from our doomed experiment, I believe these reports and arguments, and I envy the generous and respectful relationships that undergird them. But what Rick and I were doing was not truly consensual non-monogamy: I did not fully consent to all the sex and he did not fully consent to the non-monogamy. So CNM was not our problem. The misery and conflict I experienced while swinging can all be traced to the disconnections and disrespect in my marriage that long predated our swinging and long outlasted it. Swinging came to seem like the only available solution to an endlessly painful dilemma that I could not otherwise solve: How to continue to share a life with a man with whom I shared so little?

The drive to Ivan and Vanya's house was my favorite portion of a night with them. For those three hours, Rick and I had a common purpose, something to talk about that interested and excited him. I remember those drives with warmth and fondness (not so much the hungover plodding homeward); they were, I think, the closest we got to reliving the intimacy of our adventurous early years. Physically demanding, exhilarating, and a bit risky and transgressive, swinging became our married-with-young-kids version of ocean kayaking, climbing Kilimanjaro, and biking along the Rhine.

Crucially for me, swinging diverted much of Rick's sexual need else-where. We had so much sex on the weekends with Ivan and Vanya that I mostly got a free pass during the week, and weeknight sex remained in the framework of swinging. Once, we swung virtually, watching Ivan and Vanya on our screen and then performing for them. I have no idea what technology enabled such a thing in the pre-smartphone era; I entered the stage on cue and played my part. Making sex an overt performance like this was an immense relief: it normalized the performance that sex had become, painfully, in my marriage. Meanwhile, it felt strangely liberating to perform sex for people with whom there was no pretense of profound connection, rather than for a man whose intense "love" for me was pun-ishing. However much I initially resisted it, and however little I desired it for its own sake, swinging became something that made my life work. That is to say, it enabled my marriage to continue.

Tangled up with these negative motivations for swinging were posi-tive ones that led to some genuinely sweet and even beautiful memories. Our relationship with Ivan and Vanya briefly morphed into an uneven, unacknowledged, but nevertheless semi-functional kind of polyamory. It brought real intimacy to my life when I felt devastated and alone—but not through the sex that was ostensibly its purpose. In between orgiastic meet-ups, we four maintained friendly contact through email and instant messaging. Always the conversations were warm and fun and, like our sex, they took advantage of all possible combinations. As weekends drew near, Ivan and Vanya would message me and Rick individually, maintain-ing the connections, teasing upcoming pleasures, floating ideas and plans. We cooked lovely dinners for each other, and Vanya made sweet crepes for famished mornings. She and I began to exchange recipes for the high-calorie snacks we'd make for our athletic get-togethers. I still encounter "Vanya's Banana Bread" when poking around the desserts section of my accordion recipe file.

Ivan and Vanya came to feel like such a normal part of our lives that we briefly admitted them into our other life. One Sunday morning after a swinging Saturday night, Rick and I invited them to stay for the remain-der of the day. I retrieved the children from my parents, and the four of us took the kids to our neighborhood pool, where Ivan romped in the water with our six-year-old son. Back at home, Ivan showed him some soccer moves in our backyard, then he and Vanya stayed for dinner with our family before beginning the long drive home.

When I teach Gayle Rubin's sex-positive theory, I absolutely believe it: we should judge sex acts by how we treat each other in them, with what degree of respect and autonomy we show one another, not by the acts themselves or the body parts and number of people involved. Yet I see myself—the past self I'm spying on as I write this and the current self who is writing—encountering this memory with so much shame, as if, of all the cruel things Rick and I did, integrating these two parts of our lives was the most reprehensible. Ivan and Vanya were our friends, and they were never anything but kind. What Rick and I did with them belonged to the lives that adults are allowed to have separate from their kids and did not affect our parenting. So why is it so mortifying to remember Ivan and Vanya sitting at the table with my family?

I don't doubt I can attribute some of my shame to the patriarchal (which is to say heteronormative, homophobic, and highly anxious) sexual morality I was raised with. You can fight it like hell, but that stuff knows how to go to ground and pop up when you least expect it. But more so, I think the memory of that tableau is painful not because of any resent-ment toward Ivan and Vanya or embarrassment about the things we did together but because it materialized the foul state of my marriage, what a powerless outsider I was in my fake life, right in the middle of my family room. We had fun with Ivan and Vanya. But I never would have chosen to "fix" my marriage by burying my realest self and spreading the remain-der among three people, none of whom I truly loved. When I think of my children finding out about our swinging one day, I don't fear their moral judgment of inter-marital foursome sex. I hope I've taught them better than that. But I cringe at the thought of them knowing how willing I was to betray myself, how happy their dad was to convince me to do it, and how much decay moldered behind the pretty picture of our perfect family.

Later I would discover that Ivan and Vanya's marriage was fouled by a similar rot that swinging could mask but not cure. And Vanya's par-ticipation in swinging had been commandeered as surely as had mine. After we had stopped seeing Ivan and Vanya as a foursome, Rick and Vanya remained in peripatetic contact, and he relayed to me how her sad story unfolded. She had met and married Ivan shortly after moving from

Russia to the US to complete a graduate degree. Swinging was a condition of the relationship, and the relationship anchored her in her entirely new and disorienting life. Unable to understand the complexity of my own ambivalence at the time, I certainly hadn't seen the cracks in Vanya's façade of contented consent. To me, Vanya had always been the consummate swinger: welcoming, nonthreatening, equally caretaking as a sexual partner and friend. She gave me copies of her favorite books and brought me little gifts from Russia, including a beautifully painted wooden box that still sits amid other keepsakes in my study. Tucked inside is a folded square of blue paper filled with Vanya's slanted scrawl, her characteristic mixture of wry jokes and unselfconscious expressions of friendly love.

By the end of our swinging time with Vanya and Ivan, she was also in love with Rick, of course. I found this utterly unsurprising, understanding how Rick's gentleness must have felt compared to Ivan's patriarchal autocracy. It didn't bother me at all. In fact, sometimes I entertained the fantasy that Vanya and Rick would run away together, leaving me truly free. But I knew that would never happen. Rick was not in love with Vanya. Instead, once we stopped seeing Ivan and Vanya he retrenched in our own matrimonial battle, while Vanya gradually fought her way to freedom from Ivan. Rick passed along Vanya's reports from the front of that battle, which presaged what was coming for me: Ivan barring her from their joint finances, attacking her, refusing to participate in the divorce. But I heard these things from a great distance. They were about people I did not know anymore. Eventually I heard that Vanya and Ivan had divorced, and all I could feel was proud of Vanya and enormously envious.

When at the end of our swinging summer we prepared to move across the country for my new position as an English professor, we invited Ivan and Vanya to come along for the trip. We needed someone to drive one of our two cars, since I tend to nod off at the wheel, and we knew they wanted to see more of the US. What Rick and I didn't admit to each other was that we also knew their company would make the trip a lot more endurable, even enjoyable. With the kids set to join Rick and me by plane at the other end, the four of use drove and slept in swapped couples for a week. This arrangement kept spouses apart most hours of many days and seemed to suit all of us—except Rick, whose periodic anger at my absence and need for my sexual appeasement punctuated an otherwise revelrous road trip.

By the time we got to Florida, about three days in, we had begun to feel and act like an alternative family. Ivan and Vanya wanted to see the ocean, so we drove until we reached a beach, just before sunset. Sore and stiff and hungry after hours of driving, we tumbled out of the cars and headed for the surf. Our liberation from the cramped spaces met the vastness of the sky and ocean in an almost overwhelming feeling of joy. I remember seeing the same enormity register on the others' faces as I felt it myself, and the shared awe joined us in that moment in a kind of reverence. Suddenly Ivan bounded back from the car bearing boxes of food leftover from lunch, and we passed them around, eating with our hands indiscriminately from the boxes, led only by what tasted good, not caring which box had belonged to whom. It felt like a kind of communion. I felt loved and provided for by all of these people, and I did not care who belonged to whom. I've never felt anything like it before or since.

After the feast, I walked down the beach with Ivan or Vanya. My memory is of not the person beside me but the calm intimacy of it, sand on my bare feet as we strolled along an edge of rushes, the sky above a gorgeous terrine of colors and densities. Suddenly those layers opened up, and as wind and rain exploded we sprinted wildly back toward the stretch of beach where we'd parked, laughing with exhilaration. In my memory we dive into the surf, plunging under the water to escape the pelting missiles of rain, a fitting baptism after our shared communion. But that can't be right—who would do such a thing in a massive summer storm? Did I? I don't really know. But I remember it.

When we four arrived in the town where Rick and I would start our new lives, we started nesting as if preparing the house for all of us. The fridge had been left off and closed; it was filled with mold and stench and required a thorough cleaning before we could use it or the kitchen. After such a long drive, the task seemed totally beyond me. But Ivan just rolled up his sleeves and got to work, and soon we were all pitching in until that problem was solved. Every other task provoked the same group effort, the same easy solution. Our furniture would not arrive for a day or two, so the homeowners had thoughtfully left a king-sized futon mattress on the floor of the master bedroom for Rick and me to use until then. Tired from hours of cleaning and unpacking, with sex nowhere near any of our minds, the four of us climbed onto the mattress that night and slept like a family of mammals in a den. Somehow everyone seemed to hold everyone, chastely, till we yawned and stretched together in the next day's light.

That was not the end of our relationship with Ivan and Vanya, but it was the beginning of the end. They came to visit a couple of months later, on Ivan's thirtieth birthday, and we did our best to manufacture the fantastic space of freedom we'd made with them before the move. But now my life was in a much higher gear, and I had no help from anyone—no longer from my parents, and not from Rick, who was content to allow me to continue to do most of the domestic work and childcare, though my new job required more working hours than did his. I was mentally and physically exhausted all the time and could not muster the energy I once had, or faked, or both, for the swinging or the four-way relationship.

One night during that visit, Ivan approached me in the bathroom before I stepped into the shower, asking if I was okay. I was weighed down by a host of concerns that lay far outside the world we occupied with Ivan and Vanya: finding new doctors for Rick and the kids and me; finding a quality preschool and after-school care; helping my older son with his difficult transition into kindergarten; and figuring out how to manage my already overwhelming new job. I felt alone in these burdens, as Rick carried none of them, and they were not appropriate topics for pre- or postcoital conversation with our childless friends. Not understanding but wanting to express care, Ivan shocked me with a decidedly un-swingery declaration: "We love you." His required "we" felt a bit like a disguised "I," and I found it disturbing that someone who knew me so little—who knew only my body well—would say such a thing. Somehow Rick and I had created a larger relationship that repeated the alienated foundation of our own. The feeling of intimacy and family that had made the whole thing a palatable solution for my hollow marriage evaporated.

The last ecstatic moment we shared with Ivan and Vanya came a couple of months later, at the New Year's Eve party. Like our drives to meet Ivan and Vanya, the best part of that swingers' extravaganza turned out to be the preliminary warm-up in the club. When the dancing ended and the glitter balls went dim, we boarded a bus packed with swingers who called out to each other ("Didn't I see you on the pole?" "You were great in the shadow box!") and brazenly fondled each other in the dark. It deposited us at the nearby hotel where we had all checked in earlier, and everyone scattered to their rooms to set up props and drink stations. Many changed into a second, sexier outfit to prepare for the radical after-party. We felt like college kids or celebrities, or both. As usual, we four had planned to experience the party's peak as swapped couples: Ivan and I wanted to roam the hotel looking for adventures, while Rick and Vanya would stick to our hotel room. When our explorations turned up nothing interesting, Ivan and I returned to our own room and joined what was happening there—some configuration of Rick, Vanya, and another couple. Unlike the earlier dancing, when I became a lightning rod, this was something else that I did without desire. It was what I was supposed to do, so I did it until I was allowed to go to sleep.

The next day, Rick and I drove to a nearby town where my great aunt was living her last days in a nursing home. It was horrifying, as all such places are. The air reeked of urine and disinfectant, and as we wandered the corridors searching for my dear aunt's room, we encountered disoriented people with glazed eyes lurching down the hallways unattended. I did not know whether to look at my dying aunt's blank, ravaged face and glory in how powerfully alive I'd felt in that cage just hours before or register the terrifyingly short distance between that place and moment and this one. In this brave new life, was I vibrant and free? Or anesthetized, lost, and lurching.

10. WHAT WE OWE EACH OTHER

B y the beginning of 2008, I felt more than ever like Mimi Rogers's vacated body in *The Rapture*. I knew I had to do something. I tried.

Soon after that New Year's party, on a "date night" with Rick, I gathered my meager courage again and spoke aloud another dark truth: "I think we should try a separation." It had taken me weeks to be able to eke it out, and eking was all I was able to do. I was a mouse when I should have been a lion; I should have been a hippopotamus (deadliest animal in Africa!); I should have been a fucking fire-spitting dragon. I should have eaten Rick's head off in one clean crunch between cocktails and appetizers. But eking was the most I could manage. He replied with the same kind of disparagement with which he had dismissed my concerns about our relationship and sex life in couples counseling years before. It didn't matter. Two days later, at 8 a.m. on a Monday morning, Rick's doctor called and said that he had invasive cancer and needed immediate surgery. The cancer would almost certainly return at some point, and he would have to be closely monitored for the rest of his life.

Once I'd heard the whole doctor's report, I knew the rest of my life had been determined. However miserable I was in my marriage, nothing could justify leaving a man who was about to undergo a massive procedure like this one, a man whose mortality might be in question for a time and whose health might always be delicate. For the next month or so, I didn't have time to mourn the loss of an alternative future in which I might be happy and free. My job, one of many, became clear: to take care of Rick, to be by his side, to care for his physical needs and reassure him, all of which I did impeccably and with the taste of bile in my mouth. Rick's diagnosis felt like my prison sentence: life without parole.

With any question of leaving removed, other things started falling into place. We built a state-of-the-art energy-efficient house with every available bell and whistle—not just an obscene amount of high-end granite in the inconveniently large kitchen, but ten-foot ceilings throughout and marble in a master shower so big it never got warm enough to enjoy. Designing this massive house that I did not want to live in with a man I felt no emotional connection to or from became my penance for not appreciating my great fortune and for all the selfish things I had done. I threw myself into the detested project that had been assigned to me: mapping out blueprints; poring over kitchen options, fixture catalogs, and paint colors; and harnessing my obsessive perfectionism to hide my disdain for every aspect of the job. As the total cost rose, and I watched us sink our entire joint savings into the thing, building the house became an orgy of expenditure, my way of throwing into it everything we had, so there was another practical reason that I could never leave. I made these decisions for exactly the same reason that I registered in college for a public speaking class that terrified me: once I had spent the money, I knew I would not back out. I blackmailed myself into recommitting to my marriage at exactly the moment when I started to realize I had to leave.

So we upgraded the floating stairs with a custom stainless-steel railing system, a ridiculous decision I lobbied for myself. The little rods that run from rails to floor rattle in their footings every time you step on a stair. Their chatter is maddening, unfixable, and cost us $20,000. When people pity yet another marriage killed by a major home renovation, they miss the point: how building a house can manifest around you every gap, absurdity, and dysfunction upon which your life is already built.

By the time we moved into the house that seemed to contain all our past and future, we'd left by the wayside nearly everything that ideally constitutes a marriage—not just its initial purity and hope, or our emotional connection, but the very notion that it involved two autonomous people. Swinging had shown that our relationship actually required the opposite. Rick's cancer diagnosis reforged my commitment to a marriage that had been entirely emptied—of love, of union, of mutual respect—and persevered only as a shell of responsibility and performance. Between that diagnosis and the move into the new house unfolded a year during which I felt bound to this duty but freed from my loyalty to Rick. As his wife, I believed I owed him things till death, caretaking and sex primary among them. I felt I was owed some things in return. That year devolved into a nightmarish experiment: What happens to your body and heart in a marriage that has become a set of balancing scales? How many pounds of flesh can each of you heap on the other's side and survive?

Rick's surprisingly quick recovery from surgery made my reprieve from sex with him and others short-lived. With Ivan and Vanya out of reach, he started looking around for swinging options in our area. That first cold spring in our Northern hometown crawled along in a series of swinging forays that brought us no joy: the harem party, some foursome dates. Everything stayed dark and bare for so much longer than I expected. It seemed the winter would never end.

In pursuit of a little actual joy, I drove to a town a few hours away to visit my dear friend from college, a professor at another university. Wes and I had met-cute in a German language class twenty years earlier. Paired with me for conversation practice, he proffered a beginner's question, "Wie heisst deine Schule?" ("What's your high school called?"), which I politely answered. Having grown up in the same town, he knew its school districts. Wes combined his oddball humor and most of the other German words he knew to make the cogent observation, "Ah, du hast viel Geld!" ("Oh, you have a lot of money!"). Which wasn't the least bit true. He nabbed me after class to apologize, and we quickly fell into an engaging conversation, this time in English, that took us all the way back to my dorm room.

Soon we were spending all our free time together, lazing on grassy hills or haunting campus corners talking about philosophy (his major), literature (mine), music (we were both drummers), and all the things that animate college students' lives. We were best friends in an instant and only grew closer over decades during which spouses, children, and careers complicated our lives. That Wes had confessed his love and sexual attraction to me soon after we met and at various times over our long friendship, eventually adding his desire to marry me, hardly seemed to matter. We knew we loved each other, and the fact that only one of us felt romantic and sexual desire toward the other could not lessen that love. Instead, my constant rejection of his desire became one of the many things about our relationship that we fondly called "OMC." Intensely connected but platonic, we were an "old married couple" from the start.

The first night of that 2008 visit, after his family left the house, Wes came down to the basement bedroom where I was tucked away. I had sex with him. I had no idea why, because I didn't want to. I still didn't feel my friendly love for him as sexual attraction. What I did feel, very strongly, was his desire. At that time, I lived in a world defined by the pursuit of sex, in which the proper response to a man's desire was offering myself up, regardless of the presence or absence of my own desire. There, marital monogamy was a quaint, outdated fiction, not just for me and Rick but for Ivan and Vanya, for all the swinging couples we met, for Alex and James, even for Wes himself. I had watched him shepherd affairs from emotional to sexual territory often enough that I wondered whether his wife had chosen to tolerate them. In this new world, the thing that had caused me to reject him for twenty years—my lack of sexual desire for him—no longer mattered, and the other thing that might keep married friends from having sex—fidelity to their spouses—didn't exist. It was as if I could no longer find a reason not to give what he had always wanted of me. Meanwhile, sex devoid of my desire had become the only way of communicating care in my marriage. Perhaps it finally made some kind of weird sense in the context of my loving but asexual relationship with Wes.

The next morning, I worked out in his basement living room while he watched with a hunger he would have disguised only the day before. Afterward, when he approached to discuss the rest of the day, I dropped to my knees in front of him like a cheaply costumed French maid in a porn film. Again, I felt no sexual desire. I even repressed a faint repulsion. What was I doing?

I did not come of age watching porn, whose distorting effects Tracy Clark-Flory documents so vividly in *Want Me* (2021). But the swinging world I saw was certainly shaped by its tropes—not those of women-made porn, or "ethical" porn, or indie porn, but the mainstream misogynistic stuff that dominates not only the porn industry but the film industry in general. You'd often find porn playing in clubs or at gatherings, muted or moaning on TVs in corners or mounted over the bar. I suppose it was intended as an aphrodisiac. But it also provided the scripts of so much of what happened in those places: fake chivalry and a nod to female pleasure, followed by women performing every imaginable facet of male desire. Its sights and sounds and narrative arcs infiltrated your consciousness, reshaping your understanding of sex and desire, whether you wanted them to or not. While swinging, I transformed my body to fit the part, starving, tanning, and waxing myself; maintaining full highlights and blowouts; presenting myself topless, thonged, or in full-body fishnet, and suffering a spectrum of stilettos. It wasn't long before I started to perform the part that fit the costume. The swinging world provided all necessary props and stages.

At the height of the Ivan-and-Vanya fever, I even installed a stripper pole in my house. I remember the thrill of its arrival, wondering what the neighbors thought: What else could be in a pole-shaped box? Because it was easy to put up and take down, I could install it in my children's playroom on a Friday night while they slept and remove it before they woke. The athlete in me enjoyed practicing the strenuous climbs and spins that professional strippers execute with seeming ease. My wannabe porn star got into imitating Christina Applegate's Portishead routine. Once I'd learned a few moves from YouTube, I started choreographing my own sequences, calling in Rick from the living room to see. It was fun and fulfilling for a time, mostly in innocent ways. It occupied my body in a challenge I set for myself, while giving Rick and me something else to share. But in the context of our swinging life, and in performing for Ivan and Vanya or for the New Year's Eve crowd, pole dancing became another way to chase the false power that came from transforming myself into the object of others' desire.

I knelt in front of Wes like a porn star because it made me feel powerful. Here was a man who had lusted after me for twenty years, and I was about to blow his mind.

Afterward, when we were once again two old friends and mid-career college professors, he puttered around the kitchen making coffee and started The Talk. Gently, as if he were being very kind and considerate, Wes explained why we "couldn't keep doing this": not because he valued his marriage but because a new side relationship was heating up and he didn't want to jeopardize it. I was stunned speechless. I didn't point out that I didn't want to keep doing this and hadn't wanted to start doing it in the first place.

Continuing with the day's plan, we went out to lunch at the vegetarian place I loved. As we sat across from each other and chatted like we had done countless times before, the weirdness began to dissipate. I remembered who we were: best friends. The people who understood each other better than anyone else in the world, our spouses included. Eventually I found my voice and told him how deeply hurt I was. I had believed that he would value what I had given him much more highly. I thought that, in the context of our long, deep friendship, it would mean something important. Our history of nuanced conversations about every conceivable emotional complexity served us well, and we navigated this unexpectedly charged topic with grace. I left with our friendship irrevocably changed but intact.

A few months later, I received an email from Wes in which he explained that he could not see me the next time I was in town to visit a friend who also lived there. He had told his wife that he was going to be away visiting me soon, to cover the fact that he was actually hooking up with his latest affair. We didn't often find time to see each other, and it would look odd if we did so quickly after this supposed visit; his wife might ask questions. Wes was discarding an upcoming opportunity to see me to enable his new adventure. Reading that email, I suddenly realized what I had been to Wes all those years. I was not his platonic soulmate, not one half of a tragic mismatch that made us star-crossed best friends. Maybe I had been at one time. But once I had sex with him, when I thought I was giving him his life's fantasy, I became just another woman he had coaxed into sex through generous emotional investment. The only difference between me and the many other women he had seduced this way is that I had taken twenty years to break. He was the master of the long con, and I was his greatest dupe.

I never replied to Wes's email. That was over a decade ago, and he has never contacted me again, save to send his family's annual holiday letter. I assume he continues to send them to avoid tricky questions from his wife. I doubt he has any idea why I dropped out of his life. I can imagine the moral calculus that makes his treatment of me unimpeachable in his mind: I wasn't his wife, and what we did made us both cheaters, equally worthy of blame. So what did he owe me?

I had spent the winter taking care of a husband for whom I felt nothing and the spring having sex with people for whom I felt nothing in order to please him. Even my best friend had shown me that I was nothing so much as a body. I remained devastated by the loss of the email relationship with James that had made me feel like a person and desperate to find a similar salve that would enable me to suffer my marital sentence. A few months after Rick's surgery, when he was fully recovered and proclaimed cancer-free, I set out to find one.

I succeeded, immediately. It is amazing, or exactly not, how easy it is to find lonely married men who are starving for connection. They're everywhere. One of these I loved as a friend for years past our brief romantic involvement, a man who knows the fire I walked through because some of it we walked through together. I met Henry at the beginning of the summer following Rick's surgery. We moved from friendship to love affair quickly, each of us grasping at that magical thing I had found and then lost with James—another who loved art and ideas and who listened and saw us as whole people. He was a poet, and a good one; much of our bond developed through reading and discussing poetry together, often his, occasionally mine. His wife sneered at his creative practice and took every opportunity to remind him of the irrelevance of academia, his life's work. By Henry's accounts, he was as alone, unappreciated, and dominated in his marriage as I was, and he was as committed to staying put. We made an easy pair. Though it primarily took place online and in chaste conversations in public buildings, the relationship was a great boon to both of us. I was finally able to breathe again.

By Thanksgiving, Rick had discovered what I was up to. Always the clever one, he did so by manipulating me into admitting to the affair even though he only vaguely suspected it. "How did you know?" I asked. "You've been so happy lately, I knew something was up," he explained.

I promised him I would stop misbehaving with Henry, and I did. I withdrew my transgressive affections and converted our intense, life-saving relationship into a circumscribed and awkward friendship. I did this overnight, with no apology or expression of regret, only the explanation that Rick was threatening us both. According to the morality that considers sexual infidelity the worst thing you can do to another person, my sudden and heartless ending of the extramarital intimacy was the right thing to do. But today I see it as a betrayal that illustrates how ruthless I had become in assuaging my own suffering, how my need to save the marriage at all costs prevented me from acknowledging the consideration I owed Henry, regardless of the circumstances of our affection.

Years later, when I had fully extricated myself from my marriage and the entanglements that had kept it going for so long, which I did roughly simultaneously, Henry and I rebuilt an unambiguous friendship on the rubble of our short-lived affair. We resumed our poetry and teaching discussions and our mutual support. Still married, he was growing increasingly despondent in his family life. By then I was happily building a relationship with my now-partner, but Henry remained a treasured friend. I never forgot all he did to support me during my darkest days and did what I could to support him in his, which primarily meant listening as he articulated his sorrow at feeling disregarded and trapped, his fear that his children were learning to mistake scorn and mutual alienation for a healthy marriage. When he turned fifty, I spent hours making a handsewn chapbook of his poetry, wanting to mark the occasion with a reminder of the vibrant, poetic self he had buried to survive a marriage that would not acknowledge it.

A year later, his wife sent me an enraged email about our affair from over a decade earlier, which she had just discovered. She had evidently read many of the hundreds of emails we had sent in our brief time as lovers and long history as friends. She declared that I had used and manipulated her husband all that time and never cared for him except as an instrument to feed my ego. Once again, I was a selfish whore. She ordered me never to speak or write to him again. I knew Henry would apologize for her undeserved cruelty and correct her erroneous assumptions. We had been close, platonic friends for many years by then. But the first time I saw him after that email, asking for a book he'd promised to lend, he directed me to the library and ushered me out the door. He would not look me in the eye. He has rarely spoken to me since and then only when professionally required. We have never discussed what prompted his wife's email or her hateful beliefs about me, whether he shares them or pretends to in order to appease her. Like me when I abandoned him years earlier to protect my shitty marriage, he obviously thinks he owes me nothing.

Being excoriated by a woman who was not my friend and who bullied and belittled my dear friend Henry was painful enough. Knowing how badly I hurt her was painful enough. When Alex, my friend of nearly twenty years, found out about my affair with James and confronted me, also long after the affair had ended, and I had to bear her condemnation and witness her immense suffering, the pain was stunning. I don't say I didn't deserve it. In fact, you might say I had it coming. I was owed.

Meeting as we did on the brink of college graduation, Alex and I had grown up together. The night she met James I was her wingwoman, holding the rest of our crew steady at the bar while she got his number on the dance floor. We stood in each other's weddings a few years later, and I helped her write her vows. Rick had known her first in college, but through all the years of our foursome's outings and visits, she and I were the pair. Usually we went shopping, because it was her favorite and my most detested thing to do, so I often needed to do it. She routinely curated my professional wardrobe by mocking questionable fashion choices till we were in tears with laughter. Once, plucking a loud plaid jacket from my closet, she asked incredulously what I wore it with. No response could save me or the jacket. Her lovingly undiplomatic injunction still cracks me up: "And do you wear a red nose and big floppy shoes with it too?" When she had her first child and James was away for work, she flew with the baby to stay with me and Rick for weeks. I held the baby so she could finally sleep, and when she was ready I taught her those indispensable things no one tells you about, like wriggle-proof swaddling and how to nurse in public.

We were good friends. We were also very different people. I was not interested in fashion, and she was not interested in books, so we didn't have much to talk about—except the real things, the quotidian, our lives. We were very different people, but I loved her.

By the time I was falling for James, though, Alex and I had grown apart. Living in different regions of the country and occupied by our very different things, we reached a point at which the main thing we shared was marital frustration. I had listened for years as she complained about James and their painful ways of interacting. She often asked me for advice, and I thought I could help her understand him because their dynamic was so similar to mine with Rick. But since I was much more like James than like her, I thought I could see things from James's perspective. She knew their needs were at odds: he craved intellectual conversation and connection while she wanted to travel and go shopping and needed James to quietly be there and make her feel safe. Meanwhile, James had an enormous caretaking need and fear of failing at marriage, making their bond a strong one, however dysfunctional. I heard her complaints while suffering my own longing in my marriage for exactly what she disregarded in hers.

Until the night of the seven wine bottles, none of that translated into my coveting her husband. I simply never put things together like that in my mind. But after that night, and as the disintegration of my own marriage rapidly accelerated, I suddenly saw how alike James and I were in our interests, longings, and mismatched spouses, and everything shifted. The similarity of our marital dysfunctions made our transformed feelings seem almost justified. For a long stretch, James's and my unorthodox solution worked well: we asked fewer impossible things from our spouses because we were sated by each other. Rick and I were happier together than we had been for years. I could run fantasies of James in my head during sex rather than having to leave my body, making sex feel almost normal. Then came the time when Rick discovered our "happiness" required my relationship with James.

As long as I stayed in the marriage, whether Rick would tell Alex was never a question. But once our marriage was truly over he had nothing left to gain from silence. In 2010, I was divorced and had been living with the children in a basement apartment for a year and a half. James and I had been just peripatetic email friends for longer than that. It was Christmas Eve, and I was preparing to leave the house of my boyfriend's family after a lovely evening. I reached into my coat pocket for my phone and found Alex's string of hate-filled texts. As my foul past erupted once again into my painstakingly rehabilitated present, I felt instantly sick. I struggled to compose my face so I could say polite good-byes at the door. In the car, I responded to Alex with abject apology and offered to talk. It took her a few days to want to, but then we exchanged lengthy emails, followed by several nights of marathon phone conversations. She already knew pretty much everything. This is how I found out that Rick had installed keystroke-capturing software on my computer when I still lived with him. He had provided her with transcripts of instant messages and emails I had sent to James, a needlessly cruel thing to do: in punishing me, he brutalized Alex. The software he used to do both was illegal. But Rick obviously believed he owed me nothing by then.

I was completely honest with Alex while she bombarded me with fury and disgust. She was trying to work out what had happened, her husband's role in it, his feelings for me, whom to blame. Clearly she was getting a lot of obfuscation from him, for which I don't blame him much. He was fighting for his marriage, which, however dead, he still could not imagine losing. And anyway, what did he owe me? I knew exactly what that felt like. So I offered myself to Alex as a scapegoat; I took every punishment she could mete out, every insult and accusation. I apologized for things that were not mine to apologize for, on top of the mountain of things that were.

When the conversations petered out, she didn't seem to know what to do with me. And how could she? I had always been the one to help her through her life's heartbreaks. She had to establish a whole new support system to process the pain I had inflicted on her.

Soon after we talked, she shared that she was involved with another man. A few weeks later she turned to me one last time, asking for advice on how to leave her marriage. It was surreal. I tried to help her as I had always done, passing along what I had learned in leaving mine, advising her to go slow and think hard, to put the children first. She moved out almost immediately. I never heard from her again.

I've worked through much of my guilt and shame from this period, and I've put down by the side of the road great heaps of both that I should never have agreed to carry. I apologized to Rick until I saw that he would never be able to hear me. And I prostrated myself before Alex, accepted her punishment, and cried out my remorse. But I think of her moving through her life, this woman whose fragility I knew better than almost anyone, and I can hardly comprehend the extent of what my betrayal must have done to her. Her husband betrayed her as well, but I was her friend. I was the one she used to call when even her husband had hurt her. For her husband and me to have betrayed her together must have seemed monstrous to her, at least as monstrous as what Rick did to me.

When I ask myself what kind of woman could have done this to her good friend, I can't find a simple answer. The most immediate answer is that for years I had been living an utterly fragmented life. I learned to compartmentalize so well that I did it effortlessly and every second of the day. I was one person with my parents and children, another for Rick, another when swinging, another with Alex, and another when immersed in the magical world I occupied with James. Only that last version of me felt real and true. Each relationship got only the part of me that was wanted, and no one wanted the whole. And the part that felt most crucial to my sense of self was the one I gave to James, the only person who valued it.

Once, my therapist asked me what I thought would happen if I told Rick about the extent of my feelings for James. I couldn't even answer. I could not imagine surviving the devastation it would cause, though my therapist had to know I'd be forced to do it eventually. Later, the one time

James came to visit me, he said that he had never mentioned me to the analyst he was seeing for talk therapy six hours a week, as part of his own Freudian training. When I asked him why, he exclaimed, incredulous, "Because he'd tell me I have to end my relationship with you!" Neither of us could bear it. As psyches often do under stress, we splintered.

There are good reasons why my psyche was prone to splintering under this kind of stress. Some of them stem from the damaging things that were happening in my marriage but that I could not yet see. Some of them— no surprise—originate in my childhood, which at my age, and after a lot of consideration and therapy, doesn't really interest me anymore. They happened and wounded me into being the person I am; that's what being a person is. (Philip Larkin's "This Be the Verse" springs to mind here, as it so often does: "They fuck you up, your mum and dad. / They may not mean to, but they do.") So another answer to the question "What kind of woman could do such a thing?" is in some real way this: A wounded woman, a damaged woman. Which is to say, any woman.

No one believes this till they've lived the bit of life in which, against all previous evidence, they surprise themselves. When I was a college freshman, I haunted the office of my beloved humanities professor all year, collecting every morsel of enlightenment I could get. One day, after a philosophical discussion of good and evil in class, he delivered a bit of wisdom so wise that I immediately discounted it: "Everyone is capable of committing evil in the right circumstances." I don't know what "evil" haunted him, but my nineteen-year-old self knew that his maxim would never apply to me. I was too well-intentioned and vigilant to let that happen. I was a good person. It took me a long time and a lot of suffering to grow toward an understanding of what my professor meant all those years ago. I think he meant something like what Melissa Febos wrote in *Abandon Me*:

> I suspect that anyone is capable of anything under the right circum-
> stances. We don't want to believe this. . . . We are in constant collabora-
> tion with our contexts. We are more alike than we think. Not everyone
> has a bottomless pit, and not everyone will go to such lengths to fill
> it. Not everyone will use their body like a hammer, will hammer the
> body the way that I have. Not everyone needs to get so close to dying
> to find that they exist. [But] I'm not the only one.

Febos adds to my professor's insight that what prefaces the commission of "evil" is one's own suffering and often—probably especially for women— suffering to the point of eradication.

To say this is not to excuse the hurtful things I did. From my perspective, not any woman did this; I did. From Alex's perspective, not any woman did this; her good friend did. She and I both have to deal with what that means our whole lives. Part of what it means to me is recognizing that I was so unable to register and respect what I owed her, not just as my friend but simply as a fellow human being, that I was able to see loving James and hurting her as an acceptable solution to the impossible problem of needing to stay in a marriage I could not stand. And part of what it means is recognizing the existential danger of believing you owe your marriage so much, regardless of the state it's in, that sacrificing yourself and others you love seems like a reasonable, even the ethical, option.

After the cancer, the harem party, the humiliating visit with Wes, and the stunted salvation via Henry, at the end of 2008 I threw one more marriage onto the sacrificial pyre in an effort to save my perfunctory marriage and myself. This time, Rick helped swing the body into the flames.

About a month before Rick confronted me about Henry, I met another lonely, searching man. Doug was also a writer and teacher, a lover of big ideas, and miserably unhappy in a suffocating marriage to which he was tenaciously committed. I was neither the first nor the last woman he seduced as a respected husband and father of three (now four), a painful truth his wife seemed to accept either because she knew she couldn't stop him or she knew it kept him in place. After the conference where we met, he started dropping CDs by my office with thoughtfully curated playlists. Their encoded messages grew more intimate when I transferred to him the romantic energy I had withdrawn from Henry. Such faux monogamy—investing romantically in only one extramarital partner at a time—characterized each of my three affairs. We all openly acknowledged and expected it from each other, which must sound absurd but was a key feature of what we were doing: creating a "committed" relationship that we chose and enjoyed outside the marriages we no longer wanted, in order to stay committed to them. Someone outside the situation would just call such behavior "cheating." But inside the intolerable trap of a failed marriage, it felt like an enactment of intimacy ethics.

As I had done with James and then Henry, I began exchanging long, creative emails with Doug in which we wrote together the story where we could hide from our suffocating lives. Occasionally we'd steal away for a quick lunch, where we'd yearn across the table's torturous expanse, knees and hands just touching underneath, barely able to sit still in the public place we'd chosen to contain our roaring desire. When we couldn't get away from our families for days on end, he'd text on the way to the grocery store, I'd find a need for something, and we'd thrill at the sight of each other pushing a cart down a distant aisle with a kid or two in tow. By Christmas, the unleashing of our combined passion exploded into light that must have been visible from space. Rick noticed. On New Year's Day—a year after the big swingers' party and just over a month after quizzing me about Henry—Rick confronted me again. I confessed, and we had another endless, pointless, seemingly important conversation that went nowhere and solved nothing. I felt unloved, he loved me desperately, why didn't I see that? I was a horrible person. By that iteration of our pattern, I had gone so deep with Doug and fallen so far away from Rick that I could not see my way back. I didn't promise to stop seeing Doug. After some suffering and soul searching, Rick agreed to allow me to continue the relationship as long as I did not leave him.

Rick wrote Doug an email offering me up. He granted us permission to enjoy each other, asked Doug to be kind to me, even congratulated him on his good taste. Watching him write and send that email, I felt equally triumphant and nauseated. It was my pyrrhic victory, the ecstatic beginning of our marriage's actual end. Rick's acceptance of my need to see Doug in order to stay married to him, and my willingness to stay in a relationship I could only bear as long as I invested my real self in someone else, was us admitting that the marriage we had once shared—the relationship, the intimacy, the interconnection—was gone. That we did not expect to find it again.

I saw Doug on Tuesdays, when neither of us taught, which Rick, who worked from home, knew. So he also knew when I took extra time in the shower, knew where I was going after I dropped off our son at school, knew when I was headed into my bliss. The first time I left to see Doug under the new agreement, giddy as a teenager just entrusted with Dad's car, Rick cautioned me not to text while driving. I might have an accident, he said, and he couldn't stand the thought of it.

The situation was abhorrent, but all I could see was that I had been let out of my cage for a few hours every Tuesday. Soon, though, Rick slowly began to close the cage door, adding rules that would change every week. One Tuesday, he proclaimed that we could kiss but not have sex. Another, we could have sex but not say we loved each other. After that we were not allowed to do either, by which time his limitations had begun to feel silly. Doug and I met each new prohibition with a clever workaround that obeyed the law while fulfilling the desire the law could not touch. By working within Rick's system, I could tell myself that my intimacy with Doug required neither lying nor betrayal. I could see Rick's controlling prohibitions as enabling that intimacy, a kindness.

Between Tuesdays, Rick got to claim all I was not allowed to give to Doug.

The few hours of stolen bliss could not compete with the hours and days in between, when I descended into abject misery. The disorientation of shifting constantly from life to life, the feeling of being trapped in something I could neither escape nor endure, and my self-hatred for hurting Rick combined to make my self a place where increasingly I could not live. For months I thought about escaping through death or dismemberment not just every day but many times a day. The end of each work day and my required return home came as a blow, which I cushioned with fantasies of accidents severe enough to put me in the hospital for several weeks but from which I'd mostly recover. Driving home, I'd imagine the possibilities: The sudden impact, the crunch of steel, smoke billowing from under my hood. Airbags deployed, lungs burning from their packing powder, the air in the car slightly opaque and swirling with it. The whine of the ambulance drawing near. The peace of being confined to a hospital bed that no one else would be allowed to lie down in. I'd consider how much I was willing to sacrifice to buy that stretch of time: A few digits? A limb? Which one? An eye?

Perseverance through suffering runs in my blood. The day before my PhD hooding ceremony, my dad spent several hours splayed on his belly on the hardwood floor working with sticks, tape, lights, and mirrors to extract my watch and two wedding rings from the foundation of our little cottage, after my toddler had dropped them into the heat register in retaliation for the betrayal of my nursing the new baby. My father-in-law had tried for a while the day before, but as it was a tedious, uncomfortable, and likely impossible task, he gave up. My dad retrieved every lost item. His combination of obsessive doggedness and stoic tolerance for physical pain is a considerable superpower, which he passed down to me through genes and years of ideological training. At seventeen, on a blazing hot and humid summer day, I led the drum section of my high school band in a punishingly long parade during which our impressive ranks dwindled down to a few stragglers as most marchers dropped out at first-aid stations along the way. Some fainted and had to be carried off the blistering asphalt. As always, the drums never stopped playing, but by the end we were down to one cymbal, one bass drum, and me on snare. I had strep throat and a fever, so I had been pouring sweat in my black polyester uniform since before the parade began. It never occurred to me to fall out. When we reached the end of the route, I took off my harness and promptly passed out on the grass.

I seem to have inherited my mother's ability to withstand emotional suffering through the same mechanisms, while also learning that marriage would require it of me. The shaming, manipulation, and controlling behavior that characterized my marriage during those last harrowing years were as familiar to me as an old coat. They were the language of family and of love, passed down through the generations to me. Only recently, while writing this book, have I learned the appalling and heartbreaking extent to which that is also true for my mother. But that's not my story to tell.

However bad my marriage got, I would suffer, and I would stay. I would certainly not quit. Something would have to make me.

My daily car-crash fantasies soon morphed into a plan involving the hundred or so oxycodone tablets left from Rick's surgery. I read online about what would happen, how long it would take. I knew there were sufficient pills to do it. One night, after putting the kids to bed and before going to bed with Rick, I poured the little round white pills into a tempting mound in my palm. I sat there in the harsh fluorescent light of the bathroom and stared at the pills. I thought of the relief they would bring. I thought of my children. I put them back in their tall brown bottle, and the next day I told Rick what I had done and asked him to take them away.

If I had any hope at all, it was that Rick would notice that I was so distraught over the state of our marriage that I wanted to die and see that we really had to end it—that I needed him to help me; I would not do it myself, but it had to be done. All of this happened right in front of him, but he could not see it. I also started having trouble eating, as if some part of me knew I would never kill myself but had decided it could at least stop supporting my life. I had been losing weight throughout the past couple of years, first out of grief when I lost James's email companionship and then during the obsessive swinging phase. By the time Rick's cancer diagnosis redoubled my commitment to my marriage and my misery, I had little weight to comfortably lose. But I ate increasingly less often, until friends began to greet me with alarm and I was falling down in public—once in a restaurant, once on a curb—out of sheer weakness. At one point, I went most of a week without eating a bite of food. It wasn't a decision; eating was just something I could no longer do. Henry, my greatest support through this period, began inviting me to lunch hoping I'd eat if he ate with me. Mostly I would sit across from him, in one restaurant after another, crying about the marriage I could not stand and could not leave.

Struggling to feed oneself properly is almost a trope in women's memoirs, particularly those dealing with domestic abuse or sexual assault. Susan Bordo describes anorexia as one of the most visible ways that our misogynist culture writes itself on women's bodies. Women's relationship to food is always fraught: as patriarchy's designated nurturers, we are taught to feed others, not ourselves, and to view the desire to nurture ourselves as indulgent, greedy, a moral failing. Consider how often you hear a woman guiltily announce she's "being bad" while reaching for dessert or a second helping. Our choices to feed or starve ourselves express both our capitulation to societal norms and our resistance to them. The anorectic can make her body reflect an extreme of our skinny feminine ideal, the masculinity required of our current female heroes, or the male values of public life. Or she can rewrite her body as visible rejection of femininity itself by erasing every roundness and fullness. The anorectic makes herself weak and fragile, a caricature of misogyny's ideal woman, while feeling empowered by her ability to control her body and others' perceptions of it. Anorexia is another manifestation of the patriarchal structures in which women hungry for self-determination choose to punish, weaken, and limit themselves. It can also be a cry for help. By physically wasting away, the anorectic makes visible to others that inside she is disappearing, she is dying.

One night, lying in bed next to Rick, I placed my palm on my chest and was shocked to feel the nearness of my bones under my skin, the cavity of my belly plunging away from my ribs. Quietly, I said to Rick in the dark, "I think I'm losing too much weight lately." I hoped the remark would finally elicit an expression of care, evidence that he'd noticed I was killing myself trying to stay with him. Instead he replied, "I think you've never looked better."

Through all of this, I sought refuge in those hours of freedom with Doug. But they came at a price so high for Rick, and so invisible to me, that he would have to force me to fathom it. Those Tuesday hours began to be punctuated by Rick's frantic, despairing texts as he tried to articulate his pain at the knowledge of where I was. Then he started begging me to come home to him. After delaying as long as I could get away with, I would. A few weeks into the dysfunctional agreement, he showed up in Doug's driveway. You know that story.

In doing all of these things, Rick was trying to take care of himself, to endure the unbearable situation I had put him in by having affairs rather than leaving. I see that. His doomed "sharing" of me with Doug was part of his attempt to keep me happy while making me stay. There was a logic to it, just as there were good reasons why I needed another relationship in my life in order to stay. It all made sense in the upside-down world we lived in, where we owed our marriage everything, owed the institution our lives, but to each other, to those around us, and to ourselves, we owed nothing.

One of the most damaging effects of our cultural sanctification of marriage is how it trumps all other ethical matters. Preserving a marriage above all else makes us willing to sacrifice anything for its sake. It's bad enough that societal prohibition of divorce through shaming, which persists despite the fact that divorce has become a statistical norm, damages our children by consigning them to the normalized despair, alienation, and abuse that creates a new batch of emotionally stunted adults who create a new generation of dysfunctional marriages. Valuing marriage as an absolute and ultimate good can also mean denying the personhood and suffering of anyone who threatens it, from the inside or the outside. That can be a lot of people.

Every single one of us—Rick and I; Alex and James; Henry, Doug, and Wes, likely along with their wives—was willing to endure relationships that were broken at best and often utterly excruciating for the sake of preserving the public fiction of healthy marriages. At different times and for varying reasons, we were willing to sacrifice our own happiness, not to mention physical and mental health, for these performative marriages, or we were willing to sacrifice our partners, or people who had been our dear friends. In navigating the complex interrelations between the affairs and those sacred marriages, we ruined long friendships, discarded each other's real affection, invaded privacy, scapegoated, shamed, and generally treated each other without the respect we'd grant a casual acquaintance. All of us were hurting, but we had so little kindness to offer each other. Instead, in our variety of ways, we chose to cause one person's suffering in order to end our own and that of the beloved in whom we sought temporary solace. We created a lovers' twist on the trolley problem—paramours teaming up to pull the lever on a spouse, then spouses doing the same to a former paramour. In a moral system like this, the carnage never ends; it just leaps from one track to another.

Even in these situations, leaving can feel impossible because "the marriage" has become so much more than what it started out as—a loving relationship with another person. A marriage accrues heft like a snowball rolling downhill. As we move through the world, it generates material things—houses, children, retirement accounts, rooms full of objects to be painfully divided—while vital needs like belonging and approval increasingly become as attached to it as to the individuals buoyed along inside. We on the adultery tracks were throwing levers not so much to protect our original relationships as to save all that our marriages signified and guaranteed: financial resources, money for kids' college expenses, the respect and acceptance of families and religious communities, and our kids' good opinions of us, which others besides Rick threatened to ruin to keep us in line, plus the basic social, financial, and material stability that develop over years of married life, and which divorce absolutely ravages. Against all of these precious things, desperate spouses weigh the possibility—never a guarantee—of building a more fulfilling life that will be worth all the losing. It's no wonder so many people take the solace they can from connecting with other unhappily married people rather than leaving their marriages.

So much of the social and personal ugliness and loss that divorce—and affairs—exposes us to stems from this basic incompatibility between the behemoth of marriage and the delicacy of human love. As marriages snowball along they become big bullies, taking up space, granting power and privilege to the people crouched inside them, elbowing out of the way those not afforded the same protections. And they're not capable of much course correction. They mostly trundle along in the ruts left by all of those that have passed before. But the original relationship inside each one, the seed around which all the rest formed, is complicated and vulnerable. If it's still alive, it's always changing. It needs to stretch and breathe.

As recent divorce statistics suggest, women find this arrangement even more suffocating than men, likely because of the vast difference between our pretense of gender equality and the persistence of patriarchy in our social interactions and institutions. Patriarchy carved the ruts our idealistic marriages struggle to escape. During the worst years with Rick, I imagined that marriage would have been less painful for me a century ago, when everyone agreed it was entirely a social and financial institution in which I had no personhood whatsoever. I would have expected nothing for myself; I would have expected to *be* nothing except what served my husband and society. I would have had no basis for disappointment, or violation, or rage. I would have lived sequestered inside my self, not within my marriage. But as a woman in a society that pretends equality, married to a man who professed to believe in a marriage of equals without having any idea what that really meant, being married was like living in a cage that no one else could see. I was taught by our culture's faux feminism to expect things that very little in the world would ever actually grant me, that I would be routinely denied while being told I was fulfilled. For women today, being married can itself be a kind of gaslighting. Fighting to maintain one's integrity inside it is exhausting and can make you feel insane. Marriage can hold any of us squashed and captive by training us to think specifically in terms of what we owe others. But it trains women to erase ourselves altogether by teaching us that we owe more than the external things owed by men—money, labor, houses. Women owe all our intimacy—our care and emotional investment, the insides of our bodies.

What exactly, and how much of it, does any of us really owe another person, and what portion of ourselves should we be willing to sacrifice to please them? What of real value do we owe our children—beyond a fat college fund and protection from the sad truth of their parents' mutually destructive relationship? Can we give them our best selves, a model of healthy intimacy, and a peaceful home life, while consigning them to cold or seething families?

Bookstores are full of books like Eli Finkel's that aim to solve the problems of modern marriage with new interpretations and configurations. Many, like his and Carrie Jenkins's, also propose opening marriages to allow more flexibility in our romantic attachments and sexual experiences, as one way of tending to that original seed without abandoning the instrumental behemoth. Ursula Le Guin goes much further in *The Birthday of the World*, whose stories conjure alien cultures in which sex is freed from romance and both are detached from parenting. It's difficult to imagine our society manifesting these kinds of freedoms. It seems it would take light-years to become that alien to ourselves, leaving us today to figure out how best to navigate the ruts of our own landscape.

What is the inner life worth? What's worth giving up for the privilege of living on the outside as you do on the inside, of transforming beyond what your current chrysalis will allow? What material and social things would you lose—and can you afford to lose—to honor your most profoundly true self?

I wish I had allowed myself to ask these questions from inside my failing marriage, rather than needing to claw my way out in order to even see them. Imagine the suffering that would have been avoided, on so many tracks. But I no longer waste time wishing I had never met or married Rick. For one thing, because of him I have my boys, and I would walk through the hell of that marriage every day for several lifetimes in order to have them in my life and give them to the world. And for another, I have myself, the self that grew out of living through all I describe here. The thing it's hard to stop wishing is that Rick and I could have admitted the truth to each other and worked together, in sadness but in love, to peaceably pull it all apart. We did the exact opposite of that.

PART 3

DIVORCE IS NOT
THE WORST THING

The legal system is designed to protect men
from the superior power of the state but not to protect
women or children from the superior power of men.
It therefore provides strong guarantees for the
rights of the accused but essentially no
guarantees for the rights of the victim.
If one set out by design to devise a system
for provoking intrusive post-traumatic symptoms,
one could not do better than a court of law.

—JUDITH HERMAN, *Trauma and Recovery* (1992)

11. INSIDE/OUTSIDE

R ecently I read a *BuzzFeed* list called "16 Signs Therapists Say They Know a Marriage Is Doomed." I lost track of how many of those signs appeared in our couples therapy during which no one said, "This marriage is doomed." The most useful item in the list is not a "sign" and did not come from a therapist. It's advice from another poor soul who had prostrated himself to the impotent counseling gods before learning it the hard way: "Divorce is not the worst thing." Though I teach my students to evaluate their research sources and encourage my children to mindfully curate their news feeds, I still find myself compelled to read clickbait articles like this one. I find it reassuring when people I don't even know can describe some of the most painful aspects of my marriage. It makes them real, knowing they happen to other people too.

Just as our physical separation came years after the end of anything like a real marriage, our divorce began long before I could make it legally real. For me, it started the morning when, suddenly and without much thought, I decided not to wear my wedding rings. Leaving my rings on my dresser that morning was me beginning to validate my own experience. It was my inside self confronting my outside self, staring her in the eye and demanding to be seen. *There is no way in which you feel married to this man,* she said, *this man who pimped you out, this man who doesn't care that you suffer as long as he gets what he wants. So stop pretending, at least in this one small way.*

At the age of twenty, I fell in love with Zora Neale Hurston's novel *Their Eyes Were Watching God.* When I graduated college two years later and acquired my first cat, I named her Janie after the novel's inspiring central character. The book tells the story of a woman who is taught to suffer marriages to a series of men who see her only in terms of what she can do to benefit them, in exchange for her own safety and financial stability. She learns to split herself to survive them. Moments in which Janie's second husband Joe shuts her up and treats her as unworthy of an opinion "put Janie to thinking about the inside state of her marriage." When his public and private domination continues despite her resistance, and everyone in their small town allows it, she "learned to hush," and "the spirit of the marriage left the bedroom and took to living in the parlor" where it could "shake hands whenever company came to visit."

When I taught this novel after leaving Rick, I was startled to find that Hurston had given me ways of understanding what had happened to me in the twenty years since I had first read and loved it, why performing what my marriage required had alienated me so much from myself.

She also enabled me to see how I had preserved myself. Janie survives Joe intact because she realizes that "she had an inside and an outside now and suddenly she knew how not to mix them." Joe could force Janie to cover her beautiful hair and shut her smart mouth. It's not hard to imagine that a man like Joe would also have been forcing her to have sex with him, no matter where the spirit of the marriage had gone to live. But he could not make her other than she was; he could not kill the part of her that didn't love him, that knew she was a whole other person apart from the one he had use for. Having an inside and an outside means knowing on some level that the outside is not your real self. And having an inside means maintaining a place where your true self can live until it's safe for it to come out again.

Not long after I took off my wedding rings, Rick unwittingly acquainted my outside self with my inside self again when he moved me out of our master bedroom. It was about six weeks after The Worst Day of My Life, time we'd spent in alienated internal chaos dressed up as united normalcy. Photos with old friends show us poised and smiling, my dark under-eye circles the only evidence of our tenacious private distress. We hauled ourselves through long, pointless arguments, some of which ended with me dodging a thrown piece of furniture or cringing under his raised hand. I had seen Doug a few times since The Worst Day, but we were never able to re-create the bliss that had blossomed between us before. In the wake of my husband's domestic attack—in the worst symbolic gesture, he'd demolished the baby carriage—Doug had circled the wagons of his family, leaving me on the outside. So it was not Doug, but rather the promise of finding a person who would love all my parts, or of simply finding freedom from oppression, that led me finally to make a stand for myself and my future over my duty to my husband.

Rick issued an ultimatum: if he wasn't enough for me, I had to leave. Since we were united in our agreement that I would never leave him—that I owed it to him to stay—I knew he wasn't suggesting a resolution to our dysfunction so much as goading me to "behave." Still, this was the first sane and healthy thing either of us had said in a very long time, because it was true. I thought about it for a while. Then, in our impressive master bedroom whose soaring ceilings and massive windows afforded no peace, my inside self made another meek appearance in the outside world. I asked Rick politely, shyly, whether he would please "leave me alone" for a little while (read: stop guilting me into having sex with him) so I could figure out how I felt and what I wanted to do. His reply: "If you won't have sex with me, then you don't deserve to live in this master bedroom." Bad wives don't get to enjoy the perks of marriage.

I didn't protest Rick's logic, which I was too ashamed to see as demeaning and absurd. But I did wonder at his rashness. Much of the house, including the basement room where he threatened to install me if I didn't comply, was still filled with unopened boxes from our recent move. I didn't take his ultimatum seriously. So I was surprised when he greeted me late that evening when I returned from work with the question: "Have you changed your mind?" It felt like he'd been lurking in the house all day, waiting to ask me again. When I said no, Rick led me down to the basement, where we silently began the long project of moving boxes and setting up the guest bed. Once he had withdrawn up our floating stairs to his master suite, once I had ferried toiletries into the guest bathroom as if in some uncanny hotel, once I had numbly brushed my teeth and changed into random clothes snatched from the dresser during my humiliated retreat, once I had climbed into my childhood bed and settled under sheets that had only been used by visiting friends, it hit me: this is my space, and he doesn't belong here. I'm safe.

Living in the guest room in the basement of the house I had designed and just moved into was disorienting and depressing. It didn't take long for our children, by then ages five and seven, to ask why Mommy was living downstairs. I can't even remember how I tried to make sense of it for them. I do remember the deep ache of seeing their little faces at the threshold of the guest room door, quizzically peering in. And yet, not much changed for them. Though I slept in my basement hideaway, I was otherwise in the kitchen making dinner and school lunches, or reading to the boys in their bedroom, or playing with them at bath time. But for me, retreating at night to the safety of the basement became my salvation, another strange thing that allowed me to endure my marriage. I grew very fond of that room with its half-submerged view of the backyard, where I could sit in the window and watch wild turkeys and deer wander across the lawn. Finally I had a space of my own, where I could read and think and sleep unmolested. Without intending to, my husband had shown me what I had been missing all of those years while I shared a room with him: privacy, and the ability to choose what I did and did not do in bed. Every simple bedtime choice felt empowering. Simply wearing my mismatched pajamas was liberating after years of being nagged out of them. I slept the untroubled sleep of the self-possessed.

Until I didn't. I might have been stuck forever in this ridiculous new solution to our marital problem, exiled to the basement of my own house while coming up to cook, clean, and perform childcare for the man who lived upstairs, like the help in a British drama. But before long, Rick invaded the space to which he had exiled me. He began to enter my room at night, sad eyes trained on me as he proclaimed his loneliness and need. I gave in to him. Then even my safe space became a place where he could consume me.

Submitting to him seemed to be not a violation so much as what I owed him. I was rarely seeing Doug by then, but I remained ashamed of that continued "betrayal," of which Rick reminded me at every opportunity. That perverted logic kept me in line and submitting for a long time, and Rick employed it like a weapon. When I finally left a few months later, I discovered that all I needed to do to extricate myself from the entanglements that had sustained me during the worst years of my marriage was simply to get away from Rick. Once I'd decided to leave, I methodically ended every one of them.

But it was more than guilt that got my compliance. Rick's pleading invasions of my basement sanctuary triggered other feelings that made me capitulate. For a long time I could not name them. Recently, while reading Kate Manne's *Entitled*, I found words for those powerful feelings that moved me to sacrifice myself for Rick's comfort: sympathy, pity, and

care. And I found an illuminating explanation for them, though in a surprising context:

> A general ethical mandate says that when someone is in pain, we ought
> to try to soothe and assuage that pain if we can, all else being equal.
> Even if we aren't in a position to help, we should at least express our
> sympathies. And incels *are* clearly often in pain (though that pain
> may at times be overstated). But when someone is in pain precisely
> because he has an overblown sense of entitlement to the soothing
> ministrations of others, which have not been forthcoming, stepping
> in to assuage his pain becomes an ethically fraught enterprise. Even
> expressing our sympathies runs the risk of feeding into his false, dan-
> gerous sense that other people—especially girls and women—exist to
> pander to the incel's needs and to gratify his ego. So here, as elsewhere,
> we ought to resist the pressure to himpathize.

On the surface, this comparison might seem misguided, even offensive. An incel, or involuntary celibate, is a single man who blames women
for his suffering of their "withheld" sexual and romantic attention. His
relationship to women is entirely different from that of a long-married
man. And yet, the "overblown sense of entitlement to the soothing ministrations of others, which have not been forthcoming" that is felt by both
of these men, the "ethical mandate" they attempt to trigger, and the resulting "himpathy" that rewards them can be entirely the same. The rage
such men sometimes express when their entitled expectations aren't met
can also be eerily similar.

In my basement bedroom, with my autonomy gloriously restored
and then again invaded, I began to think that maybe I would really have
to leave, that it was possible I could not endure the situation for the rest
of my life. Rick's appeals for sex in the basement where he'd banished me
for resisting him upstairs made several things very clear. Removing me
from our shared room revealed how precisely Rick equated my role in
our marriage, my worth to him as a companion, and my right to share
the luxurious space in the house we had built with shared finances and
labor with my willingness to give him access to my body. The peace and
autonomy of living without him were too exquisite to give up. And his
ability to enter my space and take those from me had to end.

The first apartment I checked for the boys and me was a dingy dump with a cramped Formica kitchen and oddly sloping floors. It wasn't even a mile from the house we'd built, with its laundry room thoughtfully placed amid the three main bedrooms and a walk-in pantry adjacent to the kitchen. But it felt like a different world. Next, I tried a small old house surrounded by apple trees across the street from a farmer's market. I fell instantly in love with the cozy sleeping space under an angled ceiling on the tiny second floor, which had obviously once been an attic. I could imagine myself curled up there, an animal safe in its den, my babies breathing heavily below me. When I found out what it would cost to heat, I reluctantly moved on. I still feel the pull of that house, the first place I could imagine living peacefully with my children away from their father, every time I drive by.

Weeks passed as I continued the search. On weekends, with the kids tucked in bed after their baths, I'd hear the garage door grumble up as Rick left to troll the Main Street bars of our small college town. I would or would not hear his return. More than once he came into my room after an unsuccessful night of hunting, seeking satisfaction. I began to turn him away. One morning after a night when I had heard him leave but not return, singing drifted down the stairs as I headed up to the kitchen. He was in there making coffee, boisterous and silly. I knew immediately what had happened: he had gotten laid. Later he told me the story of that night as a plea that only revealed again how little he understood me. He'd met an undergraduate at a local bar, a senior English major at my university who would graduate the next day. He told her that his wife was a professor in her department. Knowing him, I suspect he thought he was impressing and connecting with her, failing to see how he was demeaning her and me both. They went back to her apartment and had sex. Eyes shining, he described how physically unsatisfying it had been, as if proving his love for me. I thought, that poor girl, thinking she was having an adventure.

12. HOVEL

Somewhere around this time, serendipity delivered the thing that finally enabled me to leave. I found an ad for an apartment in the basement of a house in our own neighborhood. If you walked straight from its back door across the backyard, as my boys would do hundreds of times over the next year and a half, it was only across the street from the house Rick and I had built. With two tiny bedrooms, a serviceable kitchen, and a space I convinced the homeowners to let me use for a washer and dryer, the apartment offered everything we needed in the world. And it was close enough to the big house we currently lived in together that I could think of it as a little annex. I didn't feel like I was tearing my family apart so much as enlarging the space in which we all lived in new configurations. I presented the idea to Rick that night, saying it would be good for us. Maybe if I could get away for a little while and figure things out, I would be able to come back and be happy. He grudgingly agreed.

The next night, after the kids were in bed, I walked up the street to the house with the basement apartment and signed a one-year lease. On my way back down the hill, keys jingling merrily in my shorts pocket, the realization that I was almost free began to dawn. Exhilaration bubbled up. I was Mrs. Mallard before her tragic ending. It was a short walk, and soon I was back at the driveway to our big house, where I saw a figure hulking in the night. As I approached I saw other large shapes as well. The hair on the back of my neck stood up straight as I sensed danger. As I got closer I could make out the shapes in the dark: Rick, lurking in the driveway where he'd been waiting for me to return, with several wardrobe boxes left over from our recent move. Inside were photograph albums of our years together before children, albums I had lovingly and tediously created before the ease of digital cameras or home printers. These contained our history of safaris in Kenya and the Kilimanjaro climb, our weeks backpacking around Thailand, our slow ascent of South Korea's Seoraksan at the height of the fall colors. They were the record of our early years before all that travel when we were just grad students eating beans and frozen spinach, when we were deeply in love in our first apartment that contained only garage-sale furniture, books, and our cat, Janie. Some of the albums were in tatters because Rick had torn them up. Bright red leaves, golden buddhas, and pale pink flamingos mingled in the beautiful wreckage.

Rick crouched in the dark over the open boxes with a long lighter in one hand and a can of lighter fluid in the other. His threat might have been an ultimatum connected to the lease, or simply the desire to destroy things I treasured. I pleaded with him to stop. I tried to reason with him. I begged some more. His face was again that mask of fury and disgust, and again I knew he was capable of anything. I tapped 9-1-1 into my phone and said I'd place the call if he did not stop. Lighter poised, he looked at me with eyes full of hatred and spat at me, "Do it." I did.

The police came quickly and ran through their routine, a pathetic performance of protecting a so-called victim of domestic violence. They put us in separate rooms and ticked off the required questions: Are there guns in the house, do you feel safe, does he hurt the children? I could have said anything, and the result would have been the same—an incident report describing the event as if nothing of note had taken place. Here is the entire report in its original screaming, all-caps italics:

> ON ARRIVAL A BOX CONTAINING PICTURES AND A GAS CAN WERE OUTSIDE IN DRIVEWAY. [KATE] STATED THAT HER HUSBAND, [RICK], WAS GOING TO BURN THE ITEMS. [RICK] WAS LOCATED INSIDE THE RESIDENCE AND INTERVIEWED. THERE WAS A VERBAL DISPUTE BETWEEN THE 2 PARTIES AND [RICK] WAS GOING TO BURN THE ITEMS BUT DID NOT BURN THEM NOR ATTEMPT TO.

In this account, I am implicated in the event by participating in an instigating "verbal dispute" that did not happen. Rick is distanced from the event by the emphatic description of him as being "inside the residence," far from the gas can when the police arrived, raising the question of how the gas can even got there. Meanwhile, in this report, I am the only one claiming that Rick was about to burn my photo albums. The police, despite noting the presence of the gas can, seem to be most interested in getting it on the record that Rick "did not burn them nor attempt to," as if bringing a gas can and lighter outside with a bunch of ripped-up photo albums does not qualify as preparing to light albums on fire.

In this report, the police are telling me and the world exactly what Rick has said repeatedly about his violent treatment of me and my kids: this is not domestic abuse. When he threatened to kill me, to hit me, to hit the kids—hand raised inches from our faces, car swerving inches from the telephone pole—his logic was always that he never actually completed those actions, so they had not happened. He had never been violent. No bruises, no abuse. Yet any victim of this kind of nearly completed physical abuse can tell you that almost being killed, almost being hit, almost having your precious things burned in front of you in the driveway in the dark, especially when these kinds of violent, destructive things happen repeatedly and as a concerted pattern of control, is traumatic, whether or not it leaves any visible bruises.

Once the police determined that I was not in danger—had never been in danger, their record implied—and Rick promised not to burn my belongings, they left. Then, just like on The Worst Day, the berating started: I had to know he'd never do it, he was just trying to scare me, calling the police was histrionic, it was embarrassing, I'd only done it to hurt him.

That night finally spurred me from planning to action. I knew that any time I left the house I might come back to a burning pile of my belongings, and it was impossible to feel safe with a man who had made it necessary for me to call the police. I contacted a friend with a van and explained the situation. Incredibly generously, he called into work sick the next day to help get me out of the house. For the next two days, he and I drove around town hunting down Craigslist finds, scoring rickety bunk beds, a couch that smelled strongly of wet dog, a squeaky coffee table. I bought Star Wars sheets and posters for my sons' shared room and stuck glow-in-the-dark stars all over their ceiling. We moved over most of my clothes, some of the boys' toys, a few kitchen things, my books and papers, and not much else. By the end of the second day, the apartment was more than inhabitable; it was cozy and inviting, and I was ready to launch me and the kids into it.

Over family dinner that evening, I took a deep breath and told the children that I had found an apartment very close by where I was going to live for a while. This was the hardest part so far. My therapist had helped me prepare myself for this moment by having me face the various ways my children might react, in the safe space of my relationship with her. They might yell at me and tell me they hated me. They might sob and cling to my legs and arms, trying to prevent me from leaving. Each scenario she presented hit me like a blow. I took each in, imagined myself getting through it, how I might handle it, what I could say, and I wept and wept and wept. We would wind up doing this kind of imaginative preparatory work for many stages of the divorce. Each time would be as crushing as the last, and each time would enable me to take another step.

As I began to tell my children about the apartment, Rick left the table, leaving me to handle another crisis without him, which shouldn't have been surprising. My older son, more savvy about such things by then, got right to the point: "Are you and Daddy getting a *divorce*?" And he started to cry. As I braced myself for the worst of it, he asked his next very practical question: "When are you going to the apartment?" I told him the truth, that I was considering going that night. "Where will we be?" he asked, understanding himself and his brother as a unit in this and all matters at that stage of their lives. "You can be wherever you want to be," I said. "We want to be wherever you are," he said. And it was settled.

We packed up some of their clothes and headed to the new apartment. It was the evening of July 2, 2009, warm and clear, fireflies bobbing in the shadows of yards. Rick surprised me by reappearing as we left and walked alongside us, perhaps wanting to see where we would be. When we arrived and I opened the door, the boys rushed in to delight in the Star Wars extravaganza and their exotic bunk beds, while Rick stopped at the threshold. Peering inside, he issued his proclamation: "What a hovel. You must really want to leave me if you'd live in a dump like this." The boys and I lived in that apartment, which we called "the hovel" with great affection, for a year and a half, and we were very happy there. July 2 is my Independence Day. I celebrate it every year with a bottle of champagne.

After Rick left, we punched holes in the lid of a jar, and the boys chased fireflies across the alien landscape of our borrowed backyard. Over time, we remapped the tiny floor plan to meet all our needs. I annexed living room to kitchen when I baked, spreading sheets of cooling cookies on every available surface so the whole place smelled like butter and vanilla. The kids' sword fights carried them from bedroom to bathroom, then down the hall and out into the tiny laundry area. During slumber parties, little boys in sleeping bags drew a nearly unbroken line between their bedroom and the living area, which was also my workout room in the early mornings while they slept, my study where I wrote and prepared for teaching when they were at school, and our game room at night. The apartment came with a small TV but not cable, so we spent after-dinner time playing endless games of Sorry! and the occasional round of Monopoly when my older son, who always won, could talk us into it. While I cooked, especially on fried-tofu nights, they sometimes stood in shifts on a chair, waving a magazine at the smoke alarm to avoid bothering our upstairs landlords. We were a team, and we were individually thriving as well. I still remember with such clarity the happiness I felt every time I walked in the door of the hovel at the end of the day and saw my pile of books on the little round table, my apron hanging from its hook by the fridge.

But I also felt mortified at being a thirty-nine-year-old professor begging pots and mattresses from friends, nabbing furniture with "free" signs from the side of the road, and shopping at the Salvation Army store. I was acutely self-conscious to be turning forty with my kids in the basement of a house where one of my undergraduates rented a room upstairs. Worst, I had put us all there and foisted this sudden resource reduction on my children. I had chosen to leave a man I knew would try to cut me off from our joint finances for spite. Because of me, my children had lost thousands of sunlit square feet and all the comforts and amenities that came with them. And I still couldn't explain to myself or my friends and family what had been so horrible that I had to leave.

Back then I was ignorant about every facet of domestic abuse—not just its many guises but how many women experience it and how few of us have the resources to whisk ourselves and our children away and build a perfectly lovely new home overnight. Looking back on the hovel now, I see my luck and privilege and feel not humiliation but humility and enormous gratitude.

It would be weeks before the boys would spend another night in the big house that was to become their father's. Rick didn't ask for them, and to my surprise, the kids didn't ask to be with him either. Years later, reading Rachel Cusk's *Aftermath*, I would be struck by a detail she offers about the painful weeks following her own separation:

> Sometimes, in the bath, the children cry. Their nakedness, or the warm water, or the comfort of the old routine—something, anyway, dislodges their sticking-plaster emotions and shows the wound beneath. It is my belief that I gave them that wound, so now I must take all the blame.

My children never cried about the separation or their new lives, not once, a fact that didn't occur to me until I read Cusk's memoir and was astonished by it. They nestled into the hovel as if returning to a home they'd left behind in some other life. We reshaped all the old routines to fit our newly shrunken space: we could hunt our dyed Easter eggs as easily in the small backyard of our rented apartment as we did in the shadow of the big house. This continuity seems to have brought them comfort. But the hovel also brought a beneficial change. Outside the cage of my marriage, free from the fear that thrummed in my ears and the wild longing to escape that kept my eyes trained on far horizons, I could finally be wholly present with my children. I could see them for who they were, apart from their role in my private tragedy. They were not anchors, burdens, or reasons for me to endure endless suffering. They were complicated human beings whose company I enjoyed and whom I wanted to learn more about.

Many years after the divorce, a woman greeted me at a faculty party as if we were old friends. She had lived with her husband, a professor in another department, across the road from the four of us during our first year or so in our new hometown, when the boys were three and six. This woman began to reminisce about all the funny things my children had done back then—how my older son would wander into her artist's studio and ask about all her cool materials, and she'd give him little things to do; how her husband would look up from his philosophizing and there he'd be, big eyes staring up at him; how adorable the little one was in his snowsuit, dragging his sled up the hill of our driveway. While she spoke, I was stunned silent. I could remember none of these things. I realized then how little I remember of our first two years in this town, before the boys and I moved into the hovel. What I do remember is screaming and crying, my desperation and sadness, and wanting to die. I can hardly picture my boys in that first house we rented, and this loss of them during these precious years makes me sick: Where was I? I was taking care of them in every way, cooking, cleaning, bathing, tucking in, helping with homework, attending school meetings, playing with them, sometimes even dancing in the living room, but I can hardly remember any of it, and when I do, it is only the fact of it, not the feeling. Those moments have been swallowed by all the trauma of the rest of those years. Leaving Rick, moving with my boys into our own home, restarted time for me. My memories start anew there.

One of the things I quickly learned at the hovel was that my older son, Will, desperately needed support and resources he was not getting from his distracted parents. He had been an incredibly difficult baby and toddler for reasons no one had ever been able to explain. I had to finally figure out what was causing him so much distress. His perceptive after-school teacher suggested I read a book about sensory processing disorder, and this became the first of a long list of books I read about high-needs children, difficult children, oppositional disorder, and parenting in general, each of which provided another piece of the puzzle. I researched a neuropsychologist to do extensive testing, which divulged helpful information about how his brain worked and how he experienced the world. Using this insight, I started coaching him in reading facial expressions and communicating emotions, and mandated typing training to compensate for a fine motor skill difficulty. He would not receive specific diagnoses for several more years, but the early research and testing gave us both ways of understanding what his learning and social experiences were like, why some things were hard for him, why he reacted as he did, and how to change his understanding and behavior. By the time he entered high school, he was designing coping strategies for his learning challenges. By the time he graduated, having been elected class president twice and homecoming king once, my angry, communication-challenged boy had grown into a perceptive, well-regulated young man. Now a college graduate handling an intensely demanding job with tenacity and grace, he continues to amaze me. And the hovel was key in setting him on that course.

Our separation, with the kids and me at the hovel and their dad rattling around his big house alone, evolved naturally and suited the three of us just fine. Rick did not seem to be capable of caring for himself or the kids very well at the time, so it seemed best for him too. Finally one day he said he was ready to have them over to spend the night, so I packed

some of the kids' clothes and their toothbrushes and walked them over
to the big house. The plan was to have dinner together; then I would help
tuck the kids in before leaving, to smooth the transition. We never got that
far. After dinner, with the kids off in the TV room, I broached the topic
of divorce, and Rick started on me again. As always, his appeals ping-
ponged between pathos (I miss you, I love you) and punishment (you're
a monster, you're ruining our family). By this time I had discovered that
I wasn't delusional, that leaving him was all I needed to stop wanting to
die, that living with the boys but without him was healthy for all of us. I
was kind but resolute. His entreaties gave way to fury and then suddenly
he was lying on the floor on his stomach, screaming and pounding his
fists. It sounds like the tantrum of an overgrown toddler, and I suppose
it was. But in the moment, watching a full-grown man absolutely out of
control and beating the floor to keep from beating something else, it was
terrifying. Before he could stand up, I ran downstairs, grabbed the kids
and their overnight bag, and fled back to the hovel.

Eventually Rick had successful visits with the kids, which became
regular. Things seemed to generally go fine. But he was only able to manage the kids if I was invisibly managing their needs. I went back and forth
between hovel and house, transferring the kids, bringing them the things
they would inevitably forget, sometimes reading to them and tucking
them in. When I did, I would notice the bare fridge and go out and buy
milk and their favorite foods. I would see they'd had no clean clothes for
days, and I'd put a load in the wash, then return later to transfer it to the
dryer. It sounds appalling: I was doing Rick's domestic labor, then shut-
tling off to the servants' quarters up the hill. Neither of us expected him
to be able to take care of his own children. But it was necessary. I was
helping him establish this new life that I desperately needed us to establish. I hadn't yet managed to figure out how to make the divorce happen
on my own, but I could certainly do the work required on both ends to
establish the separation.

Dante's *Inferno* opens with its narrator trying to escape the dark wood
in which he's lost by climbing a mountain whose pinnacle is bathed in
sunlight. Thwarted by a host of menacing beasts, he retreats to the forest,
where he's greeted by a ghost who promises to get him to the top of that
mountain. And the narrator does get there—but he has to travel through
nine circles of hell to do it. My long climb out of the dark wood of my

marriage was a lot like that. I didn't have a guide, but I did have a friend's wise observation on the phone late one despondent night: "Sometimes the only way out is through." Placing my foot on the path that would lead out of my nightmare was terrifying. I knew that beasts abounded. It took me a very long time to do it. Moving into the hovel was the beginning of that journey. And I would have to descend through several circles of divorce hell before emerging into the sunlight.

13. CRUEL AND INHUMANE

What no one ever told me about divorce is that, just as one person can't fix or maintain a marriage on their own, it is very difficult to make a divorce happen when only one person wants it. And though you can make the legal part of a divorce happen with some effort and a lot of giving in, there are very real ways in which you can't end the relationship if the other person refuses to exit your life. If you share children and therefore remain legally connected, your ex-spouse will have endless ways and opportunities to intrude, manipulate, and torment you. If they want to be present in your life—in your email inbox, in text messages, through summons from the court or letters in your mailbox expensively triggered from your lawyer, all demanding your attention—they can be there.

The hovel's proximity to the big house, so convenient for the kids, enabled Rick to move freely between the houses too. Periodically, he'd show up at the hovel unannounced, and I'd invite him into my tiny living room, where he'd stand awkwardly until he had exhausted whatever pretense had brought him there. Sometimes, he would ask me to hug him; once, he proposed in his terrifyingly sane, logical way that we have sex. We were both single, so why not? Sometimes I got the less sane version of him, like the night I had a friend stay with the kids while I wandered the neighborhood looking for him after a series of crazed texts. This was the furious, devastated, emotionally unstable, boundary-ignoring, sometimes violent man I needed to convince to agree to a divorce. At the time, our state didn't allow no-fault divorce. To initiate proceedings, I would be forced to accuse Rick of something that the law recognized as grounds. These were my accusation options, as taken from a legal website:

- cruel and inhumane treatment that makes it unsafe or improper for the couple to continue living together (physical or mental abuse)
- abandonment for at least one year
- incarceration for at least three consecutive years after the marriage
- adultery

This list raises all kinds of interesting questions. What do "cruel and inhumane treatment," "abandonment," and "adultery" mean in the eyes of the law, versus to me or to Rick? Is it "cruel and inhumane" to treat your wife like a sex doll, throw furniture at her, or threaten her with physical abuse, or do you have to actually beat her for your treatment to be considered cruel and inhumane? Does emotional abandonment to the point of your wife's expressed suffering over years count as "abandonment" if you're still living in the same house? Is it "adultery" if you're both having sex with other people? What if you're doing it in the same room? Does it matter who wants it and who doesn't?

I found this to be an impossible choice. According to the narrative my husband had burned into my brain, I was the only adulterer between the two of us, so I couldn't accuse him of that. And all the thrown furniture, threats, insults, illegal surveillance, and dehumanizing manipulation were caused by how much I had hurt *him*, so I couldn't accuse him of being cruel or inhumane to me. We both knew he would never abandon me, in the sense of physically leaving me or allowing me to leave, so that was out. Even if I wanted to avoid having to claim fault by living separated for a year and then filing, I couldn't legalize the separation without a court process or getting his signature on a separation agreement, neither of which he would participate in. I was stuck.

It was 2009, a woman had nearly been elected president, but I still lived under laws that prevented me from severing legal ties with a man who controlled and threatened me without risking further abuse.

I tried the nonthreatening approach. I researched mediators (quick pause as your author chuckles at the thought of Rick and me sitting in earnest collaboration in front of a mediator) and educated myself about the kinds of decisions we'd have to make. I hoped that if I did all the work, he would eventually join me in a shared, respectful process. That approach worked exactly as well as it did in saving our marriage. Every time we arranged a time to discuss the divorce—always at his house, in his space, where I felt unsafe—he found a way to avoid it. This pattern repeated for months: the family dinner, some amicable chitchat, then I'd get out my notes and he would stall, dodge, and redirect until I'd go home exhausted. When I pressed, he became belligerent and enumerated my shameful faults. After enduring nearly a year of this new version of our old dysfunction, I felt more stuck than ever. That's when I went to my writing retreat, read *The Awakening* without comprehension, and got unstuck anyway. My lawyer filed the petition for divorce in June of 2010.

The months between filing the petition and finalizing it in court were a new kind of traumatic. Rick bombarded me with emails and texts in which he berated and threatened me, demanded response, then threatened again when I didn't reply fast enough. These became his most effective methods to keep me hooked in his life throughout the separation and divorce. On the phone, he couldn't control the conversation and would inevitably become so angry that he'd lose his composure, yell for a while, and hang up. But email and text allowed him to compose long harangues full of accusations he implied he'd use against me in court. Each time one of these popped into my life it provoked a full-body response: pounding heart, shallow breath, shivering to the point of chattering teeth. Sometimes I felt I would pass out. Every time I opened my email or glanced at my phone, I braced myself.

Eventually, I developed tricks for reducing Rick's access to me. I created a filter that sent his email messages into a folder so that I could only see them when I went looking for them. I became strategic about when I forced myself to do that—right before a therapy session was best, or before I went to the yoga studio, where I could clear the adrenaline hangover from my body. I began waiting longer and longer to reply to his texts, teaching him to stop expecting me to hop to it whenever he demanded something. When we had to communicate about something immediately, I called him. That interaction was unpleasant but short.

I've spent a lot of effort over many years training myself to decrease these trauma responses, with some success. But anyone who knows anything about PTSD understands there's only so much you can do. So it was with great trepidation that, while writing this book, I read through his emails from the past fifteen years. I wanted to be able to use his own words rather than my unreliable memory of them to characterize as accurately as possible his behavior and how we understood each other through the contentious divorce process. Rereading the emails turned out to be less painful than I had imagined, because they reveal a pattern of misogynistic beliefs and actions that I was unable to see at the time. As his story begins to fade, another emerges.

Right after I left, Rick expressed sadness in his emails but was not cruel. Sometimes he pleaded for me to reconsider. Sometimes he was light and funny, enlisting old references to remind me of our long history together. He recommended a play he'd just seen with a woman he was dating. We breezily discussed logistics for the kids. We seemed to be figuring out how to stay friends and coparents while being apart.

But when I became insistent about divorcing and we began to discuss numbers for child support, things quickly got very ugly. And we were only ever fighting about those two things: he didn't push back when I asked for primary custody, and I never asked for "spousal maintenance." When we divorced, his salary was several times mine, and he got the big house, all our savings that had gone into it, nearly everything it contained, and his considerable retirement funds. The one thing my lawyer and friends convinced me to endure his threats, insults, and blackmailing attempts for was a fair amount of child support, without which I could not establish a home for the boys in our expensive school district. But first I had to initiate the divorce he refused to participate in, which forced me to cite "grounds."

I chose "cruel and inhumane treatment" as the best of bad options, not even fully believing I had the right to claim it, convinced as I was that I was the one being cruel. This legal requirement framed our divorce from its inception as a battle of blame and injury that I had been primed to lose. Rick's reaction to this accusation in a legal document was astonishing and manic, and it persisted for years. In a barrage of initial emails he called it "the greatest insult he'd ever felt from another human being," making me wish we could trade insult histories. He said I had "abused, humiliated, and dehumanized" him and that I had "shown wanton disregard for him, almost pathologically." What sent him over the moon with rage was my audacity in claiming to be the victim when clearly I was the abuser.

Then he announced he was initiating a "character war" in court to expose my guilt and "defend his honor." He told me the story he would tell the court: "I imagine it will include full descriptions of your transgressions and testimony from many people connected to all of this."

There is nothing he could have told the court then that I have not already described for you in this book. A lot of it is mortifying. You can imagine why having this story told from his point of view, as a threat of public exposure, would have gone a long way toward convincing me to comply with his demands. He exonerated himself from the one violent act for which there was a police record—nearly burning my belongings—by victim-blaming me for "not trying to wrestle the pictures away, instead choosing immediately to call the police." I should have been willing and able to fight over a man-sized box of my belongings, he implied; it was my responsibility to de-escalate his threat.

When the emotional battery didn't work, he unfurled a series of more specific threats. He would humiliate me at my university by (falsely) accusing me of a professionally unethical affair. He would seize our joint funds. He would trot out swinging photos of me in court. He would contact the men I'd been involved with and press them to tell their wives about their affairs, in some kind of weird recompense for his pain. In that email, he included the message he'd written to the men but not sent and listed the people he'd shown the message to while deciding whether to send it. He expected my gratitude for not having sent it, while illustrating that he had shared it already and could send it to others at any time. It was like pointing a gun at my head and asking me to thank him for not pulling the trigger—yet.

He never sent the email, as far as I know, though he did get the pleasure of sending Alex my way a few months later. He would blame me for the unpleasantness of that as well, for it pained him to hear from her that I had accused him of blackmailing and physically threatening me. The first he justified as "the only legal option he had," while the second was his reasonable reaction to my "dishonoring our lives together." As if his pain justified threatening to kill me and throwing furniture at me, and as if I could never have said it myself, he explained his abusiveness like this: "My god, I was coming apart. I was dying."

Perhaps you've gathered by now what I was unable to see at the time—that if he had a chance of winning in court, he would have stopped all the drama and taken our case to trial. Perhaps you've been through some version of this and so you know, as I did not, that no judge cares who fucked whom, or when, or why, in a divorce settlement. Judges just want to make the parties agree to some numbers and get them out of their courtroom. Rick could have given the judge a written affidavit detailing my affairs and leaving out his, and it would not have changed the percentage of his salary that the law dictates he had to pay to support his children. He had no leverage whatsoever—except through bullying me to give up the things the court would likely grant me.

And I *was* still vulnerable to his attempts to shame me into compliance, despite the distance I'd already traveled away from him. Living in the hovel eliminated his physical impositions but could not erase the self-punishing ones I carried with me in my mind. And before long, Rick's accusations were being compounded by a new man in my life.

Several months after moving into the hovel, I met Miller at a conference, where we quickly bonded over uninspired local beer and fizzy conversations about American literature. He was a short story writer and PhD student in the final phase of his dissertation, only a couple of years younger than I. Back home in different states, we maintained our intense conversation, falling into a version of the intoxicating mixture of email, chat, and creative-writing exchange that had powered all three of my affairs. But this time I was free. This time, the relationship could become real. After nearly a year of long phone conversations and passionate visits, Miller took the opportunity of a fellowship to live and write in a town near mine. My parents approved of his all-American masculinity, and his family embraced me immediately, not even trying to hide their hope that I would join their family. Miller seemed to be everything that Rick was not and all that I had been yearning for. He was earnest, thoughtful, and emotionally intense, loved literature as much as I did, and respected what I did with it. A year or so into the relationship, we started to fantasize a life together in which we would become family.

Miller also felt familiar—like family—in a sinister way. He made me feel judged, unacceptable, ashamed. Early in our relationship, wanting to be entirely honest with him and hoping to be loved as I am, I told him the whole ugly story of the end of my marriage. He was less appalled by my affairs, whose logic he understood, than he was by the swinging, which struck him as inexplicable and disgusting. The next morning, he announced that he had woken from a nightmare in which all of the things I had confessed to doing in my marriage were actually things I had done to him. He couldn't shake the feeling that I had betrayed him. Reminding him that I had done nothing to hurt him and he was caught in the hangover of a dream failed to end his confused mood. Again and again he brought up feelings of anger and disgust toward me and began to connect those feelings to a memory of a college girlfriend who cheated on him. Her betrayal of him and mine of Rick congealed in his mind into an ugly phantom that haunted our relationship and colored what he saw when he looked at me.

Occasionally he'd treat me as if I were the whore he was fighting in his memory. One morning he arrived at the hovel unexpectedly while I was exercising in the living room, and he reacted to the sight of me kickboxing in an athletic bra and shorts as if he'd caught me pole-dancing in a thong and pasties. "Where are the children?!" he cried, terrified they'd witness my debauchery. They were playing happily in their bedroom and in any case were quite used to seeing their mom in sports gear. When I was visiting his hometown where he was a teaching assistant and had the audacity to run in a sports bra on a ninety-degree day, he ordered me to cover up: "What if one of my students sees you?" he asked, aghast. I replied that his students probably also ran in sports gear—then I put on a T-shirt. On a summer road trip through New Orleans, I busted out my cutest sundress to take on the French Quarter and felt pretty in its mid-thigh flounces. Until Miller suggested I looked like a prostitute. We spent an entire night fighting after a friend's wedding, where I had admired an elaborate tattoo on the arm of a gay man. My forwardness in touching the man's arm made me look like a slut in front of all of his friends, he said.

Before my marriage and divorce, I wouldn't have accepted a single one of these controlling incidents, much less a year and a half of them. Miller's behavior seemed to stem from his own barely acknowledged traumatic history, and I was only loving and loyal to him. But I had learned from Rick, as I had been primed to do by my original family, that I *was* shameful, that I was selfish and unloving, that I made appalling decisions, that I couldn't be trusted. That I was a whore. For that year and a half, I had Rick reminding me of these things in regular emails and texts while

Miller periodically did the same on the phone and in the hovel. Miller's twisted vision of me made it difficult for me to resist Rick's story and the demands he attached to it, and Rick's story of me kept me vulnerable to Miller's judgment and blame.

But resist I did. Not perfectly, or even consistently, but resolutely enough to free myself from both of these men, if not yet from their misogynistic stories of me.

Entrenched in his utter denial of not just his role in our disaster but the fact that it was happening without his consent, Rick fought the divorce until the absolute end. On the day we were scheduled to finalize the settlement we'd already signed, Rick refused to come to court. I was, once again, astonished. Could he really do that, after all this, just refuse to let me divorce him? It turned out he could not. Rick's lawyer told mine that he had been screaming unhinged intransigence at her on the phone that morning; to the judge, she covered for him with the vague claim that he was "unable to attend court today." The judge said Rick was getting a good deal, and if he did not show up at the next court date to finalize it, he would be happy to adjust the terms. We all reconvened shortly thereafter, and the divorce was executed.

Months later, chastened by his displeased dissertation director, Miller fled back to his home state where he could focus on finishing his dissertation. Once re-immersed in his project, he had little energy left to connect with me, and our relationship devolved into sporadic phone calls in which I listened maternally to his grad-school woes while my own writing, teaching, and the grind and chaos of raising two children went ignored. The eight years in which I had disappeared into a marriage I would not leave finally came in handy: I saw Miller eclipsing me and ended things. I wish I had done so because I recognized and refused to accept his particular brand of abusiveness, but I hadn't gotten that far yet. Still, it was a decisive step.

After a year and a half in the hovel, the divorce finally behind me, I started looking for an affordable house in the boys' school district. Rick was surprised: "I thought you'd be looking for an apartment, maybe a duplex." He was pleased that the support he was paying would make it difficult for me to afford a house. Though living in an apartment or duplex is not a hardship, in vengefully consigning me to one, he was doing the same to his children to maintain his own three thousand square feet. For a while, he even pressed me to rent the basement of his house, the house I had designed and recently co-owned. I suppose that would have been very convenient for him, getting back as rent most of the child support he was paying every month. Maybe I'd occasionally come upstairs and cook. Maybe he'd wander down once in a while and see if I was willing to fuck him, for old times' sake.

He did briefly and resentfully rent out the basement to help pay his massive mortgage. But once he was again king of his whole domain, and once I was suitably installed in a humble house in much need of fixing, order was restored in his universe. Then, for nearly six years, emails from him were affable and even cooperative, and I was lulled into thinking we had figured out how to be friends and coparents, together doing our best to support each other and raise our children in peace.

During this period, I met my current partner, a philosophy professor at a university a thousand miles away. With the trauma of the divorce momentarily behind me, I was free to exhaust myself not with tense email exchanges and expensive lawyer meetings but romping through expansive intellectual and emotional territory in late-night phone conversations with Jack. The first time he visited, I spent many hours over two nights telling him the whole terrible, shameful story of my marriage and divorce. He listened with compassion and accepted it all, everything except my rightful claim to shame. We spent three lovely years telling each other the stories of our lives and sharing what moved and mattered to us by reading literature to each other on the phone. He was John Donne, Sóren Kierkegaard, Jorge Luis Borges, Sharon Olds. I was Olds too but also Kay Ryan, George Saunders, Mary Oliver. We met when we could at literary conferences, where he grew invested in the authors I was working on and slid seamlessly into the debates and friend groups that coalesced around these papers.

Then we went to Paris, and we simply could not come back as we had been. Walking into the Rodin Museum garden, my first time and his second, Jack pulled back at the last moment and let me step ahead. Those sublime figures, so human in their distortions and deficiencies, stopped me in my tracks, and I gasped. I felt his hand take mine, and we stood in a circuit of reverence unlike anything I'd ever experienced. Later, he said he'd wanted to see the moment when I met those statues. It was such a tiny gesture, but what it said about all he understood, felt, and saw about me was overwhelming.

In my twenties, high on the romance of new adulthood and adventure, I'd darted around Europe with Rick, basking alone in each artwork's aura until he hustled me to the next exciting thing. In my early forties, I found myself in a different kind of love altogether, one I'd longed for without really believing it existed outside the artificially intensifying constraints of affairs: one that was thoughtful, creative, and empathetic, a connection forged of symbiotic feeling. And I found myself with the only kind of partner I could love or be loved by in the long term: one who steps back and gives me space to meet and feel things on my own.

On the plane back from Paris, we found his imminent departure to his home state unimaginable. It was time to take the next step of living together, which meant becoming a family with my boys. Given the strictures of academia, in which leaving one tenure-track job usually means never getting another one, that also meant giving up not just his job and friends but his career as a professor. His PhD and years of college teaching experience would not make him eligible to do much else other than be a professor, including teaching in public high school (which requires a different degree and certification procedure), so his moving meant that his employment would always be more struggle and frustration than fulfillment. Moving also meant plunging headlong into the chaos of married-with-children life but with a woman who did not want to marry. I'm still a little stunned that he did it. Every day I'm enormously grateful. He brought to our household not just love for me but patient support of two kids in difficult situations and a model of gentle, unimposing, and truly loving masculinity. As it turned out, we would all need these things very much in coming years.

Six years of peace with Rick exploded when I had the audacity to step out of line. Over those years, I'd started saving for the kids' college educations and building my own retirement, of which the divorce left me little. My children were developing expensive tastes and expectations from their dad, making the vast difference between his resources and mine—which child support laws are intended to minimize—increasingly stressful. Meanwhile, the cost of their health insurance, which I alone paid, continued to climb. My lawyer assured me that adjusting support and health insurance payments would be straightforward, given Rick's quickly rising salary and my stagnant one. It wasn't, not at all. Starting in 2016, Rick and I were in court for three years over child support, health insurance, and our older son's college bills. Each of us paid to lawyers tens of thousands of dollars that should have gone to our children's expenses and college funds. And once again Rick waged his warfare outside the law, by rewriting the story of our marriage in emails and texts designed to cut me down before we could get into the courtroom.

This time, he wove in a new narrative, in which I was "abusing" him by using the law to take away his money and prevent his professional success. He told this story as his own survivor narrative: "I find myself hardly able to breathe as I read this court summons about child support. I need more boundaries with you. I feel deeply disrespected and used by you. I can't stand to have to interact with you and need to avoid direct contact from now on." The next day he wrote: "I feel threatened by you. I feel bullied and manipulated by you. Stay out of my house." Two weeks later he wrote: "I don't feel at all safe with you. I don't want to fake security and cordiality by having a public relationship with you." At this point he stopped acknowledging my existence at our children's school and music events. In a room full of people—our friends—and with one of my children at my side, his eyes would slide right past me as if I wasn't there.

Next, he played the damsel in distress: "My health has taken a dramatic turn for the worse. I need to eliminate as much stress from my life as possible." During these years he was routinely running marathons, as well as a fifty-mile race. As the court date approached and I insisted that he share his financial information with me, he said "This feels terribly invasive," like I was asking him to submit to a public anal exam. He refused to share his financial information unless I signed a nondisclosure agreement (he was dating a lawyer at the time). I did not have to do that, and I did not. We went to court and reported our current incomes; the judge raised child support. "I feel incredibly used by you," he wrote afterward. "You discarded me and then used me financially."

I am starting to almost enjoy reading the email record at this point. Messages that made me physically ill with fear and shame back then make me laugh out loud today. I had listed for him many rational and financial reasons why I wanted to keep the kids on my health insurance rather than switch them to his. The man who had just confused himself with a terrorized trauma survivor pressed me to acknowledge my irrationality: "This is an emotional reaction that has nothing to do with economic realities. It is wholly psychological. Please reconsider." Rereading this email, I'm transported back to the kitchen of the big house we shared, where I listen to him patiently explain that my undiagnosed mental illness was making me want to leave him.

It makes a lot of sense that reading the emails of our post-divorce battles causes flashbacks to the contentious years that preceded them: they are all of the same piece, the piece of our marriage, the whole of which had become a piece of shit. The same absolute inability to communicate with each other that led to hours of conversations in therapists' offices and living rooms and restaurants over *years*, years in which the quality of our relationship did not improve a bit, made our divorce a series of conflicts that no amount of discussion or negotiation could resolve. And he used in our divorce the same techniques that had proven so reliable in handling the intractable problems of our marriage. For him, those problems were the times when I didn't want to do something he wanted me to do, like have sex with him, or have sex with other people with him. In these email campaigns to get his way on financial matters, he first reminded me of my duty to him, then shamed me for my selfish failure to perform that duty, then showed me how much he was suffering and asked me to end it by submitting, and then bullied me and issued direct threats. When none of that worked, he told me I couldn't even understand what I was doing or what was happening to me: I was irrational, delusional, crazy.

These are the classic steps of gaslighting.

His tactics were terribly effective because I had no concept that might have enabled me to see and scorn them. Even as I managed to press on in court, these emails gutted me. It wasn't until the late stages of writing this book that I encountered the term that explains his uncanny survivor impersonation: DARVO, or, "defend, attack, reverse victim and offender." Psychologist Jennifer Freyd coined the term in 1997:

> Abusers threaten, bully and make a nightmare for anyone who holds
> them accountable or asks them to change their abusive behavior. This
> attack, intended to chill and terrify, typically includes threats of lawsuit,

overt and covert attacks on the whistle-blower's credibility [and] will likely focus on ad hominem or ad feminem instead of intellectual/ evidential issues. . . . The more the offender is held accountable, the more wronged the offender claims to be.

The term didn't get my full attention until lawyers began to lob it from both sides at the Heard-Depp defamation hearings, illustrating how DARVO can be not just a thing done by an abuser but a strategy for defending them. Depp's team invented another term to obscure the power dynamics of Heard and Depp's relationship, characterizing it as "mutually abusive," which erases any victimization and has DARVO baked into it. I can imagine that "mutually abusive" might be the kindest thing some people are willing to say about my relationship with Rick. But I hope this account illustrates crucial differences in the kinds of behaviors that can be meaninglessly collapsed into "abuse," if not proving the lie of "mutual abuse" altogether.

There are many ways to hurt someone in an intimate relationship, not all of which are abuse. You can stop loving or desiring them, and you can lie, love, or have sex with someone else. You can break their heart. These are tragic and perhaps immoral, but they are not abuse. Profound pain is their inevitable result but not their intention. They are motivated by a need to assuage the suffering self, not a desire to eradicate the other. Threatening to kill someone or to hit them, throwing furniture at them—these make someone feel physically unsafe, that their life is in danger. Threatening to publicly humiliate someone, to defame them in their workplace, to withhold needed finances—these make someone feel socially, professionally, and economically unsafe. These are *existential* threats, initiated explicitly to terrify and control someone whose suffering is not an unfortunate byproduct but the abuser's primary intention.

Part of Rick's story has always been that I never communicated to him my profound suffering, that I just withdrew from the marriage, started fucking around, and then, despite his heroic efforts to endure my wretched behavior, suddenly and unceremoniously left him. And I could never really remember a conversation we'd had about my feelings. Why hadn't I tried harder? This question has haunted me for over fifteen years. But I think I've let it haunt me because that rendition of the story is less painful than the truth. In my haunting version, our marriage failed because *I* didn't try hard enough to communicate with him, which means that if I had, he would have heard my pain and cared enough to work with me to improve our relationship. But the truth is that communication was not even possible. A conversation, like a marriage, requires two participants, each of whom respects the autonomy of the other. Lacking that, we became unable to have a real conversation or a real marriage.

When I told Rick how much it would mean to me if he would read my work, I was telling him. When I asked him not to leave the room in the middle of my sentences, I was telling him. When I attempted earnest exchanges about my devastation at our lack of emotional connection, I was telling him. When I said in our therapist's office that sex with him felt violating, I was telling him. When I told him I didn't want to have sex anymore, I was telling him. When I lay there like a dead woman as he fucked me, I was telling him. When I suggested we try a separation, I was telling him. When I cried every day, stopped eating, and confessed that I had nearly swallowed a bottle of pills, I was telling him. I told him and I told him and I told him. What I would like to ask him now is, if you loved me as much as you professed to, why didn't you listen? And how could I have said it differently to make you hear me? How about, "I feel disrespected and used by you. I feel bullied and manipulated by you." How about, "I feel threatened by you. I don't feel at all safe with you. I don't want to have to interact with you. Stay out of my house." How about, "You discarded me and then used me for sex." How about, "My god, I'm coming apart, I'm dying."

So maybe he was listening; maybe he does understand the pain and fear and despair that I spent years trying to describe to him. He certainly understood and was able to articulate them when *he* was feeling them. Yet at no time during all of those years of massive dysfunction we called a marriage, when I was expressing my pain and ultimately my resistance using my words and my body, did he once acknowledge that I hurt too. His inability to see me as a whole person who could suffer, not just the ideal he'd constructed in his mind or the body he wanted to fuck, led to both the end of the marriage and his total inability, to this day, to understand what ended it. His emails provide a kind of feminist primer in these aspects of misogyny. They document not just the steps of his gaslighting attempts but also his little-boy grief when he sees me transform, as if before his very eyes, from saint to demon, goddess-mother to praying mantis, perfect wife to monster: "You've revealed a cruelty and cold steeliness I honestly did not know you possessed."

What he will never understand is that his most powerful weapon is also his greatest curse. As long as I am not a whole person with rights and feelings, he can bully me into submission without guilt; he can dismiss my behavior as crazy and believe himself utterly victimized and innocent. And as long as I am not a whole person with rights and feelings, as long as he refuses to see that he watched me grieve the loss of our marriage for years before I left, as long as he denies that I suffered and that he did horrible things to cause my suffering, he will never understand himself or his own life. What has he learned from all of this misery? Some women are crazy. Some women are selfish bitches. They will do anything to hurt you, for no reason at all.

In the end, the only thing that allows you to move on is acknowledging that the other person is as real as you are, suffers as much, and deserves your pity and kindness. Divorce is not the worst thing. Living in a barter system, a performance, a prison, an arena of mutual destruction is the worst thing. Making your kids watch you do that is the worst thing. And coming unforged through the fire that should have melted you down to your brittle little bones and forced you to flesh back out with humility and compassion, that's the worst thing.

14. CONTROL REDUX

One morning in 2018, my yoga teacher opened class with a little story for us to meditate on as we moved through our poses. The story boils down to this: everyone has two wolves battling in their heart, one made of anger and aggression, and one that is kind, gentle, and loving. Which wolf will win? The one that you feed.

For the next seventy-five minutes I worried over this parable with more angst than my teacher had intended to inspire. It expresses a dilemma that had been troubling me for years. The parable implies a neat answer—feed the kind wolf, obviously—but my experience had shown that the question of which wolf to feed could be difficult to answer. I wanted to feed my kind wolf. After thrashing my way out of my marriage, damaging others in the process, I had mindfully rebuilt my life. I volunteered hours every week at our local food pantry and crisis hotline and gladly supported anyone in my life who needed it, including my friends and students, my children's friends, and parents I only knew from standing next to them on various sidelines. I spent years reading, meditating, and training myself to impassively receive the hurtful aggression of my high-needs child and to give back the steady love and acceptance he needed to grow past those difficulties. I had responded to Rick's post-divorce abuse by practicing lovingkindness toward him, doing my best to hold him in my heart with compassion and attend to his suffering, rather than letting our long battle turn my heart to stone, my blood to bile. I wanted our divorce to be an opportunity to become a better person—more loving, more forgiving, more generous, not less.

But kindness only makes a bully's job easier. When Rick scheduled outings with the kids on my custodial days, I allowed it. When he picked them up at unexpected times, claimed days that were not his, took them on a weekend trip over Mother's Day to meet his new girlfriend, I seethed but didn't fight. When he disregarded my suggestions and the kids' reasonable wishes or made serious parenting mistakes that left one or both of them in tears, I quietly repaired the damage and muzzled my opinions. Early in the separation I read a book about the effects of divorce on children, hoping to minimize its injuries. The experts' primary advice was to never, under any circumstances, criticize the other parent in front of the children. Children identify with their parents, they wrote, and denigrating a parent makes a child feel likewise belittled. For years I swallowed a lot of anger and did my best to convert it to understanding, while supporting Rick and his peripatetic parenting attempts.

I was surprised when Rick's abusive treatment of me bled into his treatment of our children. Isn't that the oldest story? But I still could not see that I was in fact living this oldest story, the story of domestic abuse, and of how it flows into every corner of a family.

I couldn't see at first how Rick's pattern of behavior with the kids echoed his pattern with me. But I knew in my gut that his treatment of our children was wrong. It was not what I wanted for them or what we'd agreed to when we'd discussed the kind of parents we wanted to be, back when we were full of love for each other, when we were a team. I also knew that however much I disagreed with his parenting tactics, they would not get attention from a court system overwhelmed with much more extreme cases of abuse. With no clear intention, only the need to bear witness, I began to record my children's complaints in a document on my computer, which I maintained for a little over five years. As their complaints became increasingly frequent and severe, it grew into a twenty-six-page, single-spaced account of what it looks like when a parent abuses his kids into submission without leaving physical marks. When our younger son began to beg me to get him away from his dad, I started saving all my children's texts to me, too, along with the ongoing email conversation I was having with their father.

Printed out and gathered together, these documents, texts, and emails constitute many hundreds of pages that would eventually fill a four-inch plastic binder to bursting. Like my old photo albums, that binder is buried in my closet where it can't remind me of the anguish of the custody trial and what it taught me about the legal, medical, and policing institutions that control our lives and define our freedoms: in many places, still to-day, women and children remain at the mercy of the powerful men who control these systems.

For a few years after I left, Rick's parenting was, like that of many divorced fathers, uneven but basically sufficient. I continued to do the bulk of the parenting labor—scheduling and taking the kids to all doc-tors' appointments, music lessons, and tutoring sessions; making sure schoolwork got done; planning extracurricular activities on "my" days to make sure they got to them. So Rick had little parenting work to do and got to spend his time with them doing fun things. If I sound blasé about this arrangement, let me be clear: I arrived at this grossly unequal division of labor over years of bitter resignation, as our egalitarian ideal collapsed under the crushing realities of raising children. Like so many bright-faced young feminists, I had entered into marriage and parent-ing naïvely believing my partner's earnest promises to share all domestic and childcare work equally. And like nearly all of us, I had learned that he was simply unable to see the labor being split. He did nearly half of the stuff he could see, most of the time, and called it even, congratulating himself. Handily, I couldn't see myself doing the extra work either. I just did the domestic, emotional, and parental labor that all individuals and the family unit required without really thinking about it. And by the time we split, another of the stories Rick had instilled in me was that we had always been equal parents. It took about five minutes of living apart to see how untrue that was, but it also became immediately clear that things were going to get worse, not better, as we divorced. I would have to take on more unequal parenting labor—it was the only way to make sure the unfun things got done.

Meanwhile, Rick's attention was often elsewhere, causing neglect that the kids began to notice: he forgot to pick up the little one from an after-school activity, forgot it was his custodial night and left them home alone for hours, forgot to feed them, forgot to plan promised birthday parties, forgot to take them to their friends' birthday parties and to their baseball games and to music lessons.

After I filed the petition to increase child support, the kids became Rick's favorite way to hurt and control me. He began trying to prevent them from seeing me at school or sports events that fell on his days. As a given event wound down, he'd hustle them out of the back of the auditorium or across the park, forcing me to sprint across soccer fields and parking lots to catch up with my greetings and congratulations. He issued an edict prohibiting the kids from spending any time at my house on his days, no matter how late he got home from work, even though both kids said they preferred to spend that time with me and Will reported having panic attacks during the hours alone in his dad's house. Both started asking to be at my house more and at his house less, in response to which he heightened his control, even leaving them behind while traveling with a girlfriend and instructing them to "find sleepovers" rather than stay with me.

Meanwhile, I started to hear that my children had become afraid of him. The first incident of physical harm occurred not long after we'd divorced: in response to petty misbehavior that embarrassed him, Rick grabbed Will by the face so violently that he tore connective tissue in his nose. Will bled from his nose and mouth for days and was sore for much longer. A few years later, I received a string of texts from Will that began "Help! Mom! Dad's hurting me!" Will—or Rick's inability to control him—had embarrassed Rick again, this time in front of a new girlfriend, and Rick had pulled Will out of the car by the neck on the side of a busy highway to yell him into respectful behavior. As altercations between them increased, Rick began to rely on violence and threats of violence increasingly often to control Will. Eerily, Will began to describe the same things I had experienced when I was married: the rushed charge, the raised arm, the crazy eyes, the violence acted out just up to the point that would leave physical evidence.

This increasingly obsessive control can make it look like Rick's attention was *focused* on the kids, when the opposite was true. During this period, he was not only acting like his children were a distant priority, he was telling them so. These years saw a series of girlfriends move through Rick's life, each one becoming the focus of his energy as he recreated the image of a perfect family around her. Both boys complained about how thoroughly he ignored them while requiring them to be at his house and participate in "family" activities regardless of their own increasingly meaningful social lives. When they confronted Rick about this, he earnestly explained how important the current girlfriend was, as if justifying his disregard for them. He demonstrated his girlfriends' primacy in a variety of ways, perhaps never more colorfully than by having sex at various times of day when the kids and sometimes their friends were in the house and aware of what was happening. At age fifteen, Will found this mortifying. In a series of distraught texts, he described striking up a Nerf war in the basement to distract his brother and his young friends so they would not feel the same confusing discomfort.

Both boys were beginning to see Rick's relationship with them as the performance it often was. In separate conversations and texts, each described their lives with their dad in the same terms: when a girlfriend was around he seemed to be "acting," becoming "nice" and attentive when they knew him as "mean" and disinterested. He "needed everything to be perfect" for a girlfriend and berated them, sometimes in front of friends, when they did not keep up their end of the act. In one disturbing text, Will described a day at his dad's house as "6 hours of pretending followed by 2 hours of cringing and distracting myself of not thinking what dad is doing." At only twelve years old, my younger son, Kevin, detected the sinister undertones of emotional manipulation in those performances. In a strikingly perceptive analogy, Kevin compared his dad to the John Goodman character in 10 Cloverfield Lane, a study in gaslighting. In the film, you don't know until the end whether Goodman's booming, playful, slightly off-kilter patriarch is kindly saving two young people from the end of the world or holding them captive for his own twisted purposes. Kevin said that his dad, like this character, "does things that look nice and care-taking but they don't feel that way." How did those things feel? I asked. "Scary," he replied.

When my boys made these reports, I dutifully responded as I had been told I must. I told them I believed them, acknowledged their feelings, expressed my care for their suffering. But I was careful not to criticize Rick. I told them he loved them and was being the best father he knew how to be. I encouraged them to speak with him directly about their feelings. When Will tried, he reported more threats. When Kevin tried, he said, "Dad makes me feel like I'm crazy."

Several years into this record, Will's complaints abruptly drop off. He got a part-time job and, in a text sent from Rick's house, said he planned to work as much as he could to "be away from home as much as possible." Shortly thereafter he turned sixteen, and with a license, car, and lots of good reasons for being away, Will's problem was solved. But being several years younger, Kevin remained trapped and became the focus of his father's controlling performances of devoted parenting. When Will began to break away and blossom, Kevin began to get sick.

A gifted athlete who had spent his young life playing baseball and soccer with joy and prowess, Kevin became inexplicably lethargic. He was diagnosed with pneumonia, an old case of mono, and the possibility of celiac disease. Once an endoscopy confirmed celiac and I'd switched him to a gluten-free diet, he began to feel a bit better. Then he developed intense nausea and abdominal pain. After appendicitis was ruled out, extensive infectious disease testing turned up amebiasis—an infection caused by a parasite endemic to South America, where he had ill-advisedly swum in untreated water with his dad on vacation a year before. Antiparasitic treatments are no picnic and, as predicted by his doctor, he got a lot worse before he got better. But after he'd completed weeks of harsh medication and no longer tested positive for the parasite, his pain and nausea continued and intensified.

Soon he was suffering head and abdominal migraines every moment of every day. The pain was so intense and pervasive that he could not tolerate light or being touched anywhere on his body. His right arm became so painful and numb he could hardly use it. The pediatric infectious disease specialist sent us to the hospital so he could be tested and treated; we spent two weeks there over the course of a month, trying to figure out what was wrong and how to reduce his pain. He turned thirteen in the hospital, where he underwent CT scans, MRIs, ultrasounds, and a lumbar puncture that left him reeling from ketamine, eyes wide and rolling at nightmare visions only he could see. Doctors tried every IV medication for persistent migraines they had, but these only made him horribly nauseated. Nothing worked, and nothing major seemed to be amiss. Eventually he was diagnosed with "chronic migraine" and "chronic pain syndrome," and we were directed to begin weekly treatment at a pain management clinic for kids at a hospital that was nearly two hours from our home.

As the pain continued 24-7, preventing his brain from getting the benefit of REM sleep, "chronic fatigue syndrome" was added to his list of diagnoses. He was unable to attend school for half of both seventh and eighth grades, and he spent much of that time bedridden in the dark. Caring for him and getting the resources and medical treatment he needed became my second full-time job. I pushed his school relentlessly until they enacted a 504 agreement that provided the tutors he needed for accelerated math and science classes and Spanish classes, while I became his tutor for all other subjects. Desperately trying to get him out of bed, I implemented a daily practice of restorative stretching and movement. Once or twice a week we drove the nearly two hours each way to the hospital to meet with doctors who tried many therapies to help him control his pain. As the months went by and he saw no improvement, I researched other possibilities and took him to other doctors—rheumatologist, therapist, ophthalmologist—while keeping up with the docs we had started with—infectious disease specialist, gastroenterologist, neurologist, psychologist, primary care provider—all of whom were scattered over five different towns and cities. I talked to still other specialists; I read up on his conditions. For a long time, I spent the bulk of my time and mental energy desperately trying to find someone who could figure out what had turned my smart, vivacious kid into someone who could barely walk, could not sleep but spent a good deal of his time trying, could not write, and could hardly read or think through the constant migraine and stomach pain.

Rick participated in none of this. He did not go to the hospital. He did not go to a single doctor's appointment. He did not help Kevin with his schoolwork (he tried at first, but the resulting arguments caused Kevin to refuse to accept his help). He had nothing to do with the 504 plan or tutors. Meanwhile, I emailed him long reports about every doctor's visit and lab result and kept him apprised of Kevin's school progress, for which Rick thanked me without seeming to feel the need to do more. What he did do was become increasingly controlling and abusive as Kevin pushed him away more as he became more ill. What he did was begin to tell a story in which Kevin's illness was first Kevin's fault—Rick decided Kevin was ashamed of being overweight, though no one saw Kevin as "overweight" but Rick—and later, mine. Just as he had while we negotiated the divorce, Rick told this story to me in emails as he would later tell it to the court. Because this time my character was not at issue, I didn't worry about his preposterous story. I knew I had all the evidence, hundreds of pages of it, on my side.

It was almost two years to the day between the first time Kevin asked to reduce visitation with his father and the day I filed the petition to change custody in family court. Unlike the eight years I spent unable to leave Rick, this delay was conscious and strategic. This time, the conflict was between my child and his father, and I did not want to sever that relationship; I wanted to help them rehabilitate it. I sent careful emails in which I shared my observations about Kevin's pain and gently suggested that Rick listen to him to come to an agreement about visitation they could both live with. I noted that really hearing Kevin would communicate the care he was missing and lessen his resistance. Nothing in my experience of Rick suggested that any of this would work, but I had to try. Because I also knew—though only partially, it turned out—that a custody trial with this man who had so clearly demonstrated his acumen for manipulation and bullying would be another nightmare. I wanted to spare all of us that.

The more Kevin expressed his feelings to his dad, the more abusive Rick's behavior became. Rick started forcing Kevin to do physical things that caused him pain and extreme fatigue and shaming him when he protested, calling him "baby," "spoiled brat," "king Kevin," and "princess." When Kevin reported these denigrations in texts, I was reminded how Rick had shamed Will when he was an anxious little boy who could not tolerate sitting next to strangers on airplanes: "Stop crying like a little girl and move," Rick would bark. Kevin began to recount nightmares he had at the time: in one, he was being pursued by half-human creatures he associated with his father; in another, he fled a factory where he was being violently forced to work and then arrived with relief in our front yard, where I was gardening. He developed anxious tics, including hair twisting so persistent that I had to cut out chunks of his densely knotted hair. Rick met his every attempt to escape with further policing. He took away Kevin's phone so he could not tell me or anyone what was happening at his dad's house. He routinely isolated him in his room for whole afternoons and evenings, not for misbehaving but for expressing any need or desire that opposed Rick's own. Once, in a desperate attempt to reach me, Kevin called from Rick's landline, sobbing. His dad was in a rage, and he was afraid Rick would hurt him, he said. Kevin had "stolen" the house phone and was hiding in a closet.

I was about to begin my long, slow discovery of our institutions' inability or refusal to protect children from abusive fathers. I drove to Rick's house, where I found Kevin at the front door, bag packed and hoping to flee while his dad was upstairs otherwise occupied. I told him we had to talk to his dad first; I knew enough not to get caught "violating" the custodial order. But once consulted, Rick refused to allow Kevin to leave and said he would call the police if I took him. Not believing the police would force a child to stay where he feared for his safety, I called Rick's bluff and suggested we call the police to resolve the situation. Rick moved to his next strategy. Voice dripping with condescension, as if he could not believe the melodrama Kevin and I were causing, Rick shifted responsibility to our thirteen-year-old son: "Your mom and I can't agree. You can call the police, and you'll have to explain all of this to them. Is that what you want? You want to call the police?" Kevin seemed embarrassed to be causing such a fuss and tried to shrink into the depths of the back seat of my car. But he didn't say "no." I called the police.

When the officers arrived, the female officer went over to where Kevin was sitting while Rick and I remained on the other side of my car with the male officer. He and Rick immediately enacted the secret handshake of patriarchy: Rick made knowing small talk and cracked flattering jokes, to which the officer responded, "We don't get many calls in this neighborhood," acknowledging Rick's upstanding charm. "It's a quiet neighborhood," Rick agreed. No domestic abusers here. It was in fact the same quiet neighborhood and the same house to which I had called the police only a few years before, to stop Rick from lighting my albums on fire in the driveway. When Rick walked away, I informed the officer about that previous visit. "We saw that in the residence's history," he said, as if it was the house that had terrorized me in the dark that night.

The female officer returned with her verdict that she "did not believe Kevin was in physical danger" and must remain with his dad. I was stunned. I reminded her that Kevin was very much afraid for his safety, that day and on other occasions, and told her his dad had physically hurt both kids before. She corrected me: "He's afraid of being *punished*, of being put in his room. His dad was trying to make him do homework and he said he would do it later, and his dad put him in his room." How easily she revised Kevin's terrified account into a narrative of normal parent-child conflict.

When she told Kevin he had to stay at his dad's house, he was clearly in shock. He remained seated in the back seat of my car, staring straight ahead, pale and crying. Then he repeated to the officer, incredulously, what he had told her and me already: "My dad yanked hard on my right ear and it really hurt, I had to sneak a phone to call my mom, I'm afraid of what he will do next to punish me." Her response: "Sending kids to their room is what parents do," and "He's your parent and he can punish you." Again, she revised out the rage, the screaming, the violence, the threats, and the painful ear pulling, which is a form of physical abuse, implying that all of these terrorizing actions are acceptable parenting strategies. This is what parents do and have a right to do.

I walked over to Kevin and he said again, "I'm afraid." I looked up at the female cop, who was standing right there, impassive. It was as if I had to pick up Kevin's words and carry them to her. I tried to reason with her again: "He's telling me he's afraid of his father and his father has hurt him. I don't understand why he can't just come to my house for a few hours, while his father cools down." She repeated, "He's only afraid of being punished," and Kevin repeated, "Yes, I *am* afraid of being punished. He grabbed me by the ear and it really hurt." How many things can "punished" mean? This police officer's response to my frightened, crying thirteen-year-old son: "If your dad does anything to hurt you or scare you again, you can always call 911."

In the spectrum of physical and emotional child abuse that happens all over this country, what I am describing here is relatively tame. Rick did not burn my children with cigarettes or lock them in the basement, unfed, for days. No one sexually molested them. They were never beaten. But they were routinely threatened, shamed, bullied, physically hurt, and neglected by one parent while the other parent, who wanted to give them attention and love, lived less than five minutes away. So while I understand that I am not describing horrific abuse, I want to be clear that what I am describing *is* abuse, a pattern of controlling dehumanization that was so traumatizing it was—as we would shortly find out—making Kevin sick. My children should not have been forced to endure this behavior for one second, much less for years, just because so many people with authority—doctors, lawyers, police officers, a judge—were unwilling to say the obvious: this man is harming his children and should be stopped. At the very least, the amount of time in which he could do these things should have been reduced.

A culture that accepts this kind of treatment of a child as "normal," as routine parenting, as "not bad enough" to be considered abuse and to warrant legal protection, can only perpetuate the systems of domination and manipulation that currently define our relationships at every social level: between parents and children, individuals and institutions, intimate partners, and family members. Children parented through domination and abuse learn to relate to others and get their needs met through domination and abuse. They become partners who will abuse and parents who will abuse, police officers who will abuse or look the other way when they see abuse, and judges who will abuse or enable abuse. The only language they know how to speak is power.

Author bell hooks offers a different vision for a different kind of social fabric based on love and mutual respect, one that must start with how we parent our children, how we teach them what it is to be a loving human being:

> One of the most important social myths we must debunk if we are to become a more loving culture is the one that teaches parents that abuse and neglect can coexist with love. Abuse and neglect negate love. Care and affirmation, the opposite of abuse and humiliation, are the foundation of love. No one can rightfully claim to be loving when behaving abusively. Yet parents do this all the time in our culture. Children are told that they are loved even though they are being abused.

A legal system built of people who view abuse as a parent's most effective tool will never protect our children.

Here is the entire police report filed about the incident I just described:

CALLER STATES CHILD'S FATHER IS REFUSING TO LET THEIR
13 YR OLD GO WITH HER. MATTER RESOLVED. CHILD REMAINING
AT LOCATION.

As they had done years before, the police provided a record only of what they determined *I* had done—accused their father of something and tried to take his son away. They provided no record of why I did these things, or of my son's reports of his dad's abusive behavior. These two police reports establish a record of me calling the police but not of Rick's domestic abuse. Even if the judge had looked at the evidence I would later submit for the custody trial, these reports wouldn't have helped Kevin at all.

———

Everything relating to the children, no matter how trivial, became an opportunity for Rick to assert himself against me. That Christmas, he tried to force me to change our expensive holiday flights to visit my parents by threatening court action. He declared his intention to seek fifty-fifty custody. He started attending some of the boys' medical appointments, where he misinformed doctors because he knew little about his children's medical histories but wanted to pretend to be in charge. He canceled medical appointments I had made and rescheduled them on my teaching days when I couldn't attend. He made medical appointments for them with new doctors without informing me. He insisted on driving Kevin to his therapy appointments, though they were on my nights and Kevin didn't want him to. He dragged Kevin to a family therapist to "work on their relationship" where, as in counseling with me years before, he blamed Kevin for their conflict. He pulled Kevin out of school to deliver an impassioned plea about how deeply Kevin was hurting him by asking to spend time away from him. He insisted that Kevin ride with him to a medical appointment, and when Kevin refused, he called the police to my house, expecting them to physically force Kevin into his car. They did not, and Kevin rode with me, but we were so late that we missed most of the appointment. Kevin began calling and texting nearly every time he was at his dad's house, begging to leave. His illness worsened. When he came back from a weekend at Rick's, he was intensely sick for days.

At this point, after several meetings involving me and Rick, Kevin's main doctor at the pain center, Dr. A., changed Kevin's diagnosis. What started as a "chronic pain syndrome" kicked off by the parasitic infection and its treatment had become, over the years of his dad's abuse, control, and dismissiveness, a "somatic conversion disorder." Dr. A. explained this disorder clearly to Rick and me. It happens when someone is in significant emotional distress but feels their attempts to express their suffering are unheard or disbelieved. Unable to elicit a response from a caregiver, they convert the emotional pain into physical pain—visible, somatic suffering.

My copious notes from the meetings we both attended over months show Dr. A. becoming increasingly direct and firm with Rick. She told him I had been right to call the police when Kevin was afraid and that I should do so again if I worried over his safety. Rick replied that he had "never physically harmed the kids" and that "[Kate's] version is so far from reality it's bordering on the insane." Dr. A. told Rick he had to stop forcing Kevin to comply with his demands and must communicate with him instead; most urgently he had to stop the name-calling, which was seriously damaging their relationship. Rick made a dramatic commitment on the spot to stop calling Kevin names, but Kevin reported a colorful array of new insults soon after. Dr. A. told Rick to stop trying to force Kevin to ride with him to doctors' appointments, to allow him to make his own decisions, to avoid putting him in situations where he felt unheeded and forced to submit. Three weeks later, Rick called the police to my house to force Kevin into his car.

In our last meeting with Dr. A.—before she figured out we were headed to court and cut us loose—Rick enlisted every device in his bully's toolkit to control the conversation. He interrupted, redirected, dodged questions, and assigned blame to everyone but himself. At times he used his body in that way that men do, taking up space and transgressing boundaries so you feel threatened without even knowing why. Dr. A. would have none of it: "We are not going to have the same conversational dynamic you have with everyone else when you are speaking," she firmly told him.

Unfazed, Rick switched tactics, moving seamlessly from intimidation to pathos. He stood up in the little examination room and delivered an impassioned speech about how much his son meant to him. Fat tears sprang from his eyes as if on command, and he ended with a hand-wringing plea: "You're the only one who sees us all and can help. Please tell me what I can do. *I'm begging you!*" Without missing a beat, Dr. A. looked him in the eye and replied:

> I have been telling you what to do differently for months. Look at your notes [she gestured at his legal pad, where he'd been furiously writing]. I don't know what you've been writing down there all this time. *Do those things differently.* You have to be willing to change your behavior. There is a theme of wanting to do things differently and then not doing them.

I was thrilled. I'd never seen anyone recognize Rick's charming, narcissistic performance, let alone call him on it. Dr. A. told him in no uncertain terms that Kevin's attachment to me was healthy, even necessary, given the trauma he was going through. And she told him that Kevin was "fourteen and autonomous" and needed to be treated as such, rather than be bullied and manipulated. In that moment, Dr. A. was my hero. But nothing she or anyone else did or said could change Rick's behavior.

I had long believed that disengaging from the battle into which Rick was constantly trying to draw me was the better of two bad options: submit or go to war. But it never felt right. I hated that feeding my kind wolf meant being a doormat, being shown I was powerless and, worst, being unable to protect my children from their father's increasingly damaging behavior. I asked every wise person I knew for their answer to this dilemma—doctors, meditation teachers, philosophers, counselors, friends. No one had an answer, only suggestions that I pray, meditate, be patient, let the conflicts pass. But the conflicts didn't pass, and one day Kevin came to me and asked the same questions I had been asking all of those people: What do I do when he bullies me and doesn't care how I feel? When he threatens me and scares me, how do I get away without fighting? For a long time, I didn't have a good answer for him either. Then one day I realized it was time to go to war.

15. BANSHEE

Before the custody trial even began, I started to see why having the truth on your side is not enough to win in court. You have to be able to prove it to a judge who will believe you, which requires the cooperation of people whose agendas might totally oppose yours. First, Dr. A. refused to testify about Kevin's diagnosis and its connection to his father's abusive treatment. She had been willing to stand up to Rick in her office but was not willing to stand up for Kevin in court.

Then a judge was assigned. My lawyer, Ann, delivered the news in an ominous pretrial meeting in her office, squaring her shoulders to me from behind her desk. His name fell portentously into the room. He was a misogynist, she said, of the sort that would make this case difficult to win. Our county is so full of misogynistic judges that she explained his misogyny by comparing it to that of the judge presiding over Rick's and my ongoing financial trials. The judge for the financial petitions was, she said, sexist in all the usual ways: he didn't take women seriously, didn't think they were as smart as men, ogled her ass in her business skirts when she turned her back in his court. But he really *liked* women, in the way that sexist men do, and she and the judge had a good working relationship. I suppose he saw her as one of the "good ones." But this judge for the custody trial truly hated women. Everything she'd seen in his courtroom demonstrated that he favored fathers and distrusted mothers. His past record of rulings, I would find out in the end, was deeply disturbing.

He and the opposing lawyer, on the other hand, made a congenial pair. I already knew Rick's lawyer, Johnson, from the many court dates Rick and I had been through on financial matters. He is proof all by himself that court trials are largely theater: you could see him acting, painfully, even while you could see the performance working. His chosen role was of the consummate patriarch, the leader, the holder of power. In actuality he's a small, homely man, but he could wear a suit and take up space like the big boys. In his mind he's Patrick Bateman from *American Psycho*, doling out business cards to men at dinner, then eating a beautiful woman for breakfast. His habitual manspreading was equal parts infuriating and comical. In the middle of the drab, sober courtroom, there he'd splay, chair pushed back from the table to allow plenty of space for the expanse of his meaty thighs. He sprawled like he trusted his dick to do the talking more than he trusted his mouth. While Ann and I sat poised across the aisle, upright and proper in our chairs like schoolgirls, Johnson slouched so deeply that his head wound up at table height. This demonstration of masculine power and apathy must have been effective: he was known as a very good lawyer, and Rick paid a lot for his performances. Also, his questioning in trial was sloppy to the point of embarrassing. He needed that dick, that slouch. Ultimately they really did communicate better than his words.

At every step in the trial, Rick and Johnson's strategy was to dominate, demonize, and discredit me and Kevin. No evidence Ann and I submitted to the court seemed to match the persuasiveness of their unsubstantiated patriarchal fantasy. We opened the trial with the testimony of Dr. T., Kevin's longtime therapist, who struggled valiantly for two hours to describe Kevin's pain and its causes in language that Johnson could not contort into accusations to be used against my son. Dr. T. testified eloquently to Kevin's intelligence, articulateness, and need to be heard by his father rather than controlled, threatened, and shamed by him. He clearly stated, based on years of treating Kevin and multiple conversations with his father, that Kevin's ability to make decisions about visitation was key to his emotional and physical recovery. In his cross-examination, Johnson converted Dr. T.'s demonstrably true claims into an absurd assertion that Rick should have no parental power and Kevin no boundaries, making Kevin the tyrant and Rick his victim. Johnson was DARVO-ing from the start. He capped this performance by comparing Kevin's diagnosis of somatic conversion disorder to a "fantasy" with "no medical cause," a "delusion" that I was supporting, or implanting. Sweating profusely under the obfuscating onslaught, Dr. T. asked for so many glasses of water that the pitcher had to be refilled twice.

Rick's smug satisfaction at this artful erasure of his son's suffering, and his role in it, disgusted me. But I didn't have long to ponder what kind of man could glory in calling his sick son "delusional," or how I had ever decided to reproduce with him. As Johnson continued his cross-examination of Dr. T., I began to notice the frat-boy bonhomie between the judge and Johnson as they teamed up to defend the maligned father in the courtroom. Whenever Johnson fumbled a question, the judge re-phrased it into a rhetorical one that made a neat point, usually about the unreliability of mothers or children. When Johnson failed to extract the damning testimony he needed from Dr. T., the judge inserted his own leading questions, thereby injecting all the correct answers into the pro-ceedings. "If Dad believes frequent access to Mom undermines a child's level of trust in his judgment," the judge plaintively asked, "what should the father do?" According to the man who would decide Kevin's fate, mere "access" to a mother undermines a child's trust in, and relationship with, a father. All mothers undermine; all children who cry "abuse" are being manipulated by their maligning mothers. Dads' access to their children must be protected at all costs in this situation. And all a dad has to do to enact this logic in court is to "believe" it.

Johnson's final question to Dr. T., meant to be a zinger, was ridiculous: "What if [Rick] wants [Kevin] to clean his room and he doesn't want to?" It was the courtroom equivalent of a fizzled firework dribbling sadly down, just when you're expecting a real gusher. But the judge could see where Johnson was so ineptly trying to go, and kindly got him there: "When a child says 'I'm not being listened to,' he's saying 'my wishes are not being complied with,'" the judge exhorted. With that statement he established, as part of the logic of his court, that children's requests for understanding are always veiled attempts to get their way about something, and parents and children exist in perpetual power struggles that parents rightfully win. Most distressing, the judge established that the relationship between a child and a parent is not, or should not be, based in mutual care and un-derstanding, since children are not people with feelings and rights. Those are, apparently, reserved for fathers.

On the next trial date, I took the stand to testify to the neglect and abuse Kevin had experienced from his father and the deleterious effects this treatment was having on my son. I had prepared that four-inch binder of carefully marked and organized evidence to back up my claims and had studied the materials for hours so I could easily find and reference supporting documentation. My two hours of testifying were a master class in testimonial injustice and in how men silence women (and children) and demand their submission in the name of the law.

While Ann questioned me, trying to draw out my account of Kevin's suffering and Rick's abusive parenting, the men in the room coordinated their efforts to train me into muteness. When she asked me to testify to the physical and emotional abuses the kids and I had endured at the hands of their father, the judge sustained all of Johnson's objections without explanation. None of that testimony about the abuse got on the record, though judges are required to hear testimony of abuse in a custody case. When I tried to answer Ann's questions about specific events, Johnson interrupted with pre-emptive objections to "hearsay" that I hadn't committed but that he assumed was coming. Eventually the transcript shows me interrupting and censoring myself, asking whether I can say a particular thing rather than trying to give an answer. Nearly every time Johnson or the judge cut me off, I apologized. Once I even apologized for daring to mention the exact thing I was there to testify about—my children's clearly expressed suffering at their father's treatment.

At one truly astonishing point, Rick joined the two other men in policing and interpreting my speech. Responding to Ann's question about visitation, I said, "[Kevin] was complying." Johnson admitted that he "couldn't exactly hear the word" I'd said but appealed to the judge to cut me off again, just in case. "I think she was about to tell us something that [Kevin] said," he explained. Pondering this conundrum, Johnson and the judge began to discuss what I said, was about to say, and intended to say. No one asked me. In the midst of their debate, Rick piped up from the back of the courtroom to clarify matters for everyone: "She said '[Kevin] only implied.'" Johnson was relieved: "Yeah, that's what I thought," he said. Still unasked, I offered my own account, in case anyone was interested: "I said 'comply.' I didn't say 'implied.'" No one told Rick he wasn't allowed to speak while I was on the stand.

Again and again, the men broke procedural rules and made significant errors without censure, while assiduously keeping me in line. Both Johnson and the judge repeatedly called Kevin, the person whose well-being we were all there to discuss, by the wrong name. Johnson caustically demanded to know why I was seeking sole physical custody of Kevin, when I was not. His questions continued to bumble forth in vague and inarticulate muddles. At one point, referring to Dr. T.'s two dense hours of testimony, he asked, "What did he say? In your view? Is whatever it is that he said consistent with your own views?" Each shambling question forced me to ask him to restate it so I could find something in there to answer. This elicited a lecture from the judge, delivered in simple sentences one might use when speaking to a child, about why I was not allowed to answer questions that way.

Every time I rephrased an unanswerable question, pointed out a significant error, or answered a "gotcha" question with an articulate response that made Johnson's client look like the terrible father he was, the chill in the room intensified. Sitting on the stand, I felt triumphant. How did this clown get a law degree? But the next day, after those men had communicated to Ann their opinion of me and my performance on the stand, I realized the awful truth: the more I showed them how prepared and capable I was, how smartly I evaded the traps they tried to set, how bold I was in refusing to let them shut me up, the more I pissed them off and harmed my own case.

Despite all their errors and confusions, together the three men found a way to beat me. The trial that was supposed to be about the welfare of my son turned into an exercise in putting me in my place and, more broadly, establishing men's right to control the lives of women and children. I had started as a mother confidently arguing for her son's right to escape fear and suffering caused by the father. During a pivotal exchange on the stand, I became the accused, struggling to evade the united front of Johnson and the judge, who began to circle me like velociraptors with their damning rhetorical questions. This exchange takes up nearly ten pages, about 10 percent of the transcript of that trial date. At issue was what I was willing to do to force my nearly fifteen-year-old son to spend time with a man who terrified, shamed, and hurt him. This issue—*their* issue, not the serious problem that had brought me to court—became the focus of my testimony.

Johnson asked me what I would do in various hypothetical scenarios in which Kevin might refuse to go to his father's house during visitation. For a while I dodged, pointing out that I was being asked to answer hypothetical questions. Then I discussed the things I had done, many times, in actual situations like those I was being asked to imagine: counseling Kevin to discuss his feelings with his dad, encouraging visitation. Johnson's questions grew aggressive and specific: "What would you say? What would you do?" He was trying to get on the record my refusal to force visitation on my traumatized son. "Do you think [Kevin] should be permitted to make the decision?" I did believe Kevin should be able to make this decision, but the judge had said at the start of the trial that he would never allow that. I dodged again. Finally Johnson came in for the kill: "Do you feel that you are able or unable to control [Kevin] to the extent that he would go to his father's house for his custodial time if that's what you wanted him to do?"

This question completely short-circuited me. I could not believe that I was sitting there under oath being asked if I was willing to "control" my teenage son and force him to do something that hurt him and that his own doctors said had been making him sick for years. In what nightmarish circle of family court hell was such a scenario possible? What good parent would agree to do such a thing to their child? I was being forced to choose between following the parenting principles that had brought me to court in the first place, knowing they would cause me to lose the case, or lying under oath to please the judge, which I was totally unable to do.

I was also being asked under oath whether I *wanted* Kevin to be forced to go to his father's house. Of course I didn't. Everyone in the courtroom knew that. I was spending my entire savings, subjecting myself to massive stress, and pouring most of my nonworking hours into preparing for that trial because I did not believe my son should be forced to spend so much time with his abusive father. Yet there was Johnson, posing the question to see what I would say. I sat there, boggled, for a long, charged moment. I imagine Johnson was on tenterhooks: Will she admit what she believes, like an idiot, and hand me a victory? Or will she lie—gifting me the cross-examination in which I get to prove her a liar in court? Today I'm proud of the presence of mind with which I answered that absurd, bullying question: "I don't think of parenting in these terms at all," I said. "It doesn't even make sense, the question you're asking."

The judge took the ball from Johnson and carried it over the line. He asked me what I would be willing to do to force my son to comply with visitation, regardless of "all these other conditions," including Kevin's emotional and physical health, my sense of his well-being, and his fear and suffering at his father's house. I said I'd have to think about it. "As someone who is asking me to give her sole legal custody," the judge replied, "I would hope you had done that already."

The silence that filled the courtroom then was profound. I could feel Johnson gloating from across the courtroom. The judge ended the trial session but not before allotting twice the amount of additional trial time that Johnson requested. Then he called to the bench Kevin's legal advocate, who had passionately defended Kevin's request to decrease visitation at the start of the trial. Ann and I found out why the next day: the judge told the advocate how displeased he was with my testimony and implied that the trial was already over. Johnson's gleeful email to Ann later that night put the situation more bluntly: "Does [Kate] think that she is winning? If [Rick] was seeking custody he would get it. A custodial parent telling the judge that she won't obey an order was honest but not exactly helpful." Ann advised me to settle.

After the fiasco of my overly honest testimony, I spent hours poring over what I had said and what the judge signaled he wanted me to say, and mulling over ways of saying it that felt true to me. I wrote pages of outlines and reasoning. It's painful now to see how utterly abject my submission was in those documents: I would say whatever it took to convince the judge I was not the headstrong, disobedient bitch he clearly thought I was, anything short of outright lying. I wrote and memorized long, carefully worded explanations and rebuttals; I crafted leading questions for Ann to pose so I could perform these torturous set pieces. I would wear something dowdy. I would stick my long hair into a nonthreatening ponytail. I would make less eye contact, keep my head down, play the shy, uncertain mother appealing to the powerful judge for his wise guidance in parenting my son. I would speak softly and stumble a little. I would be anything but the confident, sharp, smart, and self-assured person I am in my real life. I had learned another lesson: court is not where you go to say the truth and demand justice. It is where you perform the part that might get you a portion of what you want out of a system that does not care about the truth, does not care about justice, and certainly does not care about strident women or "the best interests of the child."

But it was too late. Against my passionate protestations that we keep fighting, Ann advised me to withdraw my petition before Johnson could call his next witness, whose testimony would bury me. That witness was the forensic psychologist I had chosen to evaluate the case and testify on behalf of Kevin about his relationships with his dad and with me. He was, I know now, part of a network of "experts" who lay the misogynist groundwork that justifies exactly the kind of silencing, discrediting, and blaming that I had been experiencing in court. A recent article about such "experts" revealed that a shocking number of them have been charged with domestic violence themselves, and quotes one of them as asserting he disbelieves "90% of all abuse accusations."

I'd chosen Dr. S., an older man, from a list of accredited psychologists because Ann said the judge knew and liked him and would listen to his recommendation. I also chose him because of his thorough methodology: I believed the evidence generated by the process would make my case for me and be well worth its considerable expense. After booking my inter-view appointments and receiving the forms I needed to fill out, I gave the project every ounce of my energy and attention, providing every scrap of information that would allow this expert to understand my child's suffering and defend him. I made Dr. S. his own binder, filled with my meticulously completed questionnaire with numerous extra pages, my twenty-six-page document listing the boys' reports of their dad's abusive behavior, Kevin's journal, and representative texts and emails as evidence of the boys' ongoing complaints and their dad's neglect and cruelty. In the report he prepared for court, Dr. S. started using my testimony against me right away, writing that "about the binder she stated, 'I know it looks insane.'" I had only made that remark because he had looked at the binder, the evidence of how diligently I was trying to protect my son, as if it "looked insane." Repeating my state-ment in the report served no function other than to quote me, in a moment of self-consciousness, as seeming to admit to my own mental instability.

I had decided at the beginning, with no little trepidation, to be abso-lutely honest with Dr. S. That's how much I trusted him and the system. I believed that if I told my whole complicated story, a highly educated and experienced expert in psychology who's performed hundreds of forensic evaluations would see the long pattern of abusiveness and how to protect Kevin from it. And I knew that anything I left out could easily be framed by Rick as evidence of my immorality or untrustworthiness. It took many hours to tell this story, one I had rarely fully told. Telling it was excruciating: I was describing sexual, emotional, and physical abuse. I was describing the death of my marriage and the anguish of my children. I was describing the most heartbreaking, terrifying, and devastating things I have ever experienced in my life.

In his report, Dr. S. characterized my earnest account as "flowery" and overexplained, which strikes me as the doctor version of "she's always so melodramatic." He labeled my mood "euthymic," a word that is usually reserved for people with bipolar disorder when they are stable. He further implied my mood dysregulation by noting several times when I cried during the interview and by quoting me describing myself as "crying a lot" at times when I did in fact cry quite a bit, such as through the abortion experience. He made my reasonable emotional reactions to my child's suffering and my own sound excessive, even hysterical.

Then he characterized my personality as evidenced by the two tests he administered to me. I am, he told the court, someone who lives in denial and rarely experiences emotional stress. I am unwilling to discuss my issues and reluctant to express feelings openly. I am not particularly energetic; I am lethargic and apathetic. I am flighty and unfocussed. I struggle to recognize even minor flaws in myself. It was disorienting enough to see myself described in terms that no one who knows me would recognize (including my therapist, with whom I shared this part of the report). But it was flabbergasting to see a man who had witnessed my emotional distress, listened to my thoughtful and self-incriminating confession, and read (presumably) the hundreds of pages in the binder I had painstakingly created for him, depict me in a court document in ways that his own evidence contradicted.

Thinking back to that interview in which I laid myself bare for him and voiced all my guilt and despair, I wonder if there is any way I could have said these things that would have sounded sufficiently contrite to make that man grant me personhood. Could I have told the story so that he'd see me as someone who regretted enormous mistakes *and* as a real person who suffered, rather than as the hysterical cartoon he constructed in his report? I ask myself the same question as I write this book, anticipating the hateful versions of me that will likely be codified in reviews and blogs and tweets. But I don't expect all my readers to have PhDs and decades of experience in psychology and counseling.

His forty-page report was littered with factual errors, misattributed and patently false quotations, and garbled transcription errors. His "Document Review" of the binder I submitted mentioned none of the evidence I provided for the boys' complaints about their father. He found, in all those pages and hours of conversation with me and Kevin, "no evidence of domestic violence."

What he did find—and any reader who has experienced a contested custody case has been waiting for this part—was parental alienation. This topic got its own bold-faced subject heading; most likely it was part of his boilerplate for these reports. "Parental alienation" has been a staple in custody cases in which abuse is alleged for over thirty years. Essentially it's the custody-trial version of DARVO. Richard Gardner, a child psychiatrist, coined the term "parental alienation syndrome" (PAS) in 1987 to describe a "mental disorder" suffered by children who had been "indoctrinated by a vindictive parent and obsessively denigrated the other parent without cause." He originated the theory to explain why children in "high-conflict" custody cases "falsely accuse" parents of sexual abuse. The American Medical Association and the American Psychiatric Association have consistently refused to recognize PAS as a diagnosis, and over time the "syndrome" part and implied mental disorder have been dropped. But the concept of "alienating behavior" has become a common framework for blaming the parent favored by a child for causing that child to "falsely" claim being abused by the other parent.

Because the vast majority of abusers are men and most protective parents are women, the concept—even as Gardner created it—is inherently misogynistic and generally gets deployed, often successfully, by abusive fathers looking to wrest custody of their children from favored mothers. A New York Times article published on the occasion of Gardner's death acknowledged as much in 2003. That article even notes that in 1992, Gardner came out in public support of Woody Allen during a custody dispute with Mia Farrow, claiming—though he knew nothing about this case—that "screaming sex abuse is a very effective way to wreak vengeance on a hated spouse." In recent years, experts have come to see "parental alienation" as, instead, a "very effective way" to deny and hide all kinds of child abuse—which is exactly what the filmmakers of the 2021 HBO documentary series Allen v. Farrow imply happened in that case. Yet "parental alienation" remains an astoundingly powerful tool for abusive fathers and their lawyers in courtrooms all over the world. In 2022–2023, *ProPublica* ran a series of reports by Hannah Dreyfus on many shocking cases in which it was used to take custody from protective mothers and award it to abusive fathers.

I first heard the history of this term and its family-court use at the Battered Mothers' Custody Conference (BMCC) in 2019. The mere fact that there are so many women in the US who have lost custody of children to their abusers to fill a ballroom *every year for over fifteen years* says a lot about the scope of the problem in this country. The fact that this annual conference features panels of women whose children have been *killed* by the abusers who won custody communicates the horrifying severity of it. I found out about this conference from another custody forensic evaluator—the one I would have hired if I hadn't been pandering to the judge's misogyny—whom I paid for a consultation after being forced to withdraw my petition. Reeling from the injustice of what had happened and terrified for the physical and emotional health of my son, I went to her to gain some understanding and learn how to help Kevin transition back to the visitation his father would force him to submit to. This doctor described the BMCC as a gathering of the nation's experts on child-custody issues and of women who had suffered the same kinds of unjust court outcomes I had just experienced. She thought attending the conference might help me to educate myself about the nature and extent of this problem, which extends well beyond me and my child.

It is sad evidence of my stubborn faith in academic pedigrees and of my unconscious suspicion of "complaining women" that I would not have attended the BMCC without this professional's strong encouragement. I was doubtful as I registered for the conference and apprehensive as I entered the ballroom of the hotel for the first time and took my seat among a sea of women. I felt like an anthropologist observing a meeting of UFO trackers. As I sat through a series of highly informative presentations by experts from an array of relevant fields—lawyers, forensic evaluators, medical doctors, academics—and heard in the discussion periods from one smart, articulate woman after another, the surprise I felt forced me to register the profound prejudice I had fought to go there. This was no room of hysterical women. These women weren't deceitful or delusional, and the experts were not marginalized "crackpots." Why had I feared, even expected that they would be? I had absorbed the misogynistic logic of the courtroom that labels women who claim their children have been abused as crazy or manipulative and denies the expertise of the professionals who defend them. I was gaslighting myself and every woman in the room in my mind. What I found, once I took off my blinders and paid attention, is that we were a diverse group in all ways—age, race, educational backgrounds, income levels—but we were all united by the intense pain of our powerlessness in a system that does not allow us to protect our children from harm, a system that more often than not actually worsens that harm. And I saw that I had a lot to learn from these people, experts and fellow mothers alike.

Facing the scope and severity of a problem that could bring so many grieving women together, some of whom were grieving the deaths of their children, was overwhelming. But it made me realize that, in managing to get out before I could actually lose custody of my child, or get sucked into several years of emotionally and financially devastating trials and appeals that I would surely lose, I was lucky, perhaps the luckiest woman in that ballroom. And it made me realize, sadly, that I am not alone in the nightmare I went through in family court. Confronting the tenacity, ubiquity, and effectiveness of the "parental alienation" defense brought me an ironic bit of peace: no amount of preparation, research, or carefully worded promises to the judge would have saved me or my son from the system.

If the trial had continued and Dr. S.'s report had been entered into the court proceedings, it would have lent expert authority for the logic of parental alienation by "undermining mothers" that the judge had injected into my son's custody trial from the start. In an interesting twist on the formula, Dr. S. held Rick responsible for initially estranging Kevin through his "lack of empathetic understanding" but then painstakingly explained why his failed relationship with Kevin was nevertheless my fault. He cited Supreme Court cases in which other mothers were similarly blamed for fathers' parental failures. In those cases, as in my own, he claimed that the fathers may have planted the "seeds" of alienation, but the "belligerence of the children toward the father grew from the soil nurtured, watered and tilled by the mother." He used the evidence I had provided him myself to argue that there was "plenty of indication, especially in the texts, that [Kate] . . . did everything she could to facilitate [Kevin's] enmity towards his father." He did not point to any particular incriminating text; there was none. He did not acknowledge the evidence of Rick trying to alienate the kids from me.

The report made chillingly clear the scope of my responsibility and the consequences of my refusal to fulfill it. Again, Dr. S. cited legal precedent to establish that it was my job not only to force Kevin to comply with court-ordered visitation but to somehow, magically, against the weight of his own experience, make him love his father again. Dr. S. handed the judge the grounds he needed to order such a preposterous thing by quoting a case in which a judge "ordered the mother to 'do everything in her power to create in the minds of [the children] a loving, caring feeling toward their father . . . [and] to convince the children that it is the mother's desire that they see their father and love their father.'" Dr. S. added that, like this other wicked mother, if I didn't or couldn't do those things, I could be charged with contempt, lose custody, or even be put in prison. This part of the report was in a different font from the rest. Any guesses how many mothers Dr. S. has threatened with the same copied-and-pasted citation?

So, let's just say this plainly. Rick had been threatening, scaring, physically hurting, yelling at, shaming, insulting, and generally traumatizing Kevin for years. Kevin was afraid of his father and angry at him for not giving a damn about his well-being, but he was so unable to get Rick to hear him that he had been sick for years. Now it was my responsibility to create in Kevin's mind a loving, caring feeling toward this man. I was being ordered to convince Kevin that it was my desire that he spend time with this man. I was being told to lie to my child, to command him to feel the opposite of what he reasonably felt in response to real suffering. I was being ordered to create a delusion in the mind of my child about his own experience and mine.

I was being ordered, at risk of imprisonment if I did not comply, to gaslight my child.

That is not a melodramatic statement. My son's grasp on reality, his understanding of what was happening and why he hurt, had been at stake all along. His continuing illness was in part an expression of his frustration and confusion at being torn between two competing narratives about his life: his own and his father's. In Kevin's experience, he was increasingly aware that his dad did not prioritize him or respect what he thought and felt, and that his dad was most concerned with gaining compliance through domination and control. In his father's story, which he told Kevin in passionate speeches, me in long emails, Dr. A. in her office, and the court via Johnson, Rick was an excellent father who demonstrated his love by administering strict demands and "fighting for their relationship." Rick delivered this narrative convincingly, despite all evidence that he was inflicting harm on his son, because he absolutely believed it, and he still does. But he also still believes he was a loving husband. The difference in the case of the custody trial is that he found an entire legal system that was designed to back up his narrative.

What is a mother in this impossible situation supposed to do? What do you say to your child, who comes to you distraught, describing in detail a new instance of his father's neglect, shaming, threats, or refusal to value him as a human being; what do you say when you've been advised by parenting books never to utter a bad word about the other parent and warned to avoid seeming to blame him? I posed this question to every expert I could access: my lawyer, Kevin's therapist, my therapist, Kevin's school counselor, several of his medical doctors. Every one of them repeated some version of the same lame thing: "Try to validate his experience without saying anything that might be construed as alienating. Remind him to express his feelings to his father directly." Then, when your child tries this tactic—at the constant, surely irritating urging of his mother and his therapist—and it results in his father's increased anger, threats, and control; when your child comes to you then, as mine did, and says, "I'm so confused; you keep saying Dad is a good dad but it doesn't feel like that to me—are you lying? Dad makes me feel like I'm crazy; I don't understand why I feel so bad when I'm with him"—what do you say that will not add to your child's gaslighting?

Eventually I realized that in my efforts to avoid being accused of "alienation," I'd been not only participating in Rick's manipulation of Kevin; I'd abdicated one of my most important roles as Kevin's parent: teaching him how to treat others, especially in an intimate relationship. By fearfully submitting to Rick's narrative, I had been teaching my son that dominating the ones you love rather than treating them as equal human beings worthy of respect and care is—for a man—acceptable, even laudable. Eventually my concern for my son's well-being and sanity, and my desire to teach him how not to grow up to treat people as his father does, became more important to me than ensuring I could not be accused of "parental alienation." Even then, I was careful never to speak my own thoughts about Rick's behavior but only to validate Kevin's thoughts and feelings about it, to let him know they were real. The fact that I was still brought down by that accusation, after betraying my values and my son's reality for so long in my efforts to avoid it, is not ironic. It is entirely predictable in a system designed to uphold the fantasy of fathers' entitled righteousness and mothers' powerless responsibility.

When Adrienne Rich wrote about "powerless responsibility" in her foundational book about motherhood, she was not writing about custody trials. But nothing captures the absurd blend of impotence and blame assigned to mothers in family court better than that phrase.

> It is [the mother], finally, who is held accountable for her children's health, the clothes they wear, their behavior at school, their intelligence and general development. Even when she herself is trying to cope with an environment beyond her control, in the eyes of society, the mother *is* the child's environment. Under the institution of motherhood, the mother is the first to blame if theory proves unworkable in practice, or if anything whatsoever goes wrong.

This dynamic is clear at every turn in the custody trial, in which I was disdained for asserting the right to determine Kevin's best interests and blamed for the inevitable outcome of his father's failure to consider them. I was held responsible for every part of Kevin's experience—his education, his health, his well-being in every way—while being denied the power to enact the changes that all my parenting involvement had taught me he needed. No one disputed that I had been the only active parent in Kevin's life; Dr. S.'s report directly acknowledged that fact. But in the end it made no difference at all, because the judge, Johnson, Dr. S., and Rick believed that my doing nearly all the parenting labor for my children's entire lives was simply my job. My years of committing to and investing in my children said nothing positive about my fitness as a parent, just as Rick's failure to do the same said nothing negative about his. Even his many acts of willful neglect were not worthy of discussion; fathers do that. The decade or so in which I had never raised a hand against my struggling older son who verbally and even physically attacked me was as unworthy of mention as the times when Rick did raise a hand to both of his sons over the stupidest, most ego-driven disagreements. As the female cop instructed my son, "Your parents have the right to punish you."

Over and over, from nearly every player in this farce of a custody trial, Kevin and I were told some version of the same things: Mothers are responsible for taking care of children. Mothers are to blame when something goes wrong, like when a child is afraid of their scary dad. Because mothers are untrustworthy (emotional, unstable, deceptive), they can't be trusted to know what their children need. Fathers maybe don't do very much to take care of their children, but their relationships with their children are precious and must be protected at all costs. When fathers yell at their children, belittle them, and frighten them, they are being good, strong dads and children need to listen to them. But they do not need to listen to their children; mothers do the listening. A dad is not capable of fostering his child's love for him, but that's okay; it's the mom's job to do that. And if she doesn't do it with a fucking smile on her face, we can put her ass in prison.

"Parental alienation" was only one of the weapons Dr. S.'s report handed to Rick. After reading its contents, Ann warned me of the other damage it was likely to do. The report opened with my "social history," and it was likely, she said, that the judge wouldn't read past it before deciding the case, if he hadn't already. In my notes from that meeting with Ann, I can see the moment that finally persuaded me to withdraw my petition, to prevent the report from being entered into evidence through Dr. S.'s testimony: "We are professional women, [Kate]," Ann said. "You know that might happen." Those lines sit inside an emphatic box in the margin of a page otherwise crowded with my dense scrawl. I'd kept writing and scheming in that meeting, unwilling to give up on the spot. But again and again I came back to the ineradicable barrier around that block of text. There was no way around it.

While domestic violence, which often transfers from partner to child, is supposed to affect custody decisions, the parents' sexual history is not, unless it can be shown to have impacted parenting. Ironically, the only one who could be accused of allowing his sex life to adversely affect his parenting was Rick, but nobody had been interested in that proof of his poor judgment. Now I was being forced to accept the fact that my own sexual history, which had nothing to do with my parenting and had been contorted into its ugly shapes in part by Rick himself, would very likely be used against me if I went forward with my petition. Rick's history of extramarital dalliances, of course, would not. And our unorthodox joint sexual history would be seen as only *my* moral failure.

On the morning of our next trial date, despite a reputation for rarely making court appearances, Dr. S. strolled right up to Rick and Johnson in the waiting area outside the courtroom as I watched in dismay. He sat down with them and started chatting like they were old chums. Aghast at such unethical behavior, Ann said later that she suspected bribery for the first time in her career. But knowing what I know now about family court, and given the tenor of Dr. S.'s report, it's not hard to imagine Dr. S. inconveniencing himself not because he was being well paid but in defense of his fellow man against another histrionic, manipulative woman.

It took minutes to abandon the petition for which I had been gathering evidence for years and feverishly preparing for months. Stunned, I followed Ann out of the courtroom and into a small meeting room where we could confer before parting ways. The case was over. I was still in shock that I'd been forced to flee when we were in the right and had extensive evidence on our side. I would remain in shock about this for a very long time. At the age of forty-eight, I was finally absorbing the truth that the world is organized according to power, not justice, and that the holders of that power, despite all of my beliefs, efforts, and desires, were still the men. And I was incredulous that a judge could get away with openly flouting so many procedures of law. Ann acknowledged his unethical bias while issuing a stern warning: "Whatever you do, don't file a complaint," she said. "Every woman who has filed a complaint against this judge in a custody matter has lost custody of her kids." A quick internet search once back home showed that to be true: for years, women have been reporting this judge's misogynistic rulings and circulating petitions attempting to remove him from the bench. At the time of my writing, several women have filed suits against him, describing experiences very similar to mine, though even more extreme. Newspapers have reported on his record of awarding custody to abusive fathers. But so far none of these attempts to remove him from the bench has succeeded, and it's hard to imagine that any ever will.

I made sure to start every court day on my yoga mat. In the quiet studio, surrounded by fellow yogis committed to feeding their kind wolves, I did my best to set aside the turmoil of the trial and be present in my body and in each moment as it presented itself. My teacher had a remarkable ability to know when I needed a bit of extra care. During shavasana, as we practiced our future corpseness, she'd gently pick up my whole head in her hands and let it rest there, as if to say, "I've got you; let go." After the trial had ended, still reeling and clenched in fear for my son's future, I told her the whole incredible story over tea. She listened with her usual calm receptiveness, then gave the yogi's response: "Accept what you can't change. Let it unfold." Though I flailed against it in the moment, I knew this ancient wisdom—the only option anyone ultimately has—lies at the bottom of everything. The painful wake of the custody trial provided many opportunities to practice it. Meanwhile, I fought to change what I could.

More empowered than ever by the weapons the court had delivered into his lap, Rick started issuing dictates. Slowly but inexorably, he reclaimed every visitation day he had coming. Each time Kevin protested a new demand—now Friday nights, now Saturdays—Rick bullied him into compliance, threatening to take away everything that made being at his house bearable and to take me back to court to see how much more custodial time he could get. A year after the trial, during the early, frightening months of the COVID-19 pandemic, with considerably different safety protocols at the two houses, Kevin made another stand against visitation. In response, Rick drove to my house, where he beat on my door and screamed on my porch while Kevin cowered in his bedroom. Once again, I prepared to call the police if necessary while filming the whole ugly scene from a front window, hands shaking and teeth chattering with the old, awakened fear. After a few more threats, delivered directly to Kevin's phone, my son came to me in tears and asked me to drive him to Rick's house to end the unbearable stress of resisting his father's fury.

Meanwhile, Rick and I were still in court about finances. Rick was trying to convince Will that it was my greed and "excessive" child support that made Rick, whose salary was now six times mine, "unable" to pay for college. He pressured Will to testify in court that I didn't need the child support, for which he promised to reward Will by paying all his college expenses (dismissing the fact that I had been diligently depositing into a 529 college savings account since the divorce and wanted to pay my portion). Rick's unremitting attacks again took over my life, invading daily with emails, texts, attorneys' letters, and phone calls. My body began to break down. A runner for thirty years, I experienced such a scarily erratic heartbeat that I had to stop running altogether. My blood pressure routinely dropped so low that I learned to sink to the ground as soon as my vision went gray—during yoga, while gardening—before I could pass out. A cardiologist wired me up while I ran on a treadmill, sent me home in a Holter monitor, then ruled out every cause except stress.

Caught in a nearly constant fight-or-flight state, weathering adrenaline storms that fried my mind and depleted my body, I embraced my angry wolf again. Soraya Chemaly's *Rage Becomes Her* playlist became my fortifying soundtrack, speaker cranked in the kitchen, profanity pulsing in my chest like a pacemaker. Sometimes all I could do was stare out the window and let the music course through me as I tried to squeeze the immensity of my rage into the me who still needed to make dinner, to talk like a human being to other people.

One afternoon, after some court date or text or lawyer's letter, I was so overwhelmed by the unfairness and pain of the situation that I entered a place beyond words, a space of total fury that would not be tucked back in. I took the rage away from my family to the farthest corner of my yard, where I sent it out in a bellow I did not recognize as coming from me. Not for the first time, my sobs became so violent that they turned into retching, as if the rage, the powerlessness, the injustice were things writhing deep inside that my body was trying forcibly to expel.

A week or so later, Jack and I sat in a room full of parents as Kevin read aloud the short story he had just written during summer camp. It was called "Banshee." A mother is shrieking, her whole body electrified by pain, and her son knows that nothing he can do will save her. He also knows that the pain is a sickness that jumps from body to body through touch. He lays his hand on her arm to comfort her. The story ends with the sound of two gun shots.

What had I taught my son?

He is no longer innocent about what is at stake when you go up against someone with more power than you, or about how much it can cost, or about your chances of winning. He knows better than a lot of people his age that the fabric of the world is power, not justice. But he also knows that sometimes you have to fight anyway. That some things, and some people, are worth fighting for, no matter the outcome. And that sometimes what looks like loss is a step onto a different path you would not have found if not for the fight.

For all its spectacular failures and unforeseen anguish, the custody trial accomplished the primary things I set out to do: to alleviate Kevin's suffering and improve his relationship with his father. Over time, Kevin started experiencing less conflict with Rick, who seemed to realize he was on the brink of losing his relationship with his son forever and adjusted his behavior. Though Kevin was still plagued by chronic illness, after the trial he gradually returned to a normal life full of most of the usual high school things. When he turned seventeen, I presented him with the keys to a humble starter car, which he drove to Rick's house for visitation. When he forgot things at my house or wanted to say hello, he just drove on over. Now a legal adult and in college, he's outgrown the circumstances that allowed Rick to threaten and control him. He's healthy and thriving. And he's declared his intent to consider some day, with a therapist, what it means that his father refused to grant him personhood or acknowledge his needs and feelings until circumstances forced him to. Right now, though, his energy is going to another transformation entirely.

I suppose you could say that though we lost the battle we won the war, but I don't like that metaphor. I never wanted to be at war with Kevin's father; I only wanted to stop Kevin's suffering. It was my reluctance to engage with Rick in the battle he was gunning for, to trigger the trap he continually set for me, that allowed Kevin's suffering to go on as long as it did. For a long time, refusing to feed my angry wolf meant capitulating to Rick's narrative in which Kevin and I had no right to resist. It meant teaching my son that he had no right to his feelings, that he should not defend himself, that he should swallow his anger and submit. I had been teaching Kevin and Will their whole lives to feed their kind wolves. But I think when Kevin saw me gray-skinned from being up all night preparing my testimony, when he saw me come home from court ragged and defeated and then go back the next day with my head up and my resolution reforged, he understood that sometimes you have to feed the other wolf. And I hope that one day, he will know how and when to feed his.

My answer to that parable about which wolf to feed turned out to be more complicated than my yoga teacher intended. I will continue to feed my kind wolf, even when it's difficult, especially when it's difficult, as long as my children and I are allowed to live unmolested. But if attacked, demeaned, bullied, or controlled, when kindness fails and the suffering continues, I will be a banshee.

PART 4
SEX IS NOT SOMETHING YOU OWE

What is marriage but prostitution
to one man instead of many?

—ANGELA CARTER,
Nights at the Circus (1984)

16. MAD

How can a mad woman help her husband to escape?
If I were not mad I could have helped you. Whatever you
had done I could have pitied and protected you. But because
I am mad, I hate you. Because I am mad, I have betrayed
you. And because I am mad I'm rejoicing in my heart
without a shred of pity, without a shred of regret,
watching you go with glory in my heart.
Mr. Cameron, come! Take this man away!

—*GASLIGHT* (1944)

Learning to be a banshee did not come easily for me. The trial exhumed my long-buried rage, but I had to figure out how to do more than disgorge it. I had to learn how to harness it. I had to understand it. To do that, I had to begin to comprehend a whole lot of things.

Despite years of self-reflection, intellectual inquiry, discussion with my closest friends, and therapy, the last devastating years of my marriage haunted me long after the divorce was finalized and the court trials ended. Estranged from my body, I had become wholly alienated from my sense of self as well. Until that surreal handful of years, I rarely questioned the ethics of social norms and institutions and dutifully followed their rules. Even through those terrible years, I took care of others to the point of sacrificing myself and gave my all to everything, including my marriage. Who *was* this selfish, damaging person? I felt worse than shameful. I was disgusting, a monster. I could neither understand the person who had done these things nor account for her, and yet she was me, a fact I struggled to live with for years. I mean that literally: as I sat in my quiet house at the end of a long day, with my children asleep and my work finally done, memories of what I have described here flooded my mind, and I wanted to die to escape them. But I bore it; I bore her, the vile creature. I lived with that monstrous woman for years, dragging her into the life I was mindfully rebuilding, knowing she was always there, a mortifying part of me. I was the mad woman in my own attic.

In tenth grade, my English teacher left a copy of *Jane Eyre* on my desk with only the intriguing message that she thought it would speak to me. Its heroine, a bookish governess, falls in passionate love with her taciturn employer, Mr. Rochester, whose mansion resounds nightly with the "snarling, canine noise" of a "wild beast" trapped on its top floor. Upon discovering that the demonic "creature" "masked an ordinary woman's face," Jane intuits the tangled web of obligation and denial binding the mad woman to the house and man she haunts. When she discovers at the altar that the woman is his wife, Mr. Rochester asks forgiveness not for imprisoning the woman but for hiding his first marriage from Jane, who leaves him. At novel's end the woman, Bertha Mason, breaks free from her cell and sets the house on fire, burning it to the ground, blinding and disfiguring Mr. Rochester, and killing herself. Impediment removed, Jane returns to marry and care for Mr. Rochester, whose injuries leave him utterly dependent on her.

On first read I was, like most high school girls I think, drawn to Jane's bold self-reliance and emotional intensity, and by the love story that ultimately allowed her to preserve both. In college, Sandra Gilbert and Susan Gubar turned my attention to Bertha Mason and the trope of the "mad woman," who represents all the socially unacceptable qualities—being outspoken, unkempt, oppositional, uncontrollable—that women must repress to live in the great patriarchal houses meant to contain them. I had lived my whole life aspiring to be Jane—quietly respectable yet self-assured, resolute in her goodness—without considering all I was giving up, silencing, imprisoning, and destroying of myself in order to do so. I emerged from my divorce feeling more like Bertha Mason: my marriage had to be a smoking ruin before I could leave. As the agent of this ruin, I was the insane, inexplicable woman, acting dangerously outside polite society—the "bad wife," a monstrous creature. And so I deserved to be burned down too. I was the thing that had to be expunged to make another happy marriage possible. But how could I survive my own expunging? And could I ever be the "good wife" again? Did I even want to be?

———————

Several years after the divorce, I started working for a local crisis hotline, which required many hours of training over several weeks. The program taught volunteers about the challenges of and resources available to people in our community who are struggling in all kinds of ways. Addiction, poverty, mental illness, suicidal ideation: each new training unit brought talks by experts and role-playing as we practiced handling the kinds of distress we might encounter on the hotline, and I diligently took notes and memorized phone numbers. Then we came to domestic violence (DV).

A social worker specializing in DV cases taught us what domestic violence looks like, how it tends to unfold, and how difficult it is to help victims extricate themselves from these situations. I learned that DV, like all kinds of abuse, describes a wide spectrum of behavior, much of it invisible and unacknowledged by society. I learned that DV is essentially a pattern of manipulation and control, and that physical battery is only the most visible, not the most common method perpetrators use. Listening to the social worker describe in detail how DV might present itself, how to spot it when its victims (usually women) will not or cannot tell anyone directly what they are suffering—when they might not even recognize they are being abused—I experienced a revelation so sudden and intense that it felt like a shock of electricity coursing through my body. I sat up very straight in my hard plastic chair. The presenter's voice, the twenty other volunteers sitting around me, and the stark white room all fell away as pieces started clicking into place in my mind. No one had ever been able to explain to me what was so confusing and painful about the dynamics of my seemingly egalitarian marriage. Yet here was a total stranger describing them as if she'd witnessed scenes out of my own life.

A year and a half later, #MeToo exploded across the country and then around the globe. It had begun eleven years earlier when Tarana Burke posted "me too" on Myspace as a delayed response to a young Black girl's description of sexual abuse. Overwhelmed by her own traumatic memories and unable to support that suffering girl in the moment, Burke was inspired to create the Me Too movement as a public response to that girl: the phrase "me too" has always illustrated both the power and the difficulty of telling our stories. In October of 2017, #MeToo and the deluge of public writing about sex it released was also, in the solitude of women's kitchens and bedrooms, in conversations over drinks between friends, quietly beginning to change how women viewed themselves and their relationships with men. How many of us were moved to revisit our sexual histories and realized, for the first time, that many of our memories were of being harassed, pressured, violated, threatened, assaulted, or raped? How many of us confessed our dark secrets or new realizations to another person for the first time?

For me, that awakening began on a night in November 2017, when I read the Babe.net article in which "Grace" detailed a sexual encounter with Aziz Ansari that she described as "violating" and he described as "consensual." The article puzzled me. Grace had been drunk in a man's apartment after a fancy dinner date; in common cultural understanding, she was basically offering herself up for the sex he would expect in exchange for the expensive meal. He had done all the things men usually do in that kind of situation—cajoling, bargaining, pressuring, guilt-tripping, forcing physical intimacy step-by-step. And yet the article took the stance that his behavior was unacceptable, that Grace had been wronged. To me, unpleasant as it was, the description of their evening together read as business as usual, as another example of the transactional nature of sex that had defined most of my dating life and much of my marriage. Why was an article depicting this normal dating scene as worthy of media attention?

My reaction grew more complicated as responses to Grace's story began to appear. Most of them empathized with her suffering and amplified her call for an apology. Ansari, at that time a beloved comedian whose work critiqued misogyny and supported female writers and performers, seemed to be on the brink of losing his career. The clarity and intensity of this public response to Grace's story exploded my understanding of the world and kicked off a reexamination of my entire sexual history. This article had identified a new kind of sexual assault—not stranger rape but not date rape either, not even something that Grace could fully identify in the moment as more than harassment. And people were taking her complaints seriously. A consensus was building that pressuring, manipulating, or guilting a woman into sex is not okay, is not just part of dating, that such behavior lies on a spectrum of sexual abuse stretching all the way, unbrokenly, to rape. I read the article at first with resentment. It seemed preposterous to me that Grace thought she had the right to cry "sexual abuse" for having suffered only a relatively tame version of what most of us have suffered countless times through our lives, of what I had endured many nights in my marriage.

And then it hit me: if what Grace described was wrong, if public opinion was recognizing that the "normal" methods men use to get sex from women are a kind of predatory abuse and must be stopped, then my husband's treatment of me was also wrong, unacceptable, harmful, abusive. And I had had no idea.

How had I, a hypereducated, seemingly empowered woman, allowed my own sexual domination to the point of losing track of my self? Though #MeToo had made this abuse visible to me, it could not explain it to me; it offered me no community of similar survivors. We've now seen best-selling memoirs, novels, and essay collections about sexual abuse in nearly every conceivable context. But what we still don't talk about when we talk about #MeToo is the sexual abuse that takes place in marriages. Studies have shown for over forty years that rape and sexual coercion are relatively common in marriage. Recent work on sexual violence routinely notes that a third of rapes are committed by a current or former intimate partner. When I began writing about sexual abuse in marriage, I raised the topic with female friends and found that every one of them had a story, her own or a friend's or relative's, about being pressured into sex in a way that made her feel disregarded, furious, or violated by her spouse or long-term partner. Why aren't we talking about this?

One reason might be that acknowledging the magnitude of this problem would be overwhelming—half of adults in the US are married, and married people have sex twice as often as single ones: do the math. Another is that we need new language for it. I don't know what to call the painful sexual experience of my marriage. Technically, it was coerced sex. It was not violent rape or physical assault: my husband employed no physical violence—beyond the unwanted sex itself—and used no weapons. He didn't have to hold me down. I wasn't blind drunk or unconscious. But "coerced sex" is what we call what happens at the end of a bad date. That's also wrong and potentially even traumatic, but in that context you can curse the asshole and jettison him from your life. Coerced sex in a life relationship can be a trauma you live through over and over and dread in between. It's suffering for which you will likely blame yourself more or less entirely, in an effort to maintain the relationship you cannot imagine leaving, especially if you share children with the perpetrator. Being systematically compelled to submit to unwanted sex over the course of a long relationship creates ongoing, seemingly inescapable trauma that can shape years or a lifetime. "Coerced sex" does not begin to describe that.

In *Girlhood*, Melissa Febos proposes the term "empty consent" to describe the "consent" women "give" when submitting to the subtle mechanisms used by men to obtain all kinds of caretaking in all sorts of situations. She wryly notes that "It has never been expected that a man ask a woman's consent before using her emotionally." "Empty consent" is submission that may look like consent to the pressuring man but does not feel like consent to the uninterested woman. It's "consent" to an asserted obligation a woman feels she can't avoid, or whose avoidance seems more difficult, or dangerous, than submission. The term adds much-needed nuance to our consent vocabulary, but I think we still need more. All the manipulative methods men use to procure such dubious consent in the context of dating, hookups, and even friendship occur at least as often in marriage. But in these long-term relationships, the power inequity—a man's right to pressure and a woman's perceived powerlessness to choose—unfolds not over the course of an evening but over years or a lifetime. "Empty consent" doesn't adequately express the brutality of such sustained and invisible domination, or sufficiently ironize the "consent" of submission that requires systematically contradicting one's own will or desires.

I consider what I experienced to be *forced consent*: submission to sex for which I expressed no meaningful consent, because I could not escape it without losing my life. The life at risk was not my physical life, but the risk was existential. The force that got my submission wasn't corporeal, but it was brutal.

After #MeToo woke me up and I published my short piece on Vox.com, I started working on this book in earnest. First, I wrote the detailed description of my experience of forced consent that appears in the first chapter. I wanted to begin from the visceral and psychic reality of this thing that had haunted me for years. Then I read everything I could find about sexual assault, rape, and consent, and was surprised to recognize my experience there. Like several writers in Roxane Gay's collection *Not That Bad: Dispatches from Rape Culture*, who describe the experience and aftermath of rape in diverse contexts—as a child, a college student, or a date; by a male family member, a male friend, or a female partner—I disassociated. Like them, I felt objectified, dehumanized, erased. Like two other writers in that collection and like Carmen Maria Machado in her memoir about queer domestic violence, *In the Dream House*, I wanted the assault to be made visible on my body. I will never forget looking up into my husband's rage-contorted face, his hand stopped mid-stroke above me, and saying, "Do it. Please do it." I could have seen with my own eyes that he was abusing me. I could have shown others and felt justified in leaving. I would have avoided a decade of self-doubt and guilt for hurting him so deeply when "all he ever did was love me," this man who had sex with me night after night, knowing I felt it as a violation. But without visible proof, and lacking language for it, I had no evidence of his abuse at all.

In the fifteen years since I left Rick, I have painfully and in fits and starts rebuilt the self I lost. I have rebuilt the boundaries Rick erased for his own benefit, replacing lines with high walls that can't be demolished and are difficult to scale. I couldn't see my own fortress until I read the account of a woman with the clarity to describe hers. A. J. McKenna wrote that "because [of] how you treated me . . . there are parts of me I hoard, parts of me I will not give away, nor sell at any price, because you tried to steal them from me." A transgender woman who was raped by another woman, McKenna enabled me to understand why I, a cis woman coerced into sex by her cis het husband, will never again love as freely or give myself as completely as I did before I was systematically violated by someone I loved.

When I finally began to extricate myself from the marriage, Rick tried to convince me I was mentally ill. He begged me to "try medication" to rid me of the "delusion" that was making me want to leave him. He did this so many times, for so long, that part of me believed him. Reading survivor narratives years later helped me see otherwise: the seething rage I had held unacknowledged in my core for so many married years was not inexplicable, or a sign of my monstrous selfishness or sexual dysfunction. It was rage at a man who said he loved me when he was totally content to shred my humanity to satisfy his sexual needs. When I began to burn down the house of our marriage, I wasn't mad, as in "crazy." Deep down, where I couldn't bear to face it, I was fucking furious.

17. DISTURBING

Why don't you write? Write!
Writing is for you, you are for you;
your body is yours, take it.

—HÉLÈNE CIXOUS,
"The Laugh of the Medusa" (1975)

J ust as Edna in Chopin's *The Awakening* had to endure an "exceedingly disturbing" new beginning to awaken, we have to set about disturbing things if we want to engender a world in which women can be truly free. We can start by debunking the comforting myths about marital sex that enable abuse and deny women's suffering.

Studies show that sexual violence in marriage is committed by every kind of man, and these perpetrators are, as Kate Manne puts it, "unremarkable, non-monstrous-seeming people." A "non-monstrous-seeming," even laudable public persona can easily mask the dangerous combination of cultural misogyny and personal narcissism that can lead to intimate partner abuse. I suspect—with only anecdotal experience to go on—that plenty of sexual abusers warrant diagnoses of narcissistic personality disorder. But Manne's point is scarier than that. She argues that misogyny is "narcissistic and delusional *by its very nature*. It transforms impersonal disappointments into embittered resentment—or a sense of 'aggrieved entitlement.'" This sense of entitlement only increases the more privilege a man enjoys in his life, so that more privilege can mean more domination of women. Men who confine their abusiveness to their private lives are unlikely to suffer consequences, because they are unlikely to be exposed. As one study put it, "Upper-class men who do not rape other men's daughters or wives—who rape their own wives and girlfriends—are unlikely to be [or, presumably, to become] involved in the legal system."

Are these public saints knowingly committing sexual violence against their wives? Plenty of studies find that some men knowingly violate women because they think they have the right, with Clarence Thomas, Brett Kavanaugh, and Donald Trump being obvious examples of both personal justification and social impunity. But I don't think that all or perhaps even most perpetrators of the kind of marital sexual abuse I am describing are aware their behavior is violating. And I don't think that making men aware of the power dynamics involved will change their behavior. As long as rape is seen as a crime about power and not about sex, not about physical violation and emotional suffering, and not about denying women equal selfhood, what will motivate men to stop? Pursuing power is the manliest thing a man can do in our culture. Instead, I write with the hope that witnessing the damage caused by such violations—and the way it extends in all directions, creating constellations of suffering—might wake up some men too. The women in Miriam Toews's novel *Women Talking* leave because they realize the abusive men in their isolated community will never change. But we can't all pack up our wagons and leave. Where would we go?

The many cultural clichés about wives' attempts to escape unwanted sex in marriage (claiming "headaches" or "monthlies"), and portrayals of the same in sitcoms and films—mostly written by men, who still dominate the entertainment industry—make it perfectly clear that men know women often do not want to have sex when their partners press for it. And these tropes have nothing to do with the subtle difference between "spontaneous" and "responsive" desire, both of which assume a mutually respectful relationship in which one person's spontaneous desire might invite the other to allow their desire to be lovingly cultivated. Instead, these stereotypes depict a man's coercion or even force of sex with an uninterested and unaroused woman, especially when they are married, as entirely within his rights. Consider how often a husband pounding away on top of his vacant wife is used in film or TV as shorthand for a stale marriage—as if having someone thrust his dick into you when you don't want him to is simply one of the things women are expected to accept in a long-term relationship. As if what women in that situation are experiencing is merely boredom, not physical violation. Worse, consider how often such scenes are framed as funny—meaning, totally normalized and unproblematic—and even worse, consider how often that happens in otherwise female-empowering vehicles. In an early scene in the 2011 film *Bridesmaids*, for example, a wife casually jokes to her female friend, demonstrating her pseudo-liberation, "You know, sometimes I just want to watch *The Daily Show* without him entering me."

If we accept that men are aware that some if not much of the sex they make happen is unwanted, then the only way to preserve our shared societal delusion that men who coerce sex are not raping women is to hold tight to the accompanying belief that a woman who submits to sex she really doesn't want experiences it as no big deal; as a small price to pay for a man's pleasure, relief, or validation; as the minor inconvenience of ten minutes lost out of her evening.

I am writing this to say: that is a terrible myth.

Our cultural depictions of coerced sex and forced consent serve patriarchy and misogyny by providing a sheen of plausible deniability that all men are welcome to employ. Men are invited to wrap themselves in these cultural myths about the normality of force and the banality of women's experience of it so they can secure their needs at the expense of their partners' suffering while maintaining the cleanliness of their public and private images. Even women who mean to draw attention to the problem of sexual abuse can fail to see this core aspect of it. One rape survivor's defense of affirmative consent, for example, sounds painfully naïve: "Since decent human beings only want to have sex with people who are into it, this shouldn't be a hard sell." Considering all the "decent human beings" who expect to have sex inside (or outside) their marriage with people who are not into it, affirmative consent appears to be quite a hard sell indeed. Or does this writer not consider all of these manipulative people "decent human beings"? In which case the world's supply of decency would suffer a dramatic reduction.

Either (1) these perpetrators of unwanted sex are inconceivably inept at reading their partners' various ways of expressing disinterest (despite popular culture's cataloging of them); or (2) they are living blissfully in denial of the real harm they are doing to other human beings (presumably ones they love), or (3) they know they are violating others and do not care, because they believe they have the right to violate them. No amount of appeals to rationality or feeling will change the minds of the third type of abuser. The first type, perpetrators who are impossibly naïve, I see as a mask for the second type. It is difficult to mistake coerced sex for desired sex. As Manne writes, "Sex women want is almost never described by them or anyone else as consensual."

So ultimately I am addressing the second type of abuser, people—most often men—who are so in denial or ignorant about the harm they are doing that witnessing the effects of their behavior might make them want to change it. Maybe being confronted by someone from whom they're not desperately trying to get something will allow them to hear it. Because I agree with that affirmative-consent writer when she says that "in the end, you have to care. You have to care about another person's wishes and feelings." Those who do, who love their partners for the independent and autonomous people they are, rather than as conduits for fulfilling their needs for love, sex, and validation, will have to stop. Or they will have to recognize that they are really the third type of abuser.

Many of the scholars I have read and cited point out the limits of the law's ability to create meaningful change on this issue. But change is possible, and Catharine MacKinnon's "butterfly politics" model for social change is especially optimistic. It views the "law and politics of gender inequality" as a kind of "complex causality" whose workings are nonlinear and unpredictable, and in which, at any moment, some "initial perturbation" might trigger systemic change. Who's to say which perturbation, when, where, and by whom might reorganize the system? The massive connectedness and speed of communication enabled by today's many social media platforms mean that anyone's offering might be the next butterfly wing: #ForcedConsentIsRape.

Virtually all writers on this topic also agree that our most effective way to perturb the system is by telling our stories—making public the truths that contradict the myths and false reality constructed by social, legal, family, educational, and cultural systems. Doing so is risky. Manne points out that women who speak out will be considered "overly dramatic"—as Fowles and I know all too well—but this is exactly why we must speak. Soraya Chemaly urges women to share their stories and "become whistle-blowers," and to prepare to be met with men's anger for daring to prioritize our own needs. Chemaly's book, *Rage Becomes Her*, argues that women's anger is useful and necessary for responding to a culture that systematically limits, objectifies, and silences us. Anger, she writes, "warns us viscerally of violation, threat, and insult." Anger requires maintaining the subjecthood that objectification by sexual oppression and gaslighting destroy. Through anger, we seek to control our circumstances and express the optimistic belief that change is possible. It is healthy, not melodramatic, to feel anger when someone has harmed you, refused to listen to you, or failed to care about your suffering. An angry woman knows who she is, recognizes abusive behavior when she sees it, and refuses to stay silent about it. An angry woman cannot be gaslighted. Instead, she tells her story and supports other women in telling theirs.

Throughout the more than ten years during which my husband convinced me that his needs were sacrosanct and mine were irrational and excessive, I felt no anger at all. I could not see his contribution to the disaster that our marriage became, so thoroughly had he gaslighted me. I could not tell a true story, only his story. But reading the stories that have come out of the #MeToo movement, and recognizing in them my own normalized but agonizing sexual experience in my marriage, has caused in me a transformation akin to awakening from a trance. I am ready to tell my own story. And I am angry.

I am angry that my husband traded my self-worth for his pleasure and validation. I am angry that he experienced my self-abnegation as physically and emotionally fulfilling. I am angry that eventually the only thing he really needed from me was sex; that my warmth, generosity, intelligence, sense of humor, kindness, creativity, and nearly endless desire to love him ultimately became irrelevant. I am angry that I was taught my whole life by my parents, his parents, teachers, and most of what I read and viewed that it is my job to take care of men, to submit to them, to do the work required to sustain every relationship, and to sacrifice everything, including myself, to do that work. I am angry that I was trained to expect so little from him and to be so easily impressed with the bits he gave me that I decided to commit my life to him. I am angry that I was made to believe that it is unacceptable for me to feel angry at his appalling treatment. I am angry that I was unable to assert myself, to say to his face, with force, what I am finally saying here: that he was killing me. I am angry that in writing that last sentence, part of me even now fears it sounds "melodramatic" though I know it is literally true. I am angry that I was brainwashed to believe that divorce is more harmful to children than subjecting them to a marriage that would teach them that misery and female self-erasure are normal parts of it. I am angry that my husband had me convinced for a decade that the end of our marriage was entirely my fault; that I deserved his fury, disgust, and punishment; that I deserved to be rejected by his family who had once been mine. I am angry that I spent years nearly paralyzed with shame. Most of all, I am angry that all of these things that I experienced are not extreme exceptions but are typical of a misogynistic culture in which women, especially in marriage, offer themselves up piece by piece to men, enduring all kinds of suffering as part of the fabric of that culture, and that *no one is talking about it*, because such behavior is considered normal. It should not be.

I have written this book not as an accusation but as a provocation—to press us all to rethink our assumptions about sex, power, choice, consent, and compliance. I hope those who have experienced forced consent—which will mostly be women, but could be anyone, in any type of relationship—will feel seen and understood, and will feel their suffering is finally made visible. Those who routinely press for sex might ask their partners whether they feel objectified or disrespected. Then, I hope they will really listen when their partners answer, possibly in distressing ways. Articulating a disconnect in sexual desires could be an opening for real intimacy and understanding, an opportunity to repair a relationship that has started to die. It might be an invitation to enact Finkel's third "love hack" with mutual respect and care. Or it might become the harbinger of an extraordinarily painful but necessary separation, because the relationship can't be brought back to life.

My hopes are grander still. I hope readers who recognize themselves in my experience, and feel able to speak without causing themselves further harm, will talk about what it felt like at the time and how it has affected them in the long term—to their friends, grown children, or current partner. And I hope they will tell their stories publicly across all kinds of media platforms. These conversations, and the stories we share, are our perturbations, our butterfly wings. Every time we speak or write honestly about sex, autonomy, and power, we create a new narrative that enters culture and disturbs it, displacing old tales and values and replacing them with new ones. These disturbances are seismic. Who can say how far their waves will travel, or how long it will take them to reshape the world? Not knowing myself, I apply my frank force to the fault line; I flutter my wings. And I ask you to join me.

18. MONSTROUS

I would give up the unessential;
I would give up money,
I would give my life for my children;
but I wouldn't give myself.

—KATE CHOPIN, *The Awakening*

O nce upon a time, a woman who freed herself from patriarchy had to be dead, mad, or monstrous. Before *The Awakening*'s Edna chose the sea's embrace over a tyrannized life, long before Sylvia Plath conjured a woman as "perfected" by death days before ending her own life, Charlotte Perkins Gilman's unnamed narrator in "The Yellow Wall-paper" escaped the infantilizing ministrations of her doctor-husband through what looks like insanity but really is her only avenue to freedom. Confined to the nursery and "forbidden to 'work'"—her husband and brother do not take her writing seriously—she projects her mind into the room instead and finds in the wallpaper pattern a trapped woman who climbs out to creep around the room. She frees herself by becoming that woman, then takes over the creeping. She wants her husband to witness her bold liberation; she wants to "astonish him." And she does: he faints at the sight of her powerful madness. She creeps right over him.

Literature is likewise full of monstrous women. One of the most famous in Western civilization is Medusa, her feminine hair replaced by serpents—agents of original sin—and a gaze that turns men to stone. Medusa has symbolized men's inability to tolerate their own objectifying weapon for thousands of years and as recently as the 2016 presidential election, when the Trump campaign sold caps and T-shirts with an image of

Hillary Clinton's screaming, snaky head atop Medusa's body. Misogynistic opponents of Angela Merkel and Theresa May made Medusa mash-ups with them as well. Once feminine but refashioned by a jealous goddess as unforgivably powerful, Medusa is freakishly masculine. She is a danger to men rather than their object; she is the ultimate castrator. Her usurping head must be cut down.

Angela Carter spent her entire literary career considering how "a free woman in an unfree society must be a monster." Certainly powerful women such as Clinton and Merkel quickly learn to expect to be depicted as monstrous. But I think Carter meant something much more essential than that. Carter's deviant heroines—her circus freaks, witchy sexpots, and husband killers—illustrate that women in patriarchy must not simply *seem* but must truly *be* monstrous if they want to come out on top. Carter's *Nights at the Circus* gleefully enacts this mandate by revealing its bold heroine as half-bird and thus only able to take the woman-on-top sexual position, which is how the book leaves her—dominant, pleasured, and laughing uproariously.

In Deborah Levy's *Hot Milk*, painful tangles with Spanish jellyfish called "medusas" punctuate a young woman's transformation out of meek subservience and into audacity, rage, and sexual appetite that she feels, and others see, as "monstrous." The medusas refigure her skin with angry welts and "sting her into desire." She begins to seek out the pain, the change, the alien ferocity. Each time she swims, she moves farther into the formless sea, passing through schools of medusa like baptismal fire. Reforged, she becomes increasingly bold: she frees a tortured dog, takes multiple lovers, and stands up to her parasitic mother and narcissistic father. The repetitive pull of the sea is a clear echo of *The Awakening*, as is the water's promise of rebirth. But *Hot Milk* offers a different possibility for women longing to break free from the suffocating molds they've been cast in: becoming a monster.

For most of my life and marriage, I would do anything to avoid being seen as a monster. I would obey, I would stay, I would lie down. I lived in the cage Rick and I made like a docile animal that would not even exit the open door. When I finally tore myself away, Rick called me a monster. Every time I asserted myself on behalf of my children or my own freedom, he reminded me of my monstrosity to activate my shame and elicit my submission as penance and corrective. It worked, because I was not really a monster, not yet. I was only a cowed woman, full of regrets and stumbling my way toward freedom.

Anger came later, as I began to locate my experiences in the vast network of misogyny and place them next to other women's stories. Still, I bowed to Rick's labels—bad wife, whore, lunatic, monster—and had no narrative that might redeem them. I felt "mad," but not enraged; whorish, but not owed my own desire; monstrously selfish but not monstrously free. It took writing this book for me to see that all along, I had been clutching at boldness, transgression, transformation, and self-determination, while refusing to allow myself to grab these things and hold tight.

Today, I am happily unmarried. I alone own the house that I share with my kids and a wonderful man who contributes his finances and labor. But every bill comes in only my name. I decide when and where to knock down walls or build them. Should Jack disappear tomorrow, my material and financial life would remain largely unchanged. This is not very egalitarian of me. It's certainly not romantic. One might reasonably see it as an overcorrection to my suffocating marriage, in which Rick and I owned everything together yet I discovered how little meaningful power I had, how little claim to my own spaces. I need to know I am never trapped and that every day Jack and I spend together is a choice. I like to think of our arrangement as a version of Beauvoir's ideal, "the mutual recognition of free beings who confirm one another's freedom." I know my need to live this way also indicates incomplete healing. But anyone who survives long-term trauma and says they are not traumatized is lying.

If my painful transformation has stung me into desire, it is the desire for autonomy and to fully inhabit my truest self, undivided by the requirements of roles that don't suit me or of people who do not see or care who I am. It is the urgent need to live outside the social expectations that dictate how I can relate to my partner or to anyone and what they can expect or demand of me. I determine who I am and what I give through love, respect, and generosity, for myself as well as others, not duty or shame. I am willfully unwilling to live inside marriage or the narratives that Rick, society, and all its institutions want to impose on me. I make my own rules and write my own story. I decide its ending, its moral, and what kind of character I get to be.

What I am is nothing so simple as hero or villain, abuse victim or bad wife, ferocious or wracked by love. I have been all those things, and

I remain each of them for someone. But at the end of this story, which is where I begin, I am something outside those neat oppositions. I have swallowed them whole and am pregnant with the wyrd potential of their eclipse. I focus my furious gaze, this record of all I have seen, and send it out to disturb and astonish. You know what I am.

I am the monster.

AWAKENING

—Narrative is the aftermath of violent events.
It is a means of reconciling yourself with the past.

—I don't want to tell my story. I want to live.

—The old story has to end before a new one can begin.

—RACHEL CUSK, *Aftermath* (2012)

M y ex-husband's version of this story goes something like this: My wife lied to me and cheated on me, with multiple men, for years. I begged her to stay, despite the horrible things she'd done to me; yet she left me and destroyed my family. And she did all this to me after I had loved her enormously for years. She became selfish, deceitful, histrionic, and capable of unthinkable cruelty. I don't know what happened. We were so happy, and then all of a sudden she changed. Either she became mentally ill, or I never knew her. What she did to me was unforgivable. She ruined my life.

Rick told me that story so many times that it became my story. Hollowed out, I was not capable of formulating my own, and his left me utterly hijacked. What he said had to be true: look at all the horrible things I had done. So why did I feel so beaten up and violated? Why was I so afraid of him, if I was the bully? But as I had for nearly twenty years, I willingly stepped into his story, in part because it was the habit of our marriage. And his story fit me like a hair shirt: I regretted the hurtful things I had done so much that it felt natural and right to choose a view of myself and my past that required constant self-loathing, self-monitoring, and penitence.

Rick is clever and gifted at making the world line up the way he needs it to. His story became his cruelest method of punishment and his most powerful tool for controlling me. Whenever I stepped out of line, he threatened to tell this story to our children. This was his ultimate weapon. I have lived in gut-wrenching fear of it for fifteen years. His story has been a gun pointed at my head, a gun I have taken out of his hand by writing this book.

But it has also been a dilemma, because most of his story's plot points are true. It took me a very long time to understand how many of its facts can be true, and yet the story itself can be false, so unlike my experience of the same years. One of the parts that I know is true for him is his intense love for me. I absolutely believe that he thought he loved me and did in fact love me to the best of his ability. I understand now that at some point he had no idea how to reach me, and I can imagine how painful it must have been when he tried and repeatedly failed. I saw him suffer in those last years of our marriage. I saw how desperately he wanted me to stay, what he was willing to do to make that happen, how hard he fought the divorce at every step. The divorce happened anyway, of course, but it happened against his will at every moment. I can imagine the tragedy of that for him, and I understand that this is his trauma, the traumatic story into which I thrust him.

Even as I have been fighting to break free of his story, I have worked to preserve my ability to understand what it means to him and how I hurt him, to not abdicate my responsibility for it. Doing so has made it hard and slow for me to see my own story. It is impossible to perceive the old woman's face and the young woman's profile in the picture at the same time. You have to look away from one to see the other. I will never stop looking away from my story to see Rick's story of me, or Alex's story of me, or my culpability for their pain. But in order to move out of his story and live in mine, I've been looking away from his for a while and trying to see what's there when I look at my past and my present with my own eyes. When I do, the plot points he clings to fade a bit, and a sky full of others asserts itself. Together, they make a very different constellation than the one he has drawn for us for so long. The new picture does not erase the mistakes I made. In my story, I'm still a liar, an "adulterer," and worst, an unforgivably duplicitous friend. But by adding the parts he can't see, I find a way of understanding my behavior that I had denied myself while always using it to understand his: suffering people cause suffering. I saw from the start the ways my husband had suffered, and I saw it as my duty to alleviate that suffering. But he could never see mine.

There's an ingenious short story made of pop quizzes that compel the reader's judgment. One quiz ends in failure; it just can't articulate a clear conflict, the basic requirement of all fiction. The imaginary author tries again with a new version, adding pages of backstory to his original quarreling characters until conflicts and possible readings of them multiply out of control. By the end we aren't sure whom to judge, why, or in what terms, but we can see that the guy we were sort of being asked to judge in the original quiz no longer deserves it. Every life is like this, as is every story. It is not possible, finally, to know enough information to accurately or righteously judge an entire other human being, whose life is as much an accumulation of heroic achievements and regretful failures as yours is. Even when you think you can, one added point could change the entire picture and your sympathies right along with it.

In Rick's story, I am easy to judge and despise, and that is who I am for him and anyone else who is satisfied by his story. I want to be, for myself and for those who want to know, love, and trust me, the fullest version of myself I can be. To that end I offer this story, whose details provide many opportunities for judgment and sympathy alike. If I deserve either of those, I deserve both, like every human being alive. Knowing this now, I find I would rather understand others than judge them and feel compassion rather than contempt. I know that generally we do those things by asking for more information, however contradictory and confusing, rather than settling for the neat narrative. And we do those things by being alert to the sources of others' suffering and knowing that none of it—not the asking and not the suffering—ever stops. All we can do is witness it, doing our best to behave with grace and forgive ourselves and each other when we do not.

I used to say that Rick and I lived on different planets, and we did, and we still do—as does everyone. Like Chimamanda Ngozi Adichie's TED Talk, "The Danger of a Single Story," the short story of pop quizzes demonstrates that no one story ever constitutes truth. Instead, every story is part of an infinite number of stories that could be told about any moment. Likewise, every person's reality is only one slice of an infinitely sliceable space-time loaf. Each slice constitutes an entirely unique

universe, defined by the viewer's position in time and space. Our best way
to cross the chasms between these universes is through acts of empathy
and imagination—stories—that create a shared universe, a world built of
shared vision, knowledge, feelings, and desires. Rick and I were not able
to do this after the first few carefree years of our marriage, and we certainly can't do it now. But I believe in his story, even in his story of me.
His is a story of enormous suffering and loss, it is entirely true for him,
and my heart hurts for him for that. But my story, this story, is also true.
Everything in it happened, even if not all of it happened in the universe
where Rick stubbornly lives.

It has taken me all these years to realize that I had the right to my own
story of my life. Writing it down has felt like a radical act of mapmaking,
of world-building. It has materialized a past where I do not want to live
anymore but that I needed to know was real. I can look at this map of the
world where I lived and know which parts I can leave behind and which
parts I need to carry a little longer, like a stone in my pocket that needs
a bit more worrying. Seeing where I've been, I understand why I am always so grateful to be free of that old place and why sometimes it is hard
to be anywhere at all.

This story, this map—like any other—can't contain every possible
plot point or perspective, and so it can't be objectively true. But if you
stand right here where I've placed you, adjust the lens, and look closely,
you will see the precise slice of the space-time loaf toward which I have
pointed this scope, words delivering the past like particles of light that
have traveled many years to reach you. In them you will see for a moment
the universe I lived in, and you will feel what you do—perhaps shock and
disgust, or maybe anger, judgment, or empathy. What you feel depends on
who you are and where you're standing. Even if you feel more offended
than moved by this particular story, I hope you will contemplate the overwhelming fact of all the points of light and all the slices, how incomplete
is any vision, and how small we are in comparison to the totality we can
never see because we are part of it. And maybe you will feel, as I do when
I look at this place I have mapped, humbled, and able to greet the rest of
the world with the humility and compassion that come from looking at
all that we are and finding the limits of what we can see.

RESOURCES

For immediate emotional support or practical help for sexual assault:

Online chat: hotline.rainn.org/online
Call 800-656-HOPE

For immediate emotional support or practical help for domestic violence:

Online chat: www.thehotline.org
Call 800-799-SAFE

RAINN.org: The nation's largest anti-sexual-violence organization, which offers information and statistics about sexual violence, survivor narratives, and support options for survivors.

Battered Mothers Custody Conference (batteredmotherscustody conference.com): Provides educational material, resources, support, and networking opportunities for mothers attempting to use family court to protect their children and themselves from abusive situations.

TaraBrach.com for mindfulness information, resources, podcasts, practice, and community.

RECOMMENDED READING

I read widely and compulsively for years—about sex, desire, consent, marriage, sexual and domestic violence, shame, trauma, and the myriad amazing ways women survive and speak about all of these things—as I struggled to understand the experiences I have narrated here, then as I searched for a form for my contribution, then as I shaped that writing and started to bring what I have learned into my teaching and research. Every day I feel gratitude for the brilliant and brave writers who enabled me to regain a sense of self, find my voice, and write this book. And live this life. Here I offer a selection of those sources, not knowing exactly what each reader might need from this or any book or where they're headed, but hoping they might find clarity and companionship in some of these voices and ideas, as I have and always will.

All About Love: New Visions by bell hooks (Harper Perennial, 2000)

The Argonauts by Maggie Nelson (Graywolf, 2015)

The Body Keeps the Score: Brain, Mind, and Body in the Healing of Trauma by Bessel van der Kolk (Viking, 2014)

Consent: A Memoir of Unwanted Attention by Donna Freitas (Little, Brown, 2019)

Entitled: How Male Privilege Hurts Women by Kate Manne (Crown, 2020)

Her Body and Other Parties: Stories by Carmen Maria Machado (Graywolf, 2017)

"Horse" in *The Wrong Heaven* by Amy Bonnaffons (Little, Brown, 2018)

Hot Milk by Deborah Levy (Bloomsbury, 2016)

In the Dream House: A Memoir by Carmen Maria Machado (Graywolf, 2019)

Know My Name: A Memoir by Chanel Miller (Viking, 2019)

Living a Feminist Life by Sara Ahmed (Duke University Press, 2017)

No Visible Bruises: What We Don't Know About Domestic Violence Can Kill Us by Rachel Louise Snyder (Bloomsbury, 2019)

Not That Bad: Dispatches from Rape Culture edited by Roxane Gay (Harper Perennial, 2018)

Rage Becomes Her: The Power of Women's Anger by Soraya Chemaly (Atria, 2018)

The Right to Sex: Feminism in the Twenty-First Century by Amia Srinivasan (Picador, 2021)

The Seven Necessary Sins for Women and Girls by Mona Eltahawy (Beacon Press, 2019)

Sex Object: A Memoir by Jessica Valenti (Dey Street Books, 2017)

Sexual Consent by Milena Popova (MIT Press, 2019)

Splitting: Protecting Yourself While Divorcing Someone with Borderline or Narcissistic Personality Disorder by Bill Eddy and Randi Kreger (New Harbinger Publications, 2021)

The State of Affairs: Rethinking Infidelity by Esther Perel (Harper, 2018)

"Thank You for Taking Care of Yourself" in *Girlhood* by Melissa Febos (Bloomsbury, 2021)

Three Women by Lisa Taddeo (Avid Reader Press, 2019)

Trauma and Recovery by Judith Herman (Basic Books, 2022)

The Vegetarian by Han Kang, translated by Deborah Smith (Hogarth, 2015)

Want Me: A Sex Writer's Journey into the Heart of Desire by Tracy Clark-Flory (Penguin, 2021)

The Will to Change: Men, Masculinity, and Love by bell hooks (Washington Square Press, 2004)

ACKNOWLEDGMENTS

I'm so grateful to my friend and colleague who, when I was just beginning to conceive of this project, urged me to be brave and write this book. He did so in a card that he wrote for me just before his death, enlisting the Audre Lorde quotation that now opens *Mad Wife*. Thanks, P. K.—I did it.

I wish I could name in print every person who supported me through all that led to this book. But I know you understand the need for this alphabet soup. If you think you're in here, you are.

My earliest readers—H., who read my first tentative pages with such affirming kindness, then suggested I read about women's rage, and who encouraged me to persevere when I felt defeated by the long, trying journey to publication: this book truly would not exist without your years of support and friendship. K. and L., stalwart companions along so many beautiful and heartening miles; and G., S., M., B., and several E.'s, L.'s, and J.'s, friends old and new: telling me that this story was compelling and important motivated me to keep working on the book. Continuing to love and respect me after reading it helped me accept everything in it as part of myself and offer it to the world. Thank you for your thoughtful feedback and empathetic witnessing.

S., to whom I've been telling this story longer than anyone: writing a book like this didn't occur to me until you said that I was the woman and writer who had to do it. I hope it does justice to all you wanted me to communicate. I could not have become the person who could write it without your patient ear, tacit affection, and gentle nudges toward painful truths I had to claim myself. I see what you did there.

"Dr. T.": Your steadfast and fearless support of my son made all the difference, however futile it felt at times. Your positive influence on him and my gratitude to you will go on long after the worst pain of those years has faded.

To the writer of every book, chapter, narrative, and article I reference here and all those I read while writing or preparing to write; to Tarana Burke, Bev Gooden, and every woman who has bravely tweeted or posted her own account of sexual or domestic violence: Had I not heard your voices, I wouldn't have known I needed to find mine. You changed my life.

I am so grateful to my agent, L., for believing in this project and fighting to get it out there, for making it stronger with perceptive questions and wise suggestions, and for treating me with such warm generosity along the way. And thank you, Kate Manne, for writing books that explained me to myself and then introducing me to L. To my feminist sisters who offered encouragement and made connections, including Soraya Chemaly, Salamishah Tillet, Jennifer Baumgardner, Nancy Miller, and R.F.; my friends/mentors/colleagues S., N., M., L., R., and A.; and my coediting coven, C. & C., and all our bold contributors, from whom I learned so much: thank you for the community and solidarity.

Being asked to excise pieces from a trauma narrative you've only recently organized into something that feels like sanity can register as an existential threat. So I am enormously grateful for the respect and tenderness with which my editor guided me through the final stages of this book. Thank you for taking a chance on a tough sell and giving my voice a chance to be heard and make a difference. Your passion for this project buoys me still. And many thanks to my eagle-eyed copyeditors for helping me clarify that voice. I am proud to be published by Beacon Press, whose long history of fierce choices continues to remind us of the power of books to do real good in the world. And thanks to my friend and colleague K. for guiding me through the wild world of trade publishing.

I am forever grateful to my yoga teachers, M. and D., whose daily reminders to let go and be present got me through the worst of it; and to Tara Brach, whose teachings underwrite my every journey. May this and all circumstances serve to awaken heartmind.

My original family, who may not always understand me or my choices but loves me nonetheless: I'm old enough now to know that sometimes love is enough.

And "Jack," who responded to this story with compassion from the start: You've patiently listened to many retellings over many years, gathering my pieces and giving them back. I might have endured what it took to get here on my own, but I would not have emerged so sound and often even joyous. Thank you for giving me the space to find myself and fight my own battles, while offering safe refuge and reinforcement along the way. It seems that every conversation we've had has led to this moment. How terrifying and wonderful to peer beyond it. How lovely to be doing that together.

NOTES

INTRODUCTION: TESTIMONY

XIII **"The beginning of things, of a world especially"**: Kate Chopin, *The Awakening*, ed. Nancy A. Walker, 2nd ed. (Boston: Bedford, 2000), 35.

XIV **nearly three every day in the US alone:** Violence Policy Center, "When Men Murder Women: An Analysis of 2018 Homicide Data," September 2020, https://vpc.org/press/nearly-2000-women-murdered-by-men-in-one-year-new-violence-policy-center-study-finds/. Since 2017, Dawn Wilcox has been updating an online database of women and girls killed by men and boys, listing their causes and circumstances of death along with their photos. For 2022, the most recent completed year when this book went to press, the database lists nearly nine hundred murdered women and girls. See https://women countusa.org.

XIX **"What I lived as feminism"**: Rachel Cusk, *Aftermath: On Marriage and Separation* (New York: Picador, 2012), 15. The term "transvestite" is dated; many people today would consider using it to describe an individual as offensive. I read Cusk as applying the term and all of its tonal complexity metaphorically to herself.

XX **Many of the women who told their stories in the early days of #MeToo:** Irin Carmon and Amelia Schonbeck, "Was It Worth It?," *New York Magazine*, September 30, 2019, https://www.thecut.com/2019/09/coming-forward-about-sexual-assault-and-what-comes-after.html.

1: FELLOW CREATURE

3 **A recent book argues:** Eli Finkel, *The All-or-Nothing Marriage: How the Best Marriages Work* (New York: Dutton, 2017).

3 **on the popular *Hidden Brain* podcast:** "When Did Marriage Become So Hard?," *Hidden Brain*, NPR, February 12, 2018, https://www.npr.org/2018/02/12/584531641/when-did-marriage-become-so-hard.

3 **women initiate divorce 69 percent of the time in the US—90 percent when the women are college-educated:** Michael J. Rosenfeld, "Who Wants the Breakup? Gender and Breakups in Heterosexual Relationships," in *Social*

Networks and the Life Course, vol. 2, ed. Duane F. Alwin, Diane H. Felmlee, and Derek A. Kreager (Cham, Switzerland: Springer, 2018), 221–43.

5 **"free! free! free!":** Kate Chopin, "The Story of an Hour," in *Literature: Reading, Reacting, Writing*, ed. Laurie Kirszner and Stephen R. Mandell (New York: Harcourt College Publishers, 2001), 44.

6 **male entitlement and the power that accompanies it can accrue invisibly over years:** This dynamic, and all the others I describe in this book, can occur in any long-term relationship shaped by patriarchal patterns, regardless of its participants' gender or sexuality; I focus on heterosexual marriage because that was my experience.

7 **sixteen times she said no; "fucking dramatic":** Stacey May Fowles, "To Get Out from Under It," in *Not That Bad: Dispatches from Rape Culture*, ed. Roxane Gay (New York: Harper Perennial, 2018), 274, 281.

8 **"Exactly how many times did I need to say no":** Fowles, "To Get Out from Under It," 274.

11 **We are taught our whole lives . . . that sex is an integral part of any romantic relationship:** Milena Popova, *Sexual Consent* (Cambridge: MIT Press, 2019), 90.

11 **Women are taught that men's drive for sex is biological and important:** Popova, *Sexual Consent*, 70–71.

11 **Sex therapists today still advise women to consent to unwanted sex in marriage in the interest of "relationship maintenance":** Popova, *Sexual Consent*, 66.

12 **women who are assaulted by a *current* intimate partner experience PTSD, stress, and dissociation at higher rates:** Jeff R. Temple, Rebecca Weston, Benjamin Rodriguez, et al., "Differing Effects of Partner and Nonpartner Sexual Assault on Women's Mental Health," *Violence Against Women* 13, no. 3 (2007): 285–97.

2: LOVE STORY

21 **a short piece on sexual abuse in marriage on Vox.com:** Anonymous, "We Need to Talk About Sexual Assault in Marriage," *Vox*, March 8, 2018, www.vox .com/first-person/2018/3/8/17087628/sexual-assault-marriage-metoo.

3: BETRAYAL

35 **not having access to abortion is far more damaging than undergoing it:** Nicoletta Lanese, "Women Denied Abortions May Endure Long-Term Health Consequences," *UCSF Research*, June 18, 2019, https://www.ucsf.edu/news /2019/06/414706/women-denied-abortions-may-endure-long-term-health -consequences.

35 **childbirth is much more dangerous than any legal abortion procedure:** Elizabeth G. Raymond and David A. Grimes, "The Comparative Safety of Legal Induced Abortion and Childhood in the United States," *Obstetrics and Gynecology* 119, no. 2 (2012): 215–19, https://pubmed.ncbi.nlm.nih.gov /22270271.

4: STAY

43 "marital sadism"; "Betrayal comes in many forms"; " a gesture of bold defiance": Esther Perel, *The State of Affairs: Rethinking Infidelity* (New York: Harper, 2017), 215–17.

43-44 we condemn marital "infidelity" more than almost any other behavior; affairs happen in every kind of marriage: Perel, *The State of Affairs*, 215, xxiv.

5: VOICES

48 "shocking," "sickening," . . . "nauseating": Nancy A. Walker, "Introduction": Kate Chopin, *The Awakening*, 2nd ed., ed. Nancy A. Walker (Boston: Bedford, 2000), 16.

49-51 "all declared that Mr. Pontellier" . . . "the voice of the sea": Chopin, *The Awakening*, 29, 26–28, 39, 40, 100, 106, 107, 34, 79, 103, 138.

6: BOILING FROG

55 "I view our bodies as a site of struggle": Susan Bordo, from *Unbearable Weight: Feminism, Western Culture, and the Body* in *The Norton Anthology of Theory and Criticism*, 2nd ed., ed. Vincent B. Leitch (New York: W. W. Norton, 2010), 2254.

60 "Her body does not seem to her to be a clear expression of herself": Simone de Beauvoir, from *The Second Sex*, in Leitch, *The Norton Anthology of Theory and Criticism*, 1268.

61 consensual non-monogamy (CNM), which includes polyamory and open marriages and is practiced by more queer people than heterosexual ones: Elisabeth A. Sheff, "Updated Estimate of Non-Monogamous People in the U.S.," *Psychology Today*, May 27, 2019, https://www.psychologytoday.com /us/blog/the-polyamorists-next-door/201905/updated-estimate-number-non -monogamous-people-in-us.

7: FREEDOM

69 "The heroine's bisexuality is merely a sexual ruse": Jack Halberstam, "The Good, the Bad, and the Ugly: Men, Women, and Masculinity," in *The Norton Anthology of Theory and Criticism*, ed. Vincent B. Leitch, 2nd ed. (New York: W. W. Norton, 2010), 2642.

73 "If we cannot at least imagine we are free"; "Freedom is never free": Deborah Levy, *The Cost of Living: A Working Autobiography* (New York: Bloomsbury, 2018), 86, 17.

8: CONTROL

75 the vast majority of swingers are . . . of child-rearing ages (thirty-six to fifty-five): Edward Fernandez, "Are Swingers Freaky and Deviant?," *Psychology Today*, October 9, 2013, https://www.psychologytoday.com/us/blog/the -swinging-paradigm/201310/are-swingers-freaky-and-deviant.

77 **Most swingers are middle to upper class, well educated, and well into their marriages:** Fernandez, "Are Swingers Freaky and Deviant?"

77 **we weren't usually the ones with the energy and drive to initiate swinging:** Edward Fernandez, "Women, Swinging, Sex, and Seduction," *Psychology Today*, November 13, 2013, https://www.psychologytoday.com/us/blog/the -swinging-paradigm/201311/women-swinging-sex-and-seduction.

10: WHAT WE OWE EACH OTHER

94 **watching porn, whose distorting effects Tracy Clark-Flory documents:** Tracy Clark-Flory, *Want Me: A Sex Writer's Journey into the Heart of Desire* (New York: Penguin, 2021).

102 **"I suspect that anyone is capable of anything":** Melissa Febos, *Abandon Me: Memoirs* (New York: Bloomsbury, 2017), 195.

11: INSIDE/OUTSIDE

116 **"put Janie to thinking about"; "learned to hush"; "the spirit of the marriage":** Zora Neale Hurston, *Their Eyes Were Watching God* (1937) (New York: Perennial, 1990), 71, 72.

119 **"A general ethical mandate says":** Kate Manne, *Entitled: How Male Privilege Hurts Women* (New York: Crown, 2020), 29–30.

12: NOVEL

123 **whether or not it leaves any visible bruises:** For a comprehensive investigation of domestic violence of all kinds, see Rachel Louise Snyder, *No Visible Bruises: What We Don't Know About Domestic Violence Can Kill Us* (New York: Bloomsbury, 2019).

126 **"Sometimes, in the bath, the children cry":** Rachel Cusk, *Aftermath* (New York: Picador, 2013), 24–25.

13: CRUEL AND INHUMANE

132 **my accusation options:** Lina Guillen, "Grounds for Divorce in [State]," www .divorcenet.com/states/ . . . / . . . _grounds_for_divorce, accessed February 27, 2021.

142-143 **"Abusers threaten, bully and make a nightmare":** Jennifer Freyd, "Violations of Power, Adaptive Blindness, and Betrayal Trauma Theory," *Feminism & Psychology* 7, no. 1 (1997): 29.

14: CONTROL REDUX

157 **"One of the most important social myths we must debunk":** bell hooks, *All About Love: New Visions* (New York: Harper Perennial, 2000), 22.

15: BANSHEE

168 **he disbelieves "90% of all abuse accusations":** Hannah Dreyfus, "A Colorado Custody Evaluator Who Disbelieves 90% of Abuse Allegations Recommended

a Teen Stay Under Her Abusive Father's Control," *Denver Post*, September 30, 2022, https://www.denverpost.com/2022/09/30/parental-responsibility -evaluators-colorado.

170 **children who had been "indoctrinated"; why children in "high-conflict" custody cases "falsely accuse":** Stuart Lavietes, "Richard Gardner, 72, Dies; Cast Doubt on Abuse Claims," *New York Times*, June 9, 2003.

171 **a series of reports by Hannah Dreyfus on many shocking cases:** Rebecca Onion, "The Controversial Parenting Theory That's Showing Up in Court Everywhere," *Slate*, September 14, 2023, https://slate.com/human-interest/2023 /09/parental-alienation-syndrome-prove-laws-hannah-dreyfus.html.

171 **the horrifying severity of it:** A total of 58,000 children per year in the US are ordered into the custody of an abusive parent after the other parent sought custody in family court; more than 650 children are killed by abusers (the vast majority of which are fathers) who act as their custodians in the US per year. See https://www.batteredmotherscustodyconference.org, which cites the American Psychological Association and American Bar Association Commission on domestic violence.

175 **"It is [the mother], finally, who is held accountable":** Adrienne Rich, *Of Woman Born: Motherhood as Experience and Institution* (New York: W. W. Norton, 1976), 52.

178 **start every court day on my yoga mat:** Dr. Bessel van der Kolk makes a compelling science-based argument for using yoga to heal from the trauma of war and all kinds of sexual and domestic abuse in *The Body Keeps the Score: Brain, Mind, and Body and the Healing of Trauma* (New York: Penguin, 2015).

179 **Soraya Chemaly's *Rage Becomes Her* playlist:** My life-saving soundtrack for those years: https://spoti.fi/2M7KHm3.

16: MAD

186 **"snarling, canine noise"; "wild beast"; "creature"; "masked . . . face":** Charlotte Brontë, *Jane Eyre*, 2nd ed., ed. Richard J. Dunn (London: W. W. Norton, 1987), 185.

186 **Sandra Gilbert and Susan Gubar turned my attention to Bertha Mason:** Sandra Gilbert and Susan Gubar, *The Mad Woman in the Attic: The Woman Writer and the Nineteenth-Century Literary Imagination* (New Haven, CT: Yale University Press, 1979).

187 **Burke was inspired to create the Me Too movement:** Tarana Burke, keynote speech, Women & Power 2019, Omega Institute, Rhinebeck, New York, September 27, 2019. See also https://metoomvmt.org/get-to-know-us/tarana -burke-founder.

188 **the Babe.net article in which "Grace" detailed a sexual encounter:** Katie Way, "I Went on a Date with Aziz Ansari," *Babe*, January 13, 2018, https://babe.net /2018/01/13/aziz-ansari-28355.

189 **rape and sexual coercion are relatively common in marriage:** In 1982, Diana Russell found that one in seven wives reported having been raped within their marriage. See Diana Russell, *Rape in Marriage* (New York: Macmillan, 1982), 2.

189 **a third of rapes are committed by a current or former intimate partner:** "Victims of Sexual Violence: Statistics," RAINN (Rape, Abuse & Incest National Network), National Institute of Justice, www.rainn.org/statistics /victims-sexual-violence.

189 **half of adults in the US are married, and married people have sex twice as often:** See Pew Research Group, "Half of Adults Are Married Today," September 14, 2017, www.pewresearch.org/fact-tank/2017/09/14/as-u-s-marriage-rate -hovers-at-50-education-gap-in-marital-status-widens/ft_17-09-14_marriage _halfof; and Linda Geddes, "Couples Are Healthier, Wealthier . . . and Less Trim," *The Guardian*, April 17, 2016, www.theguardian.com/lifeandstyle/2016 /apr/17/couples-healthier-wealthier-marriage-good-health-single-survey -research.

190 **"empty consent"; "It has never been expected that a man":** Melissa Febos, *Girlhood* (New York: Bloomsbury, 2021), 230, 241.

191 **Like two other writers . . . I wanted the assault to be made visible on my body:** A. J. McKenna, "Sixty-Three Days," and Elissa Bassist, "Why I Didn't Say No," in *Not That Bad: Dispatches from Rape Culture*, ed. Roxane Gay (New York: Harper Perennial, 2018), 85, 337.

191 **"because [of] how you treated me":** A. J. McKenna, "Sixty-Three Days," *Not That Bad*, 83–84.

17: DISTURBING

193 **"Why don't you write?":** Hélène Cixous, "The Laugh of the Medusa," in *The Norton Anthology of Theory and Criticism*, ed. Vincent B. Leitch, 2nd ed. (New York: W. W. Norton, 2010), 1943.

193 **sexual violence in marriage is committed by every kind of man; "unremark- able, non-monstrous-seeming people":** See Diana Russell, *Rape in Marriage* (New York: Macmillan, 1982), 129, 130; and Kate Manne, *Down Girl: The Logic of Misogyny* (New York: Oxford University Press, 2018), 199, 211.

193 **misogyny is "narcissistic and delusional by its very nature . . . a sense of 'aggrieved entitlement'":** Manne, *Down Girl*, 75, citing Michael Kimmel, italics in the original.

193 **entitlement only increases the more privilege a man enjoys:** Manne, *Down Girl*, 106, italics in the original, 238.

193 **"Upper-class men who do not rape other men's daughters or wives":** Elizabeth Grauerholz and Mary A. Koralewski, eds., *Sexual Coercion: A Sourcebook on Its Nature, Causes, and Prevention* (Lexington, MA: Lexington Books, 1991), 10.

194 **The women in Miriam Toews's novel *Women Talking* leave:** Miriam Toews, *Women Talking* (London: Faber and Faber, 2018).

195 **"Since decent human beings":** Sohaila Abdulali, *What We Talk About When We Talk About Rape* (New York: New Press, 2018), 45.

196 **"Sex women want":** Manne, *Down Girl*, 288.

196 **"in the end, you have to care":** Abdulali, *What We Talk About When We Talk About Rape*, 44.

196 **the "law and politics of gender inequality":** Catharine A. MacKinnon, *Butterfly Politics: Changing the World for Women* (Cambridge, MA: Belknap Press of Harvard University Press, 2019), 7.

196 **women who speak out will be considered "overly dramatic":** Manne, *Down Girl*, 227.

196 **Chemaly urges women to share their stories . . . and to prepare to be met with men's anger:** Soraya Chemaly, *Rage Becomes Her: The Power of Women's Anger* (New York: Atria, 2018), 227, 229.

196-197 **Anger, she writes. . . . Anger requires. . . . Through anger:** Chemaly, *Rage Becomes Her*, xx, 47, 5.

18: MONSTROUS

199 **a woman as "perfected" by death; "forbidden to 'work'"; "astonish him":** See Sylvia Plath, "Edge," in *Ariel* (New York: Harper & Row, 1966), 84; and Charlotte Perkins Gilman, "The Yellow Wall-paper," *New England Magazine* 11, no. 5 (1892): 647–56.

200 **Misogynistic opponents of Angela Merkel and Theresa May made Medusa mash-ups:** Mary Beard, *Women & Power: A Manifesto* (London: W. W. Norton, 2017).

200 **"a free woman in an unfree society must be a monster":** Angela Carter, *The Sadeian Woman and the Ideology of Pornography* (London: Virago, 1979), 30.

200 **"monstrous"; "sting her into desire":** Deborah Levy, *Hot Milk* (New York: Bloomsbury, 2016), 72.

200 **"the mutual recognition of free beings who confirm one another's freedom":** Simone de Beauvoir, from *The Second Sex*, in *The Norton Anthology of Theory and Criticism*, ed. Vincent B. Leitch, 2nd ed. (New York: W. W. Norton, 2010), 1266.

EPILOGUE: AWAKENING

205 **ingenious short story made of pop quizzes:** David Foster Wallace, "Octet," *Brief Interviews with Hideous Men* (Boston: Back Bay Books, 1999). After Wallace's death, women revealed his misogyny and abusiveness, though he was a self-proclaimed feminist; their revelations remind us of the limits of our vision.

205 **Chimamanda Ngozi Adichie's TED Talk:** Chimamanda Ngozi Adichie, "The Danger of a Single Story," TED Talk, July 2009, https://www.ted.com/talks/chimamanda_ngozi_adichie_the_danger_of_a_single_story, accessed April 14, 2022.